Beyond Blockchain
The Death of the Dollar and the Rise of Digital Currency

By Erik Townsend

The Audiobook version of this title can be purchased at
www.ErikTownsend.com

Copyright © 2018 Erik Townsend, All rights reserved

TABLE OF CONTENTS

TABLE OF CONTENTS 3
Chapter 1: Introduction 11
  The Digital Currency Trilemma 11
  The central prediction of this book… 13
  The Crypto Culture 13
  Two inventions that will change the world 14
    Cryptocurrency is where it all started, but nothing more 16
  The U.S. Government Malaise 17
  The *Challengers* and Reserve Currency Status 18
  Logical Replacement for USD is a Digital Reserve Currency 20
  A new "space race" is coming 21
  So what's the rest of this book about? 22
  A quick introduction to your author 23
Chapter 2: What is Money? 25
  Tripartite Definition 25
    Store of value 25
    Unit of Account 26
    Medium of Exchange 26
  Types of Money: The Societal Complacency Cycle 26
    Commodity Money 26
    Representative Money 28
    The Societal Complacency Cycle 37
  Conclusions 38
Chapter 3: The Origins and Culture of Cryptocurrency 41
  The Cypherpunk Movement 42
  Digital Currency: The Cypherpunks' greatest challenge 44
  "Crypto Community": Cypherpunks Movement goes Mainstream 45

Chapter 4: Distributed Ledger Technology 49
  Summarizing the Blockchain Distributed Ledger 57
Chapter 5: Bitcoin – The First Cryptocurrency 59
  How the Bitcoin Currency Works 59
    Bitcoin Units of Account 59
    Bitcoin Money Supply 59
    How and when are Bitcoin "minted"? 60
    How do miners get paid when the money supply is used up? 61
    Do I need to open an account to keep my Bitcoin in? 61
    How Bitcoin payments work 62
    If there are accounts, how is it like Cash? 63
    Is it really anonymous? 63
  The Millennial Generation and Crypto Mining 65
  Cryptocurrency vs. Commodity, Representative and Fiat Money 65
Chapter 6: Practical, Regulatory & Viability Challenges for CryptoCurrency
.... 71
  Issuing money has always been the exclusive purview of government 72
  Myth: Government cannot outlaw Crypto 75
  Bitcoin cannot and will not be outlawed overnight 75
  Conclusions 77
Chapter 7: Technical Challenges for CryptoCurrency 79
  Understanding Proof-of-Work 80
    Crypto "Mining": Bug or Feature? 82
Chapter 8: Nobody Stands More to Gain than Government 85
  Who benefits from Government-issued Digital Currency? 87
    Globalists seeking a single world currency 88
    Everyone who wants to outlaw cash 88
    De-Dollarization and SWIFT 89
    Governments that want more power to monitor, regulate, and control money 89

TABLE OF CONTENTS

Central bankers don't even know what they're missing! 90

To get serious about Digital Currency requires first understanding Conventional Currency! 90

Chapter 9: Fractional Reserve Banking 93

    Visualizing Money Creation 94

    Didn't they "fix this problem" after the Great Depression? 97

    Consequences of FRB 98

    "Gold Backing" under FRB 99

    FRB and Digital Currency 99

        Cryptocurrency and FRB 99

        Government-issued digital currency and FRB 101

Chapter 10: Money Supply 105

    Money supply and the economy 105

    Central bank management of the money supply 106

    Measuring the money supply 106

    Private-sector credit expansion is the primary governor of the money supply 107

    How Securitization corrupted credit markets 108

    Fitting digital currency into the system 111

        Monetary policy is imprecise, primitive, and often ineffective 113

Chapter 11: Central Banks & Monetary Policy 115

    What does the central bank actually do? 116

        Dual Mandate 117

    Monetary Policy 118

        Conventional Monetary Policy 118

        Unconventional Monetary Policy 123

    Monetary Policy in Context 126

Chapter 12: Sovereign Debt 129

    The "Risk-Free" Asset 129

    The role of government bonds as an interest rate benchmark 130

The role of sovereign bonds as a foreign diplomacy tool 131
The role of sovereign bonds as a central bank reserve asset 131
Conclusion 132

Chapter 13: Reserve Currency Status 133
International trade settlement 134
Central bank reserve assets 134
Why the U.S. Dollar still holds the title 135
Advantages enjoyed by the reserve currency issuer 137
Triffin's Dilemma 139

Chapter 14: History of the U.S. Dollar 143
Gold standard, Silver standard, or both? 143
Bretton Woods System: A whole different kind of Gold Standard 144
The Nixon Shock & Collapse of Bretton Woods 145
    1970s runaway inflation 147
Petrodollar system 147

Chapter 15: Sergei Glaziev's De-Dollarization Campaign 149
China's Yuan-denominated Crude Oil contract 151
At first, it was just the BRICS countries… 152

Chapter 16: SWIFT 153
SWIFT is a communication network, not a payment system 155
Russia Welcomes Foreign Banks to SWIFT Alternative Network 156
Conclusions 157

Chapter 17: Crypto Revisited 159
Revolutionizing the global monetary system: Is Crypto up to the task?
.... 160
    A realistic "Crypto Wins" scenario? 162
    What it would take for the crypto community to prove me wrong ... 163
My predictions for cryptocurrencies 165

Chapter 18: Other Cryptocurrencies 167
Ethereum and Smart Contracts 167

TABLE OF CONTENTS

Ripple (XRP Ledger): The crypto that's not really a crypto 168
Monero: A less transparent blockchain... 169
A brief summary of the "me too" market 170
Chapter 19: Global-Scale Digital Currency 173
    Time Horizon and the De-Dollarization Catalyst.................................. 174
    Scope of the new system... 175
        Re-engineering fractional reserve banking.. 176
        System should encompass all payment methods and credit instruments 178
        Zoned monetary architecture... 179
        Real-time Instrumentation and Monetary Policy............................... 180
        Offline Digital Cash 181
    Network scalability, availability, and parallelism 182
    Who will design and build it?.. 183
        The Challengers 183
        The U.S. Response 184
        The coming Central Bank-Fintech complex? 185
Chapter 20: Digital Global Reserve Currency: What would it take? 187
    Summarizing the strategy to dethrone King Dollar 191
    When does the new Space Race begin?... 192
Chapter 21: Gold-backed Digital Currency 195
    The next step: Government Independence 198
    Gold Standard or Gold Convertibility Standard? 200
    Conclusions 201
Chapter 22: Permissioned Distributed Ledger 203
    Permissioned Distributed Ledger still has no central "owner" 204
    Hijacking Risk in Permissioned Ledgers...205
    Breaking the Proof-of-Work Barrier 205
    Distributed Ledger State-of-the-Art: Not quite there yet 206
    Conclusions 208

Chapter 23: Smart Contracts 209
Visualizing smart contracts 210
Relevance of smart contracts to global-scale digital currency 212

Chapter 24: Digital Sovereign Bond Market 215
I'll elaborate in detail on these three points later 215
What's so great about U.S. Treasury Bonds? 215
    Size Matters! 216
    Credit Matters Even More 216
Evaluating Alternatives to U.S. Treasury Bonds 217
    German Bunds 217
    Other Eurozone Sovereign Bonds 218
    Japanese Government Bonds (JGBs) 218
    British Gilts 219
    Everything Else 219
Use Technology to Create a Better Sovereign *Bond* 220
    The Smart Contract Revenue Bond 220
    Instantaneously reverse-callable digital sovereign bonds 222
Use Technology to Create a Better Sovereign Bond *Market* 224
    Use commission rebates to incentivize liquidity providers 225
    Design the market to support central banks' priority use cases 225
Re-denominate Emerging Market debt in Digital Currency 227
Network Effect Revisited 228
The Digital Sovereign Bond Market is a Major Undertaking 230

Chapter 25: Satoshi vs. Orwell 231
Conclusions 234

Chapter 26: If I were in charge 235
The world needs an *Independent* Banco Nuevo 235
Assembling the Team 236
Growing the Organization 239
Returning to Reality… 239

TABLE OF CONTENTS

Please follow my work… 241
Appendix A: About the Author..243
Acknowledgements 249

10   Beyond Blockchain: The Death of the Dollar and the Rise of Digital Currency

Chapter 1:

Introduction

On Halloween night, 2008, the global finance community was looking over the edge into an abyss. The worst October since 1987 was finally over, but everyone feared what might come next. Veteran finance professionals and central bankers alike were questioning whether the global financial system was in the process of failing irreparably.

Everyone was in an existential panic. So when someone[1] using the pseudonym "Satoshi Nakamoto" published a white paper that day, the event went unnoticed. But my prediction is that the invention of *Distributed Ledger* and *double spend-proof digital cash* (first published in Satoshi's *Bitcoin White Paper*[2]) will eventually change the world in profound ways. And by *profound*, I mean on the scale of the Internet or the personal computer.

In the not-too-distant future, all money will be digital, and it will work differently than what we're used to. But exactly how this change will occur is anything but clear. Three competing forces will determine the outcome, and it's very possible that the balance of world power could change dramatically in the process. This book is designed to help you understand what's coming, who the most important players are, and what to watch for as the *Digital Currency Revolution* unfolds over the next ten to twenty years.

The Digital Currency Trilemma

Normally, when something new is invented, the path forward is clear and obvious: the people who invented it lead the way, and then as the innovation gains popularity the original inventors are soon joined by many others working toward the same goals. But in the case of Digital Currency, it's a completely different story. Those three major forces competing to determine the future of the global monetary system couldn't possibly have more contradictory goals, objectives, and motivations.

---

[1] Many experts now believe that "Satoshi" was actually a team of two or more people working together.
[2] https://bitcoin.org/bitcoin.pdf

Beyond Blockchain: The Death of the Dollar and the Rise of Digital Currency

The inventors of cryptocurrency are such an interesting bunch that I've dedicated an entire chapter to introducing their culture, values, and motivations. For now, suffice it to say that they see government-issued money as the problem, and everything they do is focused on promoting their cryptocurrencies as *alternatives* to government-issued money. Cryptocurrency systems are designed to use technology in clever ways to take power away from government, making it extremely difficult for law enforcement or other government officials to monitor, regulate, or control the financial affairs of private citizens.

Their inventions of *distributed ledger* and *double spend-proof digital cash* have the potential to deliver profound benefits to society. They make it possible to modernize and improve the existing global monetary system controlled by the major governments of the world. But the inventors themselves couldn't be less interested in improving the existing system. They perceive the current system as the *problem*, and their vision of the future involves their cryptocurrencies offering a superior alternative they expect will win the support of people around the world. They believe cryptocurrencies will eventually take over and become the dominant money systems, as it becomes widely recognized that cryptocurrency offers a superior alternative to government-issued money.

I don't think these aspirations are even remotely realistic. Governments won't simply give up the monopoly they've enjoyed over coining and issuing money for the last several thousand years—not without a fight, and governments will win that fight easily.

The U.S. Government stands more to gain from digital currency technology than anyone else. Ironically, they don't seem to have figured that out yet. Eventually they'll wake up and realize that digital currency technology offers the opportunity to advance their own agenda and seize far *more* control over the global monetary system.

I'll use the phrase **The Challengers** to refer to foreign governments who are sure to recognize that digital currency technology is the best means to challenge Dollar hegemony. They're extremely frustrated that the U.S. Dollar enjoys the title of *Global Reserve Currency*[3]. They feel this status gives the U.S. Government an unfair advantage over the rest of the world, and they allege that the U.S. has repeatedly abused its status as reserve currency issuer to the detriment of other nations.

---

[3] Chapter 13 will explain what is meant by *Global Reserve Currency* and why it's so important.

Chapter 1: Introduction

Who are these *Challengers*? At the moment China and Russia are the major players, but the list of countries is growing rapidly. Just during the time this book was being written, the European Union began to side with the Challengers on some matters concerning the Dollar. If the *Challengers* are able to win Europe's support, it's very possible they could use digital currency technology to dethrone King Dollar as global reserve currency. That would change the balance of world power so significantly that I've dedicated an entire chapter to explaining the meaning of *reserve currency* status and what the consequences would be if the U.S. Dollar lost that title.

The central prediction of this book...

Is that the ultimate outcome from the invention of *distributed ledger* and *digital cash* will be the replacement of the U.S. Dollar as the world's global reserve currency. That's a long-term prediction and it will take many years to occur, but it's inevitable and the process has already begun. It could come in the form of a *Digital Dollar*, which might secure U.S. hegemony over the global financial system for another fifty years. But it could also come in the form of a new global digital currency introduced by *The Challengers* for the express purpose of attacking dollar hegemony.

One thing is certain: whoever succeeds at introducing a digital currency system that becomes the new global reserve currency will win the grand prize in the form of several decades of monetary hegemony. *It's a really, really big deal.* Perhaps as big as the end of the Cold War.

My goal in writing this book isn't to predict *exactly* what's going to happen or who's going to win—that would be impossible. What I *can* do is provide all the background knowledge needed to interpret the news as it occurs, so that you can follow this story as it unfolds on the global stage over the next couple of decades.

China and Russia almost certainly already understand that digital currency is the best means available to them to reduce the U.S. Government's authority over the global economy. They may already be collaborating toward that outcome, as evidenced by both governments' strong interest in digital currency technology.

The Crypto Culture

The people who invented cryptocurrency are obsessed with the philosophy that the financial affairs of private citizens are none of the government's business—a sentiment I share. All of their efforts have focused on using technology to create a new money system designed to intentionally limit and restrict government's ability to interfere in private citizens' monetary affairs.

They have no interest in helping governments to improve or redesign the monetary systems currently running the global economy. They see the existing monetary system as the *problem*, and the governments and their central banks as the source of that problem. They don't want to *fix it*. No, their aspirations are much more grandiose. *They want to replace the existing monetary system entirely,* with a completely new kind of money that prevents governments from regulating and controlling the system.

But technology is a double-edged sword. Just as it's possible to use technology to limit and restrict the power of government, it's equally possible to use technology to design a money system that *increases* the power of government. The people who invented these new breakthrough technologies aren't stupid—they know that once governments are in the driver's seat, the agenda will be reversed to use digital currency to further *increase* the power and authority of government, not to limit it. Needless to say, the inventors of cryptocurrency have no interest in causing or helping that to occur—they are quite passionately dedicated to the exact opposite goal.

Two inventions that will change the world

The inventors of cryptocurrency made a revolutionary breakthrough in how information is stored in distributed computer networks, and by doing so they perfected an invention that had stumped computer scientists and software engineers alike for decades: true *digital cash*—the ability to transmit monetary value (not just a check, but true money value) through a computer network.

The implications of these inventions are profound, and will change the world. This new technology could be used to enhance and improve the existing monetary systems running the global economy in ways that would deliver profound benefits to society. One of my principal contentions is that sooner or later, governments will recognize and exploit the opportunity to use these inventions to redesign how government-issued money works.

The principal technology breakthrough that made cryptocurrency possible is known generically as *distributed ledger*. That phrase might be new to some of you, but I'll bet you've already heard the buzzword *blockchain*. Blockchain is the name of the distributed ledger system that underpins Bitcoin and several other cryptocurrencies.

The design focus of blockchain centers entirely on one primary goal: full *decentralization*, meaning that there is no single point of control in the entire network. The reason that's so important is that if you're designing a cryptocurrency system with the goal of making it impervious to government oversight and control, you can't have any central point of vulnerability in the network. If you did, the government could simply locate that computer and shut it down or otherwise take it off the network. For this reason, a lot of very talented software engineers put an awful lot of thought into how to make blockchain completely, totally decentralized.

What are those same brilliant software engineers doing with their time today, nearly a decade after they first invented blockchain? Some have moved on to work on a newer variation—called a *permissioned distributed ledger*. A *permissioned distributed ledger* is one that is designed to be centralized to some degree, and as a result, can achieve much better performance than blockchain.

But wait—didn't I just say the whole point of blockchain was to deliver a fully decentralized design? Yes, but the *reason* that was so important was that if you are designing a *cryptocurrency* with the goal of making it resilient or impervious to government oversight, you need that complete and total decentralization. *But if you are the government itself, and designing a government-issued digital currency system, you don't have that problem.*

I suspect the reason why some of the gurus who invented blockchain are now working on permissioned distributed ledger systems is because they see the proverbial handwriting on the wall. They know that nobody stands more to gain from digital currency technology than governments, and it's only a matter of time before governments wake up to this reality and focus on creating government-issued digital currency systems.

What will happen when governments figure out the opportunity to build their own digital currency systems? The very first thing they'll need is a really solid *permissioned distributed ledger* system. With this perspective, it's easy to see why some of the smartest guys in the crypto community are starting to refocus their energies on creating permissioned ledger products.

Most of the "crypto community" remains dedicated to its goals of designing cryptocurrency systems to *undermine* government authority. But now a few defectors have realized that government-issued digital currency is inevitable. They know it's going to be hundreds if not thousands of times bigger in scope than the entire cryptocurrency trend of the last decade, and that it's going to completely change the world we live in. They probably don't love the idea that governments are going to use technology to do exactly the opposite of what Satoshi envisioned for Bitcoin, but they know it's going to happen with or without them. So they're positioning themselves to be in the right place when major governments around the world are suddenly willing to pay for a really solid permissioned distributed ledger system. *They know what's coming.*

Cryptocurrency is where it all started, but nothing more

Now to be sure, Bitcoin and the other cryptocurrencies have become all the rage in recent years, particularly with the millennial generation. And quite a few major banks are looking seriously at *distributed ledger technology* for a variety of other financial applications. And that's all fine and well. But decades from now, we'll look back and remember Bitcoin and blockchain like we remember the *Wright Flyer*, the world's first airplane. In both cases we're talking about inventions that changed the course of human history. But when put in proper context, in the long run that means they both belong in museums.

Figure 1 The Wright Flyer, circa 1903

Don't get me wrong—I'm not down on Bitcoin. Like the Flyer, it's a milestone invention that will change the course of human history. But just like aviation technology, decades from now *digital currency* will have advanced so far that Bitcoin will seem like a primitive precursor to something that will be so much bigger and more encompassing.

Just as the Flyer was the world's first airplane, Bitcoin and blockchain were the first version of something new in the world of software. As a former software technologist, I can assure you that the first version of any software system seldom reveals how great (or not) that system will ultimately be. Consider Microsoft Windows Version 1. It always takes a few versions to advance beyond the proof-of-concept stage and engineer a world-class system.

The focus of this book will not be on *cryptocurrency*, but rather on what will come next, after governments figure out that nobody stands more to gain from Satoshi's inventions than governments themselves. I predict that they'll apply those same inventions to achieve objectives opposite to those that Satoshi envisioned for Bitcoin.

I'll certainly cover what Bitcoin is and how it works in this book, so you'll know what all the fuss has been about. But only briefly and in sufficient detail to give you an understanding of what Bitcoin achieved. But the primary focus of this book will be the much longer-term outlook for how digital currency will change the course of history.

What comes next could change the world in ways far beyond anything Satoshi ever imagined. And by the way, *we the people* better keep a close eye on the progress, and make sure Satoshi's vision of the future isn't completely replaced with George Orwell's version after governments take control of the process.

The U.S. Government Malaise

Government-issued digital currency is inevitable. The good news—the benefits to society could be tremendous. But sadly, the U.S. Government doesn't appear to have figured any of this out yet.

U.S. law enforcement agencies like the FBI have already caught on that cryptocurrencies can impair the ability of law enforcement to monitor and oversee financial transactions—in other words, cryptocurrencies do exactly what they were designed to do. And the authorities are already fighting back using contractors like blockchain forensic analysis firm *Chainalysis* to trace Bitcoin payments that some criminals errantly assumed were untraceable.

The *opportunity* for the U.S. Government to improve the global monetary system doesn't appear to have captured the attention of senior U.S. policymakers—but China and Russia are already engaged. They understand exactly how digital currency could help them dethrone the Dollar as the world's *reserve currency*. Eventually the U.S. Government will wake up and realize that China and Russia are already tooling up to use digital currency against them. When they do, everything will change rather quickly.

The *Challengers* and Reserve Currency Status

The invention of distributed ledger and digital cash comes at a time when governments all over the world are becoming increasingly frustrated with the nearly monopolistic hegemony the U.S. Dollar holds over the rest of the global financial system. A whole lot of people (including some major governments) are working very actively to remedy this.

Since 1944, the U.S. Dollar has served as the world's *global reserve currency*, meaning that most international trade is settled in U.S. dollars, and more importantly, that central bank reserve assets—a fancy name for the savings account of an entire nation—are usually denominated in U.S. dollars.

The U.S. Government derives an immense advantage over other nations as a result of its status as reserve currency issuer, because reserve currency status creates a huge artificial demand for U.S. dollars internationally (where they are needed to settle trade or to serve as central bank reserve assets). This equates directly to allowing the U.S. Government to both borrow more money (deficit spending) and to run a much larger trade deficit than other countries. If any other (non-reserve currency issuer) country were to try and do the same things, they would pay dearly for that largesse in the form of higher borrowing costs. But the U.S. is effectively immune to this consequence.

This situation has enraged foreign governments for decades. Way back in the 1960s, French Finance Minister (and later, President of France) Valéry Giscard d'Estaing famously coined the phrase *exorbitant privilege* to describe the U.S. Government's unfair advantage over other nations that derives from its status as reserve currency issuer. But there wasn't much anyone could do aside from complaining about it.

In recent years, foreign governments have become much more proactive in taking steps to try and force a change in the global balance of power. Russian scholar (and now, economic adviser to President Vladimir Putin) Sergei Glaziev is widely recognized as the mastermind behind the so-called *de-dollarization* campaign, which seeks to influence governments around the world to stop settling trade (particularly for oil) in U.S. dollars.

Mr. Glaziev doesn't mince words in his public statements—he has accused the U.S. Government of "financial terrorism", saying that the U.S. has shown a consistent pattern of abusing its control over the Dollar as the world's global reserve currency, and that as a matter of self-defense, all other governments around the world should divest their Dollar holdings and stop using dollars to settle international trade. And it's not just talk—since Mr. Glaziev was appointed formally as an economic advisor to Vladimir Putin in early 2018, Russia has been aggressively selling off its holdings of U.S. Treasury bonds.

Meanwhile, Mr. Glaziev continues to lobby other governments around the globe to do the same. China has responded by creating a new yuan-denominated futures contract allowing crude oil to be traded while bypassing the U.S. dollar entirely in settling those transactions. To an increasing extent, nations everywhere seek to find ways to distance themselves from dependence on the Dollar.

The Dollar is the *currency* which forms the backbone of the global financial system, but to make international payments of dollars, an international *payment system* is needed. SWIFT is the *international wire transfer network*, and it facilitates almost all international trade settlement.

SWIFT has recently become the subject of quite a bit of controversy, because the U.S. Government has been withholding access to SWIFT as a tactic to impose sanctions against countries like Iran. It recently threatened to do the same with Venezuela, if that country doesn't play ball with U.S. policy negotiators. For some time, Russia and China have been calling foul on this practice, arguing that the U.S. Government has no right to unilaterally deny other nations access to the global financial system. This is one of the many reasons they have been actively promoting the campaign of *de-dollarization* for several years now.

It's not just Russia and China. In August 2018, the German government issued a statement calling for a new international payment system *independent from the U.S. Government.* Now, to my thinking, that's pretty big coming from Germany, a long-time U.S. ally. Sure, Russia and China have been accusing the U.S. Government of wrongdoing for decades—but for an ally like Germany to take Russia and China's side of the argument and publicly say that the world needs a global payment system free from U.S. oversight is a pretty newsworthy development.

One month later, the European Union's foreign policy chief stood shoulder to shoulder with the Iranian foreign minister at the United Nations in New York City, and announced their intentions to develop a new payment system for the express purpose of bypassing SWIFT to prevent the U.S. from overstepping its authority over other nations' financial affairs.

In summary, a long list of nations and very influential people around the world are getting more and more frustrated with what they perceive as the U.S. Government abusing its status as global reserve currency issuer. They're ready for a new world order in which the U.S. doesn't have nearly as much control over the global financial system.

Logical Replacement for USD is a Digital Reserve Currency

Let's return to the topic at hand—digital currency—with the benefit of this context about what's going on geopolitically. The main point is that a whole lot of people want very badly to find a way to dethrone the U.S. dollar, and to create an alternative to SWIFT—one which the U.S. Government has far less control over.

There's no doubt in my mind that the best way for them to achieve their goals would be to design and build a global-scale digital currency system. Remember that the cryptocurrency pioneers have already invented the needed technological innovations (distributed ledger and double spend-proof digital cash).

Now imagine that you're the governments of Russia and China. You have believed for decades that the United States has abused its monetary authority since World War II, and that the Dollar should be dethroned from the power it enjoys over the global financial system. Your competitive advantage derives from being able to think and plan on a longer time scale than Western governments whose election cycles demand shorter-term policy initiatives.

Why wouldn't you make it your top priority to assemble a *Manhattan Project*-like team to design and build a global-scale government-issued digital currency system, thus using technology superiority rather than military might to defeat the Goliath of financial power you've been fighting for the last seventy-five years?

Now I know what you're probably thinking ... Secret "Manhattan Project" style efforts? Clandestine foreign government initiatives designed to undermine the power of the U.S. Government? Is this going to be a serious book about digital currency or just more "conspiracy theories"? Admittedly the last few paragraphs sound a bit conspiratorial—even to me!

But please ask yourself... If what I've said is just a bunch of nonsensical conspiracy theory, then why is the People's Bank of China (the Chinese central bank) actively hiring blockchain engineers (a widely publicized fact), and why are they being so quiet about what these people are actually working on? Why did Sergei Glaziev—the father of de-dollarization—recently give a keynote speech at a blockchain conference in Europe? And why did the Chinese central bank file more patents relating to digital currency than anyone else in 2017? *Something's going on here.*

A new "space race" is coming

Space travel was anticipated by science fiction writers and futurists more than one hundred years before it became reality. But nobody took it seriously. In the 1950s, everyone knew about flying saucers, ray-guns, and little green men from Mars. But it was just science fiction.

Until October 4th, 1957, that is. When Russia's *Sputnik* satellite orbited the earth, suddenly it wasn't science fiction any more. *It was science reality, and the Russians were in the lead.* The military implications were staggering—whoever controlled space could easily win the Cold War. The U.S. Government's new top priority was to figure out how Russia got the lead, and how to take it back. *Suddenly, nothing was more important.* The space race was on.

A new *space race* has already begun, and the grand prize goes to whichever nation is first to develop and roll out a global-scale government-issued digital currency system which will serve as the world's global reserve currency for many decades to come. It's only logical to expect other nations to engineer such a system for the express purpose of displacing the U.S. dollar. The *Challengers* are a real threat the U.S. Government.

I'm convinced The Challengers are already hard at work on this agenda—and when the U.S. Government finally wakes up and smells the coffee, it will respond with a massive initiative of its own to compete. The new-era *space race* will be on.

What will happen to cryptocurrencies—which were designed to serve as an *alternative* to government-issued money? It's going to be very interesting to find out. One very real possibility is that governments will seek to outlaw cryptocurrency completely, because they'll want their own government-issued digital currencies to enjoy a monopoly.

Many people in the crypto community believe that cryptocurrencies will evolve to reach a global scale, and that the replacement for the U.S. dollar as global reserve currency will be Bitcoin or another cryptocurrency. I don't think those expectations are realistic for several reasons, but anything is possible.

If the crypto community wants to have a crack at one of their cryptocurrencies eventually becoming the global digital reserve currency system, it will need to start paying much closer attention to the design of conventional currency systems, and create a cryptocurrency to offer features more attractive than the Dollar for denominating central bank reserve assets. One of my goals in writing this book was to provide at least an initial understanding of the factors that influence conventional monetary system design and reserve currency selection.

Suppose that I'm right and we do eventually get to the point where the U.S. is pitted against Russia and China in a race to create the world's new digital global reserve currency. Who will the rest of the world side with? Just a few years ago it would have been a safe assumption that Europe would side with the U.S.—but remember that outrage over the SWIFT system that led Germany to make its August 2018 announcement. The world is becoming sick and tired of the U.S. having near-complete control.

A global digital currency system backed by the U.S. Government would almost certainly have the effect of dramatically *increasing* the degree of authority and control the U.S. already enjoys over the world financial system. On the other hand, any digital currency issued and controlled by *The Challengers* would dramatically *decrease* U.S. hegemony, while giving Russia and/or China much *more* power. Who is the rest of the world more likely to side with? The answer is far less clear today than it would have been just a few years ago.

So what's the rest of this book about?

First I'm going to give you a brief introduction to the history of money and currency systems, as this is essential to understanding digital currency in proper context. Next we'll cover *Distributed Ledger Technology*, and blockchain in particular. Then I'm going to introduce you to Bitcoin—the first cryptocurrency. I'll explain its features as well as offering considerable criticism about its longer-term viability. I'll also explain why nobody stands more to gain than Governments themselves when it comes to what digital currency technology has to offer.

But that's just the warm-up. From there we're going to go deep on money theory. Eight full chapters will give you a clear understanding of exactly how currency systems operate, and exactly what it means for a currency to serve as the world's global reserve currency. From there we'll return to digital currency, starting with a review of some of the advances made by other (non-Bitcoin) cryptocurrencies.

Finally, we'll take a deep dive into where digital currency is headed, and I'll present my own arguments for why I believe the "secret sauce" that will propel a digital currency system to the coveted status of global reserve currency will actually be the design of an integrated *digital sovereign bond market*. I'll also explain why I believe there is great risk of an Orwellian outcome, in which governments design digital currency systems to assert too much power and control over the governed.

A quick introduction to your author

I was a *distributed systems architect* and a software entrepreneur in my first career, so all the enabling technologies used to create cryptocurrencies are very familiar to me. I sold my software company and retired at the age of thirty-three, but soon "flunked retirement", got bored, and reinvented myself as a finance guy. In my second career I managed a hedge fund based on a macroeconomic investment theme. I've also spent quite a few years studying the International Monetary System. A particular fascination of mine has always been the U.S. dollar's hegemony over the rest of the financial system, and more specifically, how long it can last. These days I host a free weekly macroeconomics podcast called MacroVoices.[4]

Having this background first as a distributed systems technology expert, and then as a financial markets professional and devoted student of global macroeconomics, gives me a unique perspective on digital currency. While my finance buddies struggle to get their heads around cryptocurrency and figure out what the technology "geek speak" means, it's mostly old news to me. Similarly as I see the cryptocurrency experts easily out-do my own knowledge of distributed systems (which is now twenty years out of date—I retired from software in 1998), I can't help but notice that despite their superior grasp of the latest software technology, these guys usually have little understanding of the true significance of the global reserve currency status, and why the Dollar still enjoys it, or why so many powerful people around the globe are working hard to change that situation.

I believe that I can see the long-term digital currency story more clearly than almost anyone. At risk of sounding arrogant, ever since cryptocurrency became a "thing", I've felt like my peers can't see the forest beyond the trees. They're excited about this new investment asset class

---
[4] http://www.macrovoices.com/

called crypto and that's fine—except almost everyone is missing the much bigger story.

That's enough about me for this chapter. For those of you who care to learn more, I've written a full summary of my professional background in both distributed computing technology and in finance in Appendix A.

Chapter 2:
What is Money?

Ask most people whether they know what money is, and they'll look at you as if you'd gone crazy. After all, *everyone* "knows" what money is—we all use it every single day and it plays a central role in our lives. So the very notion that anyone, anywhere, might not know what money is would seem absurd.

But ask those very same people even the simplest questions to test their understanding of what money actually is, and they will usually have no idea. Why specifically do these colored pieces of paper issued by the government have so much more value than ordinary paper? How much money is there in total? What factors cause the total amount of money in existence to change? Does the government control how much money exists directly, or only indirectly? What mechanism does the government use to regulate the supply of money? Most people can't answer.

Tripartite Definition

The *tripartite definition of money* states that a currency system must satisfy three key criteria to serve as money:

Store of value

Money must offer a way to store value (savings) and preserve the purchasing power of those savings. In other words, the value of money, as measured by its ability to purchase other things, must remain relatively constant.

Some people correctly argue that currencies including the U.S. dollar which exhibit *inflation* over a long time period are not completely suitable as money, because inflation erodes the purchasing power of that money and therefore defeats its viability as a true *store of value*, at least over the long term.

The *Federal Reserve*, the central bank of the United States, was created in 1913 and given the mandate of maintaining "stable prices". In the 106 years since the Fed's inception, the U.S. dollar has lost more than 97% of its purchasing power—and no, that's not a typo—97%. But in the eyes of central bankers, this is considered a success, because that loss of purchasing power has, for the most part, occurred gradually over a long period of time with only a few relatively brief periods (such as the 1970s) when purchasing power eroded very quickly in the face of sustained high rates of inflation.

Many people have argued that the Fed's policy of encouraging low but consistently positive inflation rates (currently targeting 2% per annum) is a form of hidden tax which robs the people of most of the value of their savings. That criticism is well justified.

Unit of Account
Money must provide a way to keep track of the value of assets and liabilities. By breaking the primary unit of currency (the dollar) into equal-sized sub-units (cents) of relatively small value, the exact price or value of any asset or liability can be accurately accounted for.

Medium of Exchange
Money must provide a way for people to buy and sell goods and services without the need for barter (trading one product or service for another). This means that the currency itself must be sufficiently portable that it can be carried on one's person, and used to purchase goods and services. For this reason objects of value which cannot practically be carried around (such as fragile bird's eggs) cannot serve as money. Conversely, metal coins which are durable and easily identified are well suited to serving as money.

Types of Money: The Societal Complacency Cycle
Ok, so the "textbook definition" of money is that it must serve as a store of value, a unit of account, and a medium of exchange. Fair enough. But how does money actually derive its value and what does it actually represent? The answer is quite fascinating: throughout recorded history, societies have moved from *commodity money* to *representative money* to *fiat money*, and then (usually after a war or other major economic dislocation), the *fiat money* system collapses and the cycle starts anew with *commodity money* once again. I'll define these different kinds of money, and then explain what drives the cycle.

Commodity Money
The first type of money is known as *commodity money*. As the name implies, the idea is that some commodity which has *intrinsic value* is used as money. Considered perhaps the earliest known example of a unit of currency, dating back to 3000 B.C, the Mesopotamian *shekel* was equal to

approximately 160 grains of barley. Various cultures around the world have used everything from seashells to animal furs as money. The whole idea is to use something that has *intrinsic value*—people want to own the commodity itself because it can be used for other purposes, so they assign value to it.

Without a doubt the most popular and successful form of *commodity money* has always been metal coins, with gold and silver coins generally being preferred as the high-value denominations, and copper or other base-metal coins used for small denominations. The first known example of a society minting gold and silver bullion into coins with recognizable identifying patterns dates back to Lydia in the 6th century B.C.

A key concept to understand is that for more than 5,000 years, gold and silver have consistently proven themselves as a durable *store of value*. A fine suit of men's clothing costs approximately one troy ounce of gold, and that price has remained roughly constant for thousands of years. Nothing else on earth begins to compare with gold and silver bullion's proven track record as a reliable *store of value*. Furthermore, since these metals are dense and durable (and don't rot or mold like the barley used in ancient Mesopotamia), they are extremely well suited to being minted into coins and used as *commodity money*.

Commodity money derives its value principally from the *scarcity* of the commodity, and nothing is better suited to the job than gold bullion. Every single ounce of gold that has ever been mined in the history of the world would fit into just two Olympic-sized swimming pools. That's how rare gold itself is, so it's practical to carry a very large amount of monetary value in gold coins. For example, assuming a $1,200/ounce market price, one million U.S. dollars worth of gold bullion weighs about 57 lbs. (26kg)—an amount a single person could theoretically carry. In contrast, the same dollar value in Mesopotamian shekels would fill several railway cars full of barley!

Precious metals are preferred over diamonds and other precious gems because their value can be quickly determined simply by weight. A 1-ounce gold bullion coin is always worth exactly the same amount as two half-ounce gold coins. But when gemstones are used as money, determination of one stone's value compared to another is a very subjective process, and thus invites fraud.

While various other commodities have been used as money at various times in history, only gold and silver have consistently demonstrated their reliability as a *store of value* through thick and thin, including major wars and societal collapses. For these reasons, so-called *sound money advocates* have long argued that nothing but gold and silver coin should ever be used as money.

A phenomenon that has repeated over and over again throughout history is that when societies collapse or governments are destroyed after losing major wars, society almost always reverts to commodity money. For example, at the end of World War II, when national currencies were collapsing and paper money had no value, soldiers improvised and began using cigarettes as money. When all else fails, any commodity that has value and for which demand exists can be used as *commodity money*.

Representative Money

Representative Money is a close cousin to commodity money. Its origins trace back to the way that goldsmiths first began to offer depository services during periods of history when commodity money was in use. While in theory one person could lift a million dollars worth of gold, the silver coins were much heavier for the same purchasing value, and the copper coins were a real bear to carry around. In the era of pure commodity money, when gold and silver coin served as the primary money system, that money was heavy and impractical to carry.

Goldsmiths began offering secure storage services that worked like a coat check in a restaurant. You would go to the goldsmith and leave them a 1-ounce coin to store in their vault for safe-keeping, and the goldsmith would give you a claim check that read "This claim check can be redeemed for a 1-ounce gold coin at XYZ Goldsmiths". Eventually commercial banks would replace goldsmiths as the issuers of these claim checks. At first, the idea was just to be able to go back and claim your own gold coins which had been left in the bank or goldsmith's vault for safekeeping.

But people soon realized that the claim check had exactly the same value as the coin. So long as XYZ bank (or XYZ Goldsmith in the early days) had a good reputation, why would a merchant insist on payment with a heavy, awkward gold coin when it was so much easier just to accept the paper claim check, which entitled the merchant to later stop by XYZ bank and redeem a whole pile of gold coins that the claim checks *represented*?

These claim checks were originally known as *bank notes*, a phrase later shortened to the word *banknote*, which is the technically correct name for what most people call a "dollar bill"—a unit of paper currency. In the beginning, *banknotes* were issued by commercial banks. Later on, the system would be nationalized and the government would take over the function of issuing them.

It's absolutely critical to understand that nobody in their right mind would have accepted a piece of paper as money for the sake of the commodity value *of the paper itself*. That wasn't the point—everyone knows paper isn't worth very much. A *bank note* was a very special paper which *represented a claim* on a gold or silver bullion coin. That little piece of paper was literally "as good as gold" because it could be taken to the issuing bank and exchanged for a gold bullion coin at any time.

The Gold Standard: Modern Age Representative Money
There was a problem with the *bank note* system of representative money: if one particular bank were to fail (say, after a robbery), the bank notes it had issued would become worthless, causing losses to many innocent people. Governments responded by nationalizing the depository services that were previously offered by goldsmiths and then banks, at the same time guaranteeing that the government would always honor the claim. The bank-issued "bank note" was replaced by the government-issued *banknote*—the *dollar bill*.

The original version of this system worked just like the prior system of bank notes issued by commercial banks: For each and every *banknote* in circulation, the government had gold or silver bullion in a vault somewhere. This system became known as the *gold standard*[5], meaning that the government issues paper money, but every single paper *banknote* is "backed" by gold or silver bullion in a government vault.

Most governments issuing paper money under a gold standard offered a *redemption privilege*, meaning that any citizen who chooses to can show up at a government treasury office at any time, turn in their paper money, and receive gold or silver bullion in return right then and there, no questions asked. Once again, the paper money truly is "as good as gold", because every single paper banknote *represents* a unit of physical bullion stored in a vault somewhere, which the holder of the paper money can exchange into physical bullion form at any time.

Because a true *gold standard* requires that every paper banknote be backed by physical gold or silver bullion, the money supply of such a

---

[5] Technically, the phrase "gold standard" refers to money being defined as gold itself. But in practice, in modern times, the phrase "gold standard" includes representative money systems in which every single unit of paper currency is backed by actual gold bullion in a vault somewhere.

currency system is limited in exactly the same way it would be limited under a pure *commodity money* system. The only way to increase the amount of money in circulation is to mine more gold or silver bullion, and add it to the vault. Only then can more representative banknotes be printed to correspond to that bullion.

This means that the government has no way to increase the supply of paper money in circulation unless gold mines are able to produce and refine more gold bullion. And that begs a very important question: *Is it a good thing or a bad thing that the government is unable to increase the paper money supply under a gold standard?*

No surprise, the answer is a highly subjective matter of opinion.

So-called *sound money advocates* have long argued that the discipline a gold standard enforces on the government is the single most important *benefit* of the system. They argue that governments are always prone to spending beyond their means, so therefore, giving any government the ability to arbitrarily print more paper money out of thin air is asking for trouble. Their conclusion is that the only "honest" representative money system is a true *gold standard*, and that any system which allows government to increase the money supply in any way other than mining and vaulting more gold and silver bullion to support the additional paper money supply equates to defrauding the public.

The opposing view is that government *needs* the ability to arbitrarily increase the money supply to contend with national emergencies. John Maynard Keynes, a very prominent economist in the early 20th century, suggested that the gold standard was the *principal cause* of the Great Depression of the 1930s. To this day, many Keynesian economists state this view as if it were an immutable fact: The cause of the Great Depression was the gold standard in place at the time, because it meant that the government was helpless to increase the money supply to fight deflation in the economy.

To make such an assertion as a *matter of fact* is about as credible as saying that the anti-war movement of the late 1960s and early 1970s was caused by *The Beatles*. In each case there is a plausible argument to justify such an *opinion*, but to state it as unequivocal *fact* is ludicrous. But economists are an odd bunch. They describe their field as a *soft science*. I've worked with quite a few scientists in my career, and I know *science* when I see it. The field of Economics bears more similarity to religion than to science.

The key point to understand is that there's considerable disagreement on whether governments being powerless to increase the money supply without mining more bullion is a bug or a feature.

Gold Convertibility: The first step in exploiting societal complacency
Assume that most people in society either remember when commodity money (gold and silver coin) was in use, or if nothing else, their grandparents told them about it. So everybody still understands that for a paper banknote to truly have any value there has to be some gold bullion in a vault somewhere backing it. That's what the *gold standard* means, right?

But this is one of those "fine print" games. Suppose the government figures out that very few people in society are going to actually redeem their paper banknotes for physical bullion. The government exploits this condition of *societal complacency* by quietly replacing the *gold standard* with a *gold convertibility standard*. This is precisely the change that economist John Maynand Keynes was influential in bringing about after the Great Depression.[6]

What's the difference? Under both systems, every person holding a paper banknote still has the legal right to show up at a government office and demand that it be redeemed for the gold or silver bullion it *represents*. But there's just one little detail most people don't even notice—the government doesn't actually have anything close to enough gold to allow everyone to redeem all the banknotes (dollar bills) the government printed and placed in circulation.

Sure, they have some gold on hand to placate those few people who feel inclined to exercise their *conversion right,* but in reality there isn't anywhere close to enough gold to cover all the paper money in circulation. *The consequence of this is that if a large percentage of the populous suddenly wanted to redeem their paper money for gold, the government would be forced to change the rules and deny the redemptions.* The only way they can service redemptions is if those redemptions remain an unusual occurrence—demand is low.

So the difference is that the government doesn't have to possess enough gold to equal the banknotes distributed. Only enough, "just in case".

---

[6] The gold exchange standard applied to the Dollar by the 1944 Bretton Woods treaty was more restrictive than described here, and applied only to foreign governments. I'll elaborate on this in Chapter 14.

The reason that few people object to the change from *gold standard* to *gold convertibility standard* is that in both systems they *are* guaranteed by law the right to redeem their paper banknotes for physical gold or silver bullion at any time.[7] So long as they have that *right*, who cares how much gold the government has? Surely the people running the government are responsible adults, and they must be ensuring that at least as much gold as is needed is always available, right?

The reality is that the value of everyone's money is actually the total value of all the gold and silver in the vaults divided by the number of paper banknotes (and their stated value) in circulation. If the government increases the money supply by 10% by printing up more banknotes, they are devaluing everyone's savings by 10%, because there is now the same amount of bullion backing *more* paper banknotes. But few laymen grasp this concept. They still have a banknote that is worth the same number of dollars, so they see no reason for concern.

The risk is that the government will print so many banknotes that smart people will insist on taking their gold back. This is exactly what happened to the U.S. dollar in the late 1960s. The Dollar (which had been under a true gold standard prior to the Great Depression) had been changed to a gold *convertibility* standard after the Great Depression, thanks in large part to the efforts of John Maynard Keynes.

At first there was only a little more paper currency in circulation than the gold required to support the banknotes distributed, so there was no problem. But by the late 1960s, the U.S. Government had so badly abused "deficit spending"—mostly to fund the Vietnam War—that investors around the world recognized that the Dollar was no longer worth the gold it supposedly represented.

The result: the French government exercised its legal right to convert their U.S. dollar holdings to gold bullion at the guaranteed fixed conversion rate of $35 per troy ounce of gold bullion. Suddenly it became clear to the U.S. Government that a "run on the gold reserves of the nation" was underway. What was really going on was that astute French officials recognized the dollar had been devalued by the U.S. Government's reckless overspending on the Vietnam War without increasing taxes to pay for that expenditure. They knew that to protect their own citizens, it was in their

---

[7] These statements are true of a gold convertibility standard generally, but the Bretton Woods system applied to the U.S. Dollar from 1944 to 1971 was more restrictive and did not apply to private citizens. Chapter 14 will explain this in detail.

Chapter 2:
What is Money?

best interest to exercise their legal right to redeem their dollars for gold while they still could.[8]

This all came to a head on August 15th, 1971, when President Nixon famously "suspended temporarily" the convertibility of dollars for Gold, effectively defaulting on the Bretton Woods treaty which had served as the foundation of the International Monetary System since 1944. Forty-seven years later, that "temporary" suspension remains in effect today, and free market price discovery shows that the actual value of the Dollar has since declined to 1/1200th of an ounce of gold (as of this writing), as opposed to the 1/35th of an ounce conversion rate that had been guaranteed under the Bretton Woods gold convertibility standard.

To my thinking, changing from the gold standard to a gold *convertibility* standard is the first step in a progressive societal confidence game. The cycle began with everyone agreeing that it didn't make sense to treat anything as *money* other than gold and silver coin, or a banknote *that was actually backed by gold or silver coin.* And that made perfect logical sense.

But now suppose that this system remains in place for several generations—to the point that nobody living remembers the days when physical bullion coins (commodity money) were still in common use. Everyone is used to paying with paper—for our entire lives, paper has worked as money. *Nobody has reason to question its value.* We all pay for things with paper—and get products and services in return.

Eventually, only a few people in society still understand that the paper itself has no real value unless it is backed by corresponding bullion in a vault somewhere. And that leads to a societal complacency which is likely to soon be exploited. The first step in that exploitation is to replace the gold standard with a gold convertibility standard. To almost everyone, it seems as if nothing has changed. Their paper money is still guaranteed by law to be convertible to gold any time they want the gold. Why should they worry?

The answer is that the 1971 outcome was entirely predictable. In fact, quite a few people predicted that exact outcome when arguing against John Maynard Keynes when he lobbied the international community to move from a gold standard to a gold convertibility standard offered exclusively to foreign governments. But rightly or wrongly, Keynes won the argument at the time.

---

[8] There were also geopolitical factors, such as the U.S. response to the Suez crisis, which may have affected France's decision.

Fiat Money: Completing the Societal Complacency Exploitation
Fiat Money is the kind of money which has been in circulation throughout most of the world ever since Nixon's "temporary suspension" of the gold convertibility standard in August of 1971. Fiat money has no backing or *conversion right* whatsoever. Quite literally, fiat money is paper currency with an *intrinsic value of zero*, which derives all of its purchasing power from the government enacting *legal tender laws*, which stipulate that this paper money must be accepted to settle all public and private debts. This is precisely the reason that each and every U.S. banknote (dollar bill) has the words *"THIS NOTE IS LEGAL TENDER FOR ALL DEBTS, PUBLIC AND PRIVATE"* printed on it.

What this actually means is that if anyone were to object to the fact that, after August 15th 1971, the dollar's "guaranteed" convertibility to gold at a fixed rate of $35 per ounce was suddenly no longer guaranteed (or honored at all), well, tough luck. If they are owed $350 under the old system where that $350 was worth 10 ounces of gold, they still have to accept $350 of *Legal Tender* instead, which was now convertible into exactly nothing. By law, nobody had the choice to say, "Hey, I don't want to take your payment in dollars because last week $350 dollars were as good as 10 ounces of gold, but this week they're just pieces of paper". Under *legal tender* laws, if *legal tender* has been offered and refused, the court will consider the debt to be extinguished.

Now I know what you're probably thinking: how could any of this possibly be true? Recall that this story began with everyone in society agreeing that it never made sense to accept anything other than gold and silver coin (or a banknote redeemable for that same gold and silver coin) as money. And that wisdom was informed by knowledge of prior fiat money experiments collapsing in a way that caused everyone to lose their savings! So given that predisposition, how could it ever be possible, even over a period of a million years, that people would eventually just calmly accept that the gold-convertible *representative money* system had suddenly been replaced one day (Aug. 15, 1971 to be precise) by a new system where money was nothing more than paper—that was redeemable for precisely *nothing?* And not just any system, but the *same fiat money system* that had led to numerous past currency collapses throughout history!

Am I really asking you to believe that an entire society would just accept such a profound change without serious objection? Just because the President issued an executive order one day, forcing everyone to accept *fiat money* despite its *intrinsic value* of precisely zero? Yes.

Chapter 2:
What is Money?

The explanation is that it doesn't take a *million* years, but it does take quite a few years. By that time, society has been conditioned for several generations to accept paper currency as having the same value as real money. From that day in 1971 when President Nixon moved the U.S. from *representative money* to *fiat money*, there was no longer a true *representative money* system—but nobody really noticed because the concept of paper money always having value, regardless of any changes to the monetary system supporting it, was entrenched in our thinking.

For your entire life, those colored pieces of paper in your wallet had always worked— been accepted as payment for goods and services. You had no reason to question their value unless you really thought it through carefully, which few people did. And unless you happened to be a monetary history buff, you would have no way of knowing that in almost every case in the past where governments created fiat money systems, eventually the value of that money collapsed to zero.

President Nixon wasn't about to panic the world by telling the truth and admitting that the U.S. government had borrowed and spent beyond its means, prompting rational governments around the world to convert their U.S. dollar holdings to gold. Instead he blamed 'international money speculators' for causing 'volatility' in markets, and assured the American People that a 'necessary' measure to deal with these 'speculators' was to 'suspend temporarily' the convertibility of dollars into gold.

There was no announcement that the *intrinsic value* of every dollar of your savings had just been changed from 1/35th of an ounce of gold to *zero*. Similarly there was no announcement that this change would pave the way for more reckless government spending and would ultimately unleash the Great Inflation of the 1970s, which proved debilitating to the global economy. And to be sure, President Nixon didn't find it necessary to mention in his television address that this action amounted to defaulting on Bretton Woods, the international treaty serving as the foundation of the International Monetary System since the end of World War II.

Based on what President Nixon actually said on television, most people saw no cause for concern. The President was just dealing with some pesky 'speculators'. The green dollar bills in their wallets still bought a six-pack of beer. No big deal—what's the problem?

Sound money advocates are fond of quoting the statistic that there have been more than 3,000 fiat currency systems in recorded history, and every single one of them has eventually collapsed to its intrinsic value: zero. The implication is that anyone still holding their savings in those currencies *will* lose those savings. However, it stands to reason that most people preserve at least *some* of their savings by spending the last of their money or converting it to another currency before the final collapse.

Obviously the statement that every single fiat currency has always collapsed to zero is not accurate. The French Franc didn't collapse to zero before it was replaced by the Euro, for example. Likewise there was a period around the Civil War when the U.S. Greenback was pure fiat, but was then converted back to a gold redemption standard. It didn't collapse to zero value in the interim. And of course the fiat currency systems like the Dollar and the Euro we use today haven't collapsed *yet*. The real claim being made by sound money advocates is that when governments have replaced commodity or representative money systems with pure fiat, *eventually* the fiat currencies collapse and *then everyone loses savings still held in those fiat currencies.*

That's a sobering perspective when you consider that since 1971 almost all of the world's currency systems have been based on pure *fiat money*. Most people today would scoff at any implication that our money could suddenly become worthless. Sure, maybe hundreds of years ago there might have been examples of these *fiat money* systems collapsing to zero value and everyone losing their life's savings in the process. But surely, nothing like that could ever occur in the United States ... could it?

Actually, it *has* happened in the United States, several times. There were several colonial fiat currency systems which collapsed entirely prior to the signing of the *Declaration of Independence*. Everyone holding those currencies lost all of their savings. After the Revolutionary War began in 1775, the U.S. Government's official currency was known as the *Continental Dollar*, a pure fiat currency. By 1781, *Continentals* had become completely worthless. This painful experience with fiat currency led to the addition of the *gold and silver clause* to the U.S. Constitution (Article 1, Section 8). This clause expressly forbids the individual *states* from "making anything but gold and silver coin legal tender in the payment of debts".

The idea was to make sure the states would never get away with trying to issue a fiat currency ever again. Apparently nobody thought it necessary to include the federal government in the list of organizations that needed to be held accountable under the Constitution to avoid another mishap with *fiat money*.

The Societal Complacency Cycle

This cycle has repeated over and over throughout recorded monetary history, but we never seem to learn our lesson. As noted earlier, the sound money crowd claims that every single prior example of a *fiat* money system has eventually collapsed to its intrinsic value of *zero*, and everyone holding savings in that currency lost 100% of the value of those savings. That sort of thing makes an awfully strong impression on people, and the result is usually that after such an event, society rightly insists on using nothing other than gold and silver coin as money—because for thousands of years it has always performed flawlessly as a *store of value*. Suddenly those sound money advocates who had previously been dismissed as goldbug nut-cases look like the smartest guys in the room.

The collapse of the *Continental Dollar* currency in 1781 led not only to a return to *commodity money*, but to the addition of a clause to the newly formed U.S. Constitution, prohibiting the states from ever allowing anything other than gold and silver coin to serve as money. There are many other examples of essentially the same thing happening throughout history.

The cycle is always the same. After the catastrophic collapse of any fiat currency, nobody in their right mind is willing to even consider using anything but gold and silver coin as money. That societal attitude lasts for a generation or so, but then those coins become awfully heavy to carry around. It's a pretty easy sell to persuade a society to again let go of holding gold and silver coin in favor of a *representative* money system under the gold standard. After all, every single unit of currency is backed by real bullion in a vault somewhere. The paper banknotes are just a convenience that allows everyone to carry something lighter in their pocket, while the gold and silver coins they represent remain safely in a vault.

Once the shift is made to *representative money*, the day-to-day experience of everyone in society is that these colored pieces of paper issued by the government reliably operate as money. Maybe at first, the "old timers" still remember the last fiat collapse, and they caution their children never to trust anything but a true gold standard. But in the long run their wisdom is lost. After a few more generations, paper money still works just fine. The fact that the only reason it apparently works so reliably is that the paper money *was* backed by a true gold standard is a subtle nuance that's lost on most people. The complacency this breeds opens the door for government to change to fiat money.

Sometimes the shift from a true gold standard to pure fiat occurs in a single step, and in other cases a gold *convertibility* standard has existed between the gold standard and the fiat system. But the one thing that seems to remain constant throughout history is that the shift to pure fiat almost *never* happens when there are still plenty of people living who remember the last collapse. So long as these "old-timers" are around to warn society of the dangers of pure fiat currency, it's seldom been adopted. It's only once they're gone that government-issued, worthless paper money is once again accepted.

Whether the shift from *representative money* to *fiat money* occurred in 1965, 1971, or 1976 is a matter of opinion that comes down to arguing semantics of exactly what constitutes fiat money. But one way or another, the whole world has been running on *pure fiat* since 1976, if not earlier.

If you doubt me, by all means fact-check what I've said here. Regardless, it should now be clear why the "crypto community" thought that an alternative to government-issued fiat currency might be a good idea.

As you start to assimilate an understanding of digital money, you'll begin developing a model of how digital currency compares to other kinds of money—including any historical context—and how it might fit in based on where we are in the commodity-fiat cycle. As you read on, keep in mind your understanding of *commodity, representative,* and *fiat* money systems.

Conclusions

Astute readers may have noticed that only a few of the questions I posed in the second paragraph of this chapter have been answered thus far. I fully intend to answer all of those questions—I'm quite passionate about doing so. But here's the rub: You need to know *quite a lot* about conventional money systems to grasp the full extent of opportunity that exists for digital currency to completely change the world. But I know that most of you are too excited to learn about *digital* currency to endure much more background material before getting to the meat of what digital currency is all about.

So next we're going to explore just the basics of cryptocurrency, the first incarnation of *digital currency.* After that, you'll have a solid introduction to both digital *and* conventional money systems.

Then it will be time to really "go deep". We'll cover all the monetary and conventional currency concepts you need to understand in full detail, including a thorough discussion of what a *global reserve currency* is, and why right now is a particularly ripe moment in history for something else to come along and take that title away from the U.S. dollar. Then finally, we'll move well beyond the current generation of cryptocurrencies and discuss what the future is likely to hold for global-scale digital currency systems, who is likely to build them, and what features and benefits they're likely to offer above and beyond today's conventional currency systems.

40   Beyond Blockchain: The Death of the Dollar and the Rise of Digital Currency

Chapter 3: The Origins and Culture of Cryptocurrency

We'll be delving into what Bitcoin and blockchain are and how they work, but first, it's really important to understand some context—what led to their invention and what motivated the inventors. Likewise, it's important to grasp that cryptocurrency is not just technology, and it's not just a new form of money. An entire *culture* has evolved around cryptocurrency. Knowing its origins and ideology will help make sense of why its inventors are not the slightest bit inclined to support a government-issued digital currency.

Why is all of this business about the *culture* of cryptocurrency significant? Because the crypto guys *passionately* believe that cryptocurrencies will evolve to replace conventional currency systems, and that governments will no longer be in charge of the money system. But I think it's very unlikely to go the way they expect, and that the inventors of cryptocurrency will eventually regret their invention when they realize how it will ultimately be used.

An analogy is the experience of Swedish chemist Alfred Nobel. Nobel was an ardent inventor. His most famous achievement was motivated by a desire to improve safety in the mining industry. In Nobel's day, miners used raw nitro glycerin as an explosive to break up large rock formations. Nitro glycerin in raw form is incredibly unstable and dangerous, and fatal mining accidents were commonplace. Nobel worked on finding a better way and discovered that nitro glycerin could be made far more stable if it was absorbed in an inert material, such as sawdust. He patented the invention of "dynamite" in 1867. His brothers Ludvig and Robert used dynamite to become leaders in the early days of the oil industry, making all three men very rich.

When Nobel's brother Ludvig died in 1888, several newspapers erroneously published Alfred Nobel's obituary—Alfred was still very much alive and well—condemning him for all of the death resulting from the weaponization of dynamite. Nobel was so distressed by the thought that this would be how he would be remembered that he bequeathed a substantial part of the fortune he'd amassed to create the *Nobel Prize*, designed to recognize people who used their inventive talents to do good for humanity.

So what's the analogy? Cryptocurrency, the people who invented it, and the culture that has arisen around it, are all focused on one thing: using technology to *reduce* the power of government to monitor and control private citizens' financial affairs. But just like dynamite, my prediction is that others will use these inventions for purposes opposite those intended by the inventors. They'll use digital currency to *increase* the power of government. And Satoshi's inventions will have made it all possible.

This is inevitable. The proverbial cat is out of the bag, and the inventions of *distributed ledger* and *double spend-proof digital cash* are now well-known. It's only a matter of time before governments use these inventions to create government-issued digital currency. That could markedly improve the antiquated global monetary system and deliver terrific benefits to society. But it will also enable governments to attain increased control over private citizens' financial affairs.

I certainly don't endorse the latter outcome, and I agree with the crypto crowd that if government is in charge, the result is likely to seriously threaten individual liberty. But while that part concerns me, I'm convinced government-issued digital money is coming. The benefits could be tremendous for society. The crypto community would do well to get involved, because it *will* happen with or without them—and their involvement might help the ultimate outcome look a little closer to Satoshi's vision of the future than George Orwell's version.

The Cypherpunk Movement

So how did all of this come about? A group known as the *cypherpunks* formed in San Francisco in 1992. Its purpose was to unite like-minded people who shared the belief that privacy is an essential human right in a free society, and that responsible citizens should use encryption technology wherever possible to protect themselves from governments abusing their power and violating the individual's rights.

The basic values and beliefs of cypherpunks are laid out in Eric Hughes' 1993 missive, *A Cypherpunk's Manifesto.*[9] Perhaps the most controversial cypherpunk is Julian Assange, founder of Wikileaks.

---

[9] https://www.activism.net/cypherpunk/manifesto.html

Chapter 3:
The Origins and Culture of Cryptocurrency

The cypherpunks movement began almost a full decade before 9/11, so needless to say the increase in government monitoring of private citizens' financial transactions since 9/11 has only further enraged the cypherpunks.

The cypherpunks' first major achievement was to make military-grade data encryption technology available to everyone. Cypherpunk Phil Zimmerman created *Pretty Good Privacy*[10] *(*a.k.a *PGP),* a free computer program that gave anyone a level of data encryption technology similar to what the U.S. Government uses for military operations. Suddenly everyone from libertarian privacy buffs to organized criminals had access to the same kind of secure data communications the CIA used for its covert operations.

The cypherpunks have often been willing to break the law when they believe the law itself to be a violation of their rights. In the case of PGP, when that program was first created, encryption technology was classified as a *munition* and therefore illegal to export beyond U.S. borders without a license.

After a long legal battle, the cypherpunks found a very clever way to work around this: *they printed the program out on paper,* and argued the computer program was a written *work of art*, protected under the 1st Amendment of the U.S. Constitution. They won that legal battle, and thus made military-grade data encryption technology available to the world.

That was prior to 9/11. I doubt they'd have won today, given the changes we've seen in public attitude toward allowing government more authority to regulate such matters in the name of fighting terrorism.

The early activities of the cypherpunks could be categorized as *defensive warfare.* The cypherpunks believed they were victims of crimes perpetrated by governments *breaking their own laws* to violate the privacy of their citizens.

Then cypherpunk Julian Assange took the battle to the next level with Wikileaks. Where prior cypherpunk activities were defensive in nature, Assange went on the offensive. He targeted governments he suspected of breaking their own laws, then broke some of those laws himself to collect and publicize evidence of criminal acts being committed by those governments and their law enforcement agencies.

So how should we think about these cypherpunks? Are they just shady characters with a long criminal record who should be punished for the many times they've broken the law? Or is it more accurate to characterize

---

[10] https://en.wikipedia.org/wiki/Pretty_Good_Privacy

them as patriotic heroes of modern society, risking their own freedom to protect the rest of us from corrupt governments?

Much of the evidence Wikileaks discovered was obtained by breaking the law, making Wikileaks itself guilty of crimes. Whether legally obtained or not, that evidence has been damning, and clearly shows a consistent pattern of governments (and law enforcement agencies in particular) breaking their own laws in the course of enforcing the law on others.

So *are* Wikileaks and the rest of the cypherpunk movement heroes or villains?

In the eyes of many, Assange and NSA Whistleblower Edward Snowden are public enemies who should be hanged by the neck until dead in a public ceremony. To others, they are the greatest patriotic heroes of our time, and deserve full Presidential pardons for any crimes committed in the course of doing the right thing for humanity. Some have even suggested they deserve a Nobel Prize. It's truly amazing that society can be as divided as it has become in recent years with respect to how we should view people who break the law to expose the government's corruption—which in many cases has been irrefutable.

So the first really big accomplishment of the cypherpunks was to give everyone access to military-grade encryption technology. And to be sure, that has enabled some significant criminal activity. For example, drug cartels routinely use PGP to protect their communications.

But encrypted communications was never that big of a technical challenge. The algorithms were quite well known in computer science circles. The cypherpunks had to fight City Hall (and the NSA and CIA) to legalize *export* of PGP, but figuring out how to engineer an e-mail encryption program in the first place was never particularly difficult.

Digital Currency: The Cypherpunks' greatest challenge

The cypherpunks always knew the real *coup d'état* would be to figure out a way to bypass the commercial banking system and make it possible to make *payments of money* (including international payments) from one party to another in such a way that the government would never know.

Most undertakings require spending money to make them happen. Whether the activity is an illegal drug-running operation, or a perfectly legal campaign to promote public awareness of government corruption, you can't make much progress without spending money. And the instant you do, law enforcement has plenty of tools to monitor and trace those

Chapter 3:
The Origins and Culture of Cryptocurrency

payment transactions back to you. That's one of their most effective techniques to track down all manner of bad guys.

Does that make a government-resistant payment system a bad thing? It's well known that a black market has developed where you can buy illegal drugs on the dark web, pay for them in Bitcoin, and the criminals will express mail your drugs to you. I'm told you can also buy myriad other illegal services on the dark web—including hiring a hit man—and pay for those illegal services in Bitcoin. Do we want this kind of thing to be possible?

Regardless of which side of this philosophical divide you or I might stand on, one thing is clear: the cypherpunks see themselves as heroes. They view governments as the real criminals, and saw it as their patriotic duty to invent and popularize first PGP (encryption) and now cryptocurrency to help society protect itself from government abusing its power.

Providing secure *communications* was easy. But a secure payment system that would hide money transfers (including international payments) from prying government eyes? Now that's a much harder problem to solve. The primary challenge was to perfect an invention that software engineers and computer scientists had been struggling with for years: *Digital Cash*. Now, you might be thinking that systems like PayPal have been around for many years, but that's not true Digital Cash—I'll explain that distinction later.

After more than twenty years of trying to perfect a true digital cash system, someone finally figured out how to overcome a key design challenge known as the *double-spending problem*. This was a significant breakthrough, and fear of government retribution may have been one reason why whoever finally solved the problem decided to publish their work pseudonymously—Satoshi Nakamoto.

"Crypto Community": Cypherpunks Movement goes Mainstream

Many people have become interested in cryptocurrency for many different reasons. To a large extent, the so-called *crypto community* bears a lot of resemblance and shares philosophical values with the cypherpunks who worked so hard figuring out how to perfect digital cash.

In cypherpunk culture, adopting a pseudonym or "screen name" is very common. In fact, using your real name in online forums can undermine your credibility within the cypherpunk community. Obviously, you don't understand the privacy risks. If you ask someone to e-mail you privately in a cypherpunk discussion forum, you provide them with your *PGP public key* to encrypt the message. What's a PGP Public Key? Dude, if you don't already know, you *must* be one of those people who "doesn't get it" yet.

The crypto community isn't quite as hardcore, but lots of the same cultural values carry over. Many in the crypto world use pseudonyms for everything they do, while others such as researchers who hope to promote, say, their next book are much more likely to use their real names.

Now you might wonder, if some of these people routinely live behind pseudonyms and encrypt all their e-mail communications, surely they must be engaged in criminal activity. After all, unless they have something to hide, why would they behave that way? The answer is they believe governments violate everyone's privacy all the time, and the only defense is to encrypt everything—yes, even when they have absolutely nothing to hide.

The widely held view is that every citizen has not only the right, but some would go so far as to argue the *civic duty,* to protect everything they do from prying government eyes. They conduct themselves as anonymously as possible in every aspect of their online lives and in their financial affairs, because they believe it's an obligation to resist what they see as completely unjust overreach of government authority.

The crypto community's distrust doesn't end with governments. It applies to all large institutions, including big banks. The widely held view of the crypto crowd is that society would be a lot better off with less centralization, and less control of our lives by centralized authority figures of any kind. That includes governments, big banks, and anything else centralized.

Cryptocurrency – a truly brilliant feat of software engineering, by the way – was created to provide both a currency (money) system and an electronic payment network that allows both domestic and international payments to be made in that currency, almost anonymously.

The view of cryptocurrency's inventors and many of its users is that any centralized authority is the enemy of free society, and that the people of the world have the right to protect themselves by using cryptocurrency as an alternative to the government-issued money system that forms the basis of the international commercial banking network.

The main point I want to impress upon you is that cryptocurrency isn't just something some guy invented one day to satisfy his own personal paranoia. Rather, it's something a very well organized movement (the cypherpunks) literally toiled for decades trying to perfect—and not just to make a few bucks. No, their aspirations were far greater in scale. They wanted to change the world and make it better (in their perception) by creating a superior alternative to government-issued money.

These people are on a *mission* to free society from what they see as ongoing abuse by corrupt governments. Regardless of whether you personally agree with that view, please understand that these people are serious, they're passionate, and they believe they are saving humanity from great injustice. They are deeply invested emotionally, and in terms of spending money, time and effort, all to create something they *believe in*. Something that offers people the choice to free themselves from government oppression, and to exercise their right of privacy in their financial affairs.

Ok, why am I making such a big deal over this? Because when someone like me comes along and says that nobody stands more to gain from the inventions of distributed ledger and digital cash than *governments*, that kind of talk borders on treason in the eyes of many in the crypto community. The governments are the bad guys—the establishment. Down with the establishment!!! And for me to suggest that a *good* opportunity exists to radically improve the global financial system by creating government-issued mainstream digital currency systems, that's the absolute last thing most people in the crypto community want to hear. That's centralization!

Label me as the enemy if you must, but please consider the facts. Like it or not, Satoshi's inventions are now widely publicized and well understood. They have already been used to create several new money systems.

The crypto community believes in its mission—with religious conviction. That mission is to create an alternative to government-issued money. They fully expect to show the rest of the world that this is a better way. And they expect that as soon as they do, the good people of the world will come together and all start using cryptocurrency instead of government-issued money. They are firmly of the belief that the world will be a better place when that happens, and are quick to dismiss the counter-argument that governments will probably outlaw cryptocurrencies entirely as soon as they figure out how much of a threat they truly pose to government's monopoly.

They're so dedicated to this mission that they don't have time (nor do they even care) to discuss minor details like the fact that for several thousand years of recorded monetary history, governments have controlled who issues the money, and that governments aren't likely to give up that license any time soon. The crypto community for the most part believes that they're already well on the way to replacing government-issued money with something much better.

My view is quite different. To my thinking, the only reason cryptocurrencies have gotten away with coining their own money for a full decade now without being shut down by governments is that government is so slow, inefficient and bureaucratic that they have yet to even figure out what cryptocurrency is and the full extent of the risk it poses to their control over society. When they eventually do, storm clouds will form over cryptocurrency, and all those rainbows and unicorns will disappear very quickly.

But until that happens, few in the crypto community are interested in even discussing what I think is a far more likely outcome—that governments will embrace digital currency for their own use while outlawing cryptocurrency. I'm convinced we're ultimately headed toward re-engineering the mainstream global monetary system to benefit from digital currency technology. Society badly *needs* the crypto community involved, otherwise the ultimate outcome will be enough to scare George Orwell out of his grave!

The crypto community needs to embrace the age-old wisdom, *if you can't beat 'em, join 'em.* After all, joining them is the only way to influence the outcome. But my sense is the crypto community has yet to realize *they can't beat 'em.* When they figure that out the hard way, I hope to persuade at least some of them that any government-issued digital currency initiative will be a whole lot better for society with their direct involvement than without it.

Chapter 4:
Distributed Ledger Technology

As I explained, the cypherpunks democratized secure message encryption technology in the early 1990s, and they'd been trying to figure out how to make *digital cash* work since about the same time. But the latter problem proved extremely difficult to solve.

You might be thinking, "Wait a minute, PayPal is basically a type of digital cash, and it's been around for a long time, so what's the problem?" But really, true digital cash never existed before Bitcoin. PayPal and dozens of similar systems work like a *check*. The electronic payment (check) has to be drawn on one PayPal account and deposited into another PayPal account. That means both parties to the transaction must have an account, and when the transaction occurs, a permanent audit trail is created showing the date and amount of the payment, and it identifies the participants.

The cypherpunks wanted to create an electronic payment system that worked like *cash*, as opposed to working like a *check*. They wanted the ability to take any amount of money and store the actual value in a file on a computer (or on a USB flash drive or even in an e-mail attachment[11]). In other words, just as you can hand a random stranger a hundred-dollar bill and walk away with no record of the payment having been created, and even without either party knowing the other's identity, the cypherpunks wanted to create true digital cash. They wanted a form of money that could be stored on a computer file and spent as easily as giving that file to someone else, without the need for either party to draw from or deposit into an established account linked to their legal identity.

At first glance it probably sounds like the challenge would be in figuring out how to design an electronic currency system that is functionally similar to cash. But designing the currency system itself (Bitcoin) was the easy part. Sure, the Bitcoin design includes some very creative technology innovations. For example, it uses *public/private-key encryption* to create something akin to a numbered Swiss bank account, where the identity of

---

[11] The mechanics of a Bitcoin payment don't actually involve sending a file containing money to the recipient of the payment. I'm describing it this way to illustrate the concept, and the actual details will be explained in the next chapter.

the account owner is never registered with the bank and a password is used to control the funds. But as creative as that might sound, it was pretty simple for the cypherpunks to figure out how to make such features work. They are expert at computer encryption technology, and for software engineers of their caliber, creating a really cool digital currency system was straightforward.

The big challenge came in figuring out how to store the data in a decentralized computer network. That was the hard part, and that's what took them well over a decade to figure out. Once they solved that problem, the rest was relatively easy. The phrase *Distributed Ledger* refers to a completely new kind of secure computer database. The distributed ledger system that underpins Bitcoin and several other cryptocurrencies is called *blockchain*. And it represents a breakthrough in computer science.

Before the invention of distributed ledger, virtually all computer systems used a *centralized architecture*, meaning that the database which contained all the information associated with the system was owned by some central authority. That central authority had more power and control over the data than anyone else. Blockchain changed all of that, and made Bitcoin and other cryptocurrencies possible.

The best way to comprehend the benefit of blockchain is to start by understanding why the old way of doing things wasn't good enough. Creating a digital currency system using a *centralized architecture* is very simple and straightforward. This diagram shows how it would work:

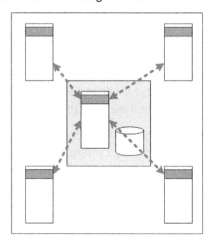

Figure 2 Digital Currency System with Centralized Architecture

Chapter 4: Distributed Ledger Technology

This diagram shows five computers, but there could be any number of computers participating in the network. The computer at the center of the diagram is a *server* with a master database (called a *ledger*) which keeps track of who owns each unit of digital currency in the system. Each time someone "spends" a digital "coin", a cryptographic security check makes sure the guy who spent it was the same guy the database had recorded as the last person to receive that coin. The recipient uses a cryptographic password of their own to register themselves as the new owner of that coin, and this is recorded in the central database. Nobody but the new owner of the coin will be able to spend it, because only they know their password, which effectively locks the coin from being transferred.

Simple, couldn't be easier—any competent IT professional could design a system like this with minimal effort. But such a centralized design is completely useless, for several reasons:

1. The central database represents a single point of failure (vulnerability). If that central server computer ever burned up in a fire, the entire currency system would be lost and everyone would lose their savings.

2. Even if there was no fire, a government agency wanting to shut the system down could simply raid the building and seize the computer. Remember, the cypherpunks' goal was to create something immune to being shut down, even by the government or its law enforcement agencies.

3. Anyone with physical control over the server computer could hack the central database and steal everyone's coins and keep them for themselves.

4. There is no reason for everyone using the currency system to ever trust any one party to have the keys to the entire kingdom. In a centralized design like this, whoever controls the computer at the center of the diagram literally controls everything. Why would anyone ever want to participate in such a system? Remember, the cypherpunk/crypto culture is extremely distrustful of any central authority figure.

5. If the server computer goes offline due to a power outage or for any other reason, the entire currency system will be disabled until the master server computer is turned back on. This results in unacceptable reliability.

So clearly the centralized architecture just plain doesn't work. To address the problem the cypherpunks wanted to solve, we need to switch to a *peer-to-peer* network topology, as depicted below:

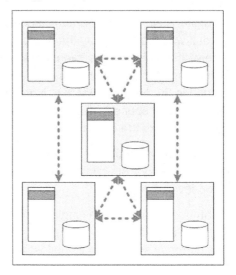

Figure 3 Peer-to-Peer Distributed Ledger Architecture

In this topology, every computer can talk directly to any other computer, and there is no central database or central point of control in the entire system. This makes the software design a little more complex, but it's absolutely necessary to achieve the cypherpunks' goal of creating an alternative to government-issued money that is completely decentralized.

If, hypothetically, we could safely assume that every computer in the network is running the software it's supposed to be running, and that nobody is trying to hack the network or collude with other unscrupulous members of the network, then it would be relatively straightforward (from a software design standpoint) to build a digital currency system in this peer-to-peer network topology.

But needless to say, we cannot make any such assumptions. In fact, we absolutely must assume the exact opposite—that there will always be unscrupulous actors who are trying to hack the system and steal everyone else's digital cash. We must therefore assume that at least some of the computers in the network are running modified software designed to perpetrate a crime. Well, guess what? From a software design perspective, the problem just went from fairly trivial to nearly impossible to solve.

Chapter 4:
Distributed Ledger Technology

To make this work, we need to introduce some sort of police force to keep the rest of the network honest. Each time someone tries to record a transaction in this distributed peer-to-peer network, we need someone else to validate that no coin is being double-spent, and approve that transaction before it goes through. The diagram below illustrates this concept:

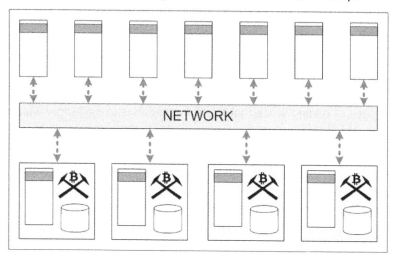

Figure 4: Blockchain Network Architecture. Transaction nodes (upper tier) may or may not have a copy of the ledger. Mining nodes (lower tier) each have a copy of the ledger and are responsible for adding new blocks of transactions to the blockchain.

The top tier of computers in this diagram represent the participants who are sending and receiving payments between one another, and the shaded boxes represent the aforementioned police force—the network participants whose job it is to verify and validate every transaction to make sure no monkey business is going on before adding it to the permanent ledger. In the blockchain distributed ledger system which underpins the Bitcoin cryptocurrency, these cops are known as *miners*. Their job is to add new blocks of transactions to the ledger after making sure everyone is playing by the rules, that nobody is trying to double-spend the same coin, and so forth.

The blockchain architecture also includes the concept of *full nodes*, which are computers that have a copy of the ledger, and keep the miners themselves honest by making sure that all the blocks added to the blockchain follow all the rules. The job of the miners is to assemble blocks of valid transactions and add them to the blockchain, but the *full nodes* are ultimately responsible for making sure all the transactions are valid and all the rules are being followed.

Remember, there can be no central authority in this network, so the miners cannot be special "authority figures" like real-world police who get their badges and guns as a result of government authority. We have to design the network so that anybody who wants to be a miner can be, and since we very much need these miners to keep the network safe, we're going to have to figure out a way to make it worth people's time and effort to participate in the network in this role.

Again, we have to assume the absolute worst, and design the system to accommodate the possibility that the bad guys trying to get away with fraudulent transactions have also inserted dirty miners into the network for the purpose of adding those fraudulent transactions to the ledger without proper scrutiny. Suddenly the software engineering task is much more complex.

There is a fairly obvious (to a distributed systems designer like myself) way to make this work. I'm going to spare you the gory technical details and just say that by using something called a *consensus algorithm* and encouraging plenty of people to participate in the role of miners, you could *almost* make this work. The gist of it would be that for any transaction to go through, the *majority* of the miners and full nodes have to agree that the transaction is valid. That's where the *consensus algorithm* comes into play. Think of it like a jury that has to vote to find the defendant "not guilty" before the transaction is allowed to occur.

Why did I say this approach would *almost* work? Because there's a clever way to cheat a consensus algorithm that's well known in the world of distributed systems design. It's called a *Sybil attack*, also commonly known as a *51% attack*[12]. Here's how it works: The network is designed so that any transaction can only be approved if a *majority* of the miners and full nodes agree it's legitimate and no fraud is being perpetrated. At first glance, that solves the problem. Surely there can't be that many bad apples in the basket to beat a system like that ... or could there be?

Computers are pretty inexpensive, especially when you consider that the Bitcoin cryptocurrency (all of the outstanding Bitcoin) has a total value in the hundreds of billions of dollars. For someone trying to hack the network and steal that kind of money, spending a few hundred thousand bucks is a

---

[12] To be perfectly accurate, "Sybil attack" and "51% attack" are not interchangeable or synonymous terms, and gurus in the technology use such terms very precisely to describe specific kinds of attacks. But for the purposes of this book, they both refer to the general approach of one person or a small number of people ganging up on the rest of the network by creating the false appearance of being a large number of unrelated actors on the network.

drop in the bucket, and that buys an awful lot of computers—a lot of *miners*. Meanwhile, it's very easy to program a single computer to register itself with many different *internet protocol* (IP) addresses, making it appear to the rest of the network like a whole bunch of different computers.

Suppose we already have 1,000 honest miners in the network, but it's really not that difficult for the bad guys to simply add another 2,000 *dirty* miners tipping the balance their way. The consensus algorithm will favor the corrupt miners, fraudulent transactions are approved, and the bad guys win!

It might seem like all you'd need to do is limit the number of miners on the network and ensure their integrity. But again, no central authority decides who's in and who's out, and remember that anyone who feels inclined to be a miner can sign up to be one—even a bad one. Instead, the system has to be designed with *incentives* so that the good miners will always outnumber the bad. But how?

This exact problem is the crux of why a decentralized digital cash system took so long to figure out. All these concepts are very well understood in the field of distributed software design—and they appear to lead to a dead end. It would appear from a software engineering standpoint that we're stuck. There's just no obvious way to make this system work reliably, because the good miners could always be outnumbered by bad miners in a Sybil attack.

The breakthrough that changed everything was Satoshi's invention of *blockchain*, more generically known as a *decentralized distributed ledger* system. Satoshi put a lot of thought into those incentives and how to create barriers of entry to prevent Sybil attacks.

The first step is to pay the miners very well, so that plenty of good guys want to sign up. By the way, the reason the cops in a blockchain network are known as "miners" is that they get paid in Bitcoin for their role, and it's really good pay. Remember, the miner's job is to review the transactions that are pending settlement, verify that nobody is trying to double-spend the same coin, and then add them to the ledger after making sure everything is on the up and up.

When a miner assembles a full folder of verified transactions, it's called a *block*. That block can now be added to the list of all the previous blocks of valid transactions. Hence the name *blockchain*. About once every ten minutes, a new block is added to the Bitcoin blockchain. And the miner who adds that block gets paid 12.5 Bitcoin under current rules.

When you consider that Bitcoins were bought and sold for nearly $20,000 apiece at the height of the 2017 price rally, that means that once every ten minutes, somewhere in the world a miner is making a quarter-million dollar paycheck for ten minutes' work! No wonder everybody wants to be a miner.

So what's the hitch? This sounds too good to be true. The answer is that being a miner is very competitive. A whole lot of miners want that payday, and they're all working hard to earn it. But only *one* gets paid. Who gets chosen, when the system has no central authority to make such decisions?

These miners are a bunch of serious math geeks. The way you compete with your fellow miners is that the system requires each miner to first assemble a block of validated transactions—that's the easy part— then each miner has to do a very difficult cryptographic math problem before being allowed to add the block to the blockchain. *Whichever miner finishes the math problem first gets to add his block to the blockchain and collect the 12.5 Bitcoin.*

The whole idea is that while it might be easy to get bad miners into the network and jig the consensus, it would be very hard to find a whole bunch of bad guys *and* consistently do the math problems faster than any of the good miners. This is the core innovation of blockchain; making the miners do something very difficult and *earning* the right to add the next block to the blockchain and get paid. It's a system designed around merit.

A common misconception is that calculating the solution to this big complicated math problem (which is known as *Proof-of-Work*) is somehow necessary to keep the network secure—that's simply not the case. The big math problem is just *busywork*. The answer to the math problem is never used for any useful purpose other than to make sure the miner adding the next block to the blockchain had to work really hard to prove himself.

The really clever part of this is that although solving the busywork math problem is incredibly compute-intensive and requires a massive amount of computing power, it's very simple for the *full nodes* to check any miner's work and keep everyone honest. If the miner cheated and added a block containing transactions that double-spend coins, the full nodes will easily detect this. In fact, it will take them a small fraction of a second to check if someone cheated. This is possible because of a well-known technique known as a *one-way algorithm* that's been used in computer cryptography for decades.

Chapter 4: Distributed Ledger Technology

The upshot of all this is that to be a bad miner, you need an enormous amount of computing resources—the only way to win the contest and complete a block faster than the other miners is to invest some serious money in a super high-performance computer system known as a *mining rig*. To successfully mount a Sybil attack, *all* the bad miners would have to possess expensive, super-high performance computers just to have a chance at adding a fraudulent block to the blockchain. But even a rookie *full node* running his Bitcoin software on a used laptop he bought at a yard sale has the power to spot a dirty miner and keep him honest. The key to Satoshi's brilliant design was using mathematics to make the job of being a corrupt miner incredibly demanding, while keeping the job of spotting those corrupt miners incredibly easy.

There's a penalty for all of this, and it's a really big penalty. An incredible amount of computing resource is needed just to add the next block to the blockchain. This is precisely the reason that you've probably heard stories about the Bitcoin network consuming more electricity than entire nations. There's nothing inherent to maintaining the ledger itself that requires anything close to that much computing power or electricity consumption—it's the fail-safe of solving the busywork math problem chewing all the juice. But it's the only way anyone has figured out (so far) to make being a bad miner so much hard work that nobody can mount a successful Sybil attack.

My prediction is that someday, someone will find a more efficient way to achieve the same safeguard. When they do, Bitcoin and other blockchain-based cryptocurrencies will become far more efficient. And you can be sure that plenty of really smart people are already working on exactly this problem.

Summarizing the Blockchain Distributed Ledger
Here are the key points to remember:

- Creating a digital cash system using a *centralized architecture* would have been both quite easy and quite pointless. To achieve the cypherpunks' goal of creating a money system that was resistant, if not impervious, to being hacked by bad guys or shut down by the government, a fully decentralized, peer-to-peer network topology was needed.

- For the entire history of the computer industry, every system and every database has been owned and *controlled* by someone. But the notion of a computer database that *no single person or organization controls*, where the integrity of the database is assured by the design of a peer-to-peer network—that's something that never existed before Satoshi invented *blockchain*.

- *Distributed Ledger* is the generic name for Satoshi's invention of a computer database that has no owner and no central point of control or administration. The data itself is distributed across a network. There is no owner and everyone keeps one another honest when making updates to the database. Nobody in the network has any more authority than anyone else.

- Cryptographic math tricks make being a bad miner thousands of times more compute-intensive than catching a bad miner in the act of cheating. This makes launching a successful Sybil attack nearly impossible.

- The first distributed ledger (invented by Satoshi for Bitcoin) is known as *blockchain*. Its design is fully decentralized.

- Currently, blockchain is very inefficient and consumes a lot of electricity. The reason is that the "proof-of-work" algorithm used to keep the miners honest intentionally imposes a huge amount of "busy work" to make the miners prove themselves before they can add a block to the blockchain. Very smart people are already working to find a more efficient way to solve the problem.

- Blockchain could never work without a really enticing reward to motivate the *miners* to police the network. Each time a block is added to the blockchain, the miner who added the block gets paid 12.5 Bitcoin for his efforts. The other miners are all competing to be the one to complete the next block by finishing the busy-work math problem before anyone else. The winner of the math contest wins a prize of 12.5 Bitcoin. This occurs about once every ten minutes.

Chapter 5: Bitcoin – The First Cryptocurrency

My goal for this chapter is only to introduce you to Bitcoin at a high level. Entire books have been written about the alphabet soup of acronyms and concepts associated with trading Bitcoin tokens, and you should look to those books if that's your interest. I only plan to help you understand what Bitcoin is and how it fits into a much bigger picture. I'll strive to keep it short and to the point so that we can more on to more interesting topics.

How the Bitcoin Currency Works

The hard part was figuring out how to make the distributed ledger work reliably. That's what took so long, and to be sure, distributed ledger represents a breakthrough in the field of computer science. The very notion of a database that has no owner and where nobody has any more authority than anyone else is revolutionary. My expectation is that distributed ledger technology will find myriad applications well beyond digital currency.

Once the problem of keeping the data secure and hack-proof had been solved, the rest was fairly easy. Bitcoin is a *digital currency* system. Be clear on that: It's not a digital *payment* system like PayPal which delivers funds in an existing currency such as U.S. dollars or Euros. Bitcoin is a *currency system* unto itself, with its own money supply. When you send someone a payment using Bitcoin, the price is not in dollars or any other conventional currency—it's in Bitcoin, which is a unit of digital currency.

Bitcoin Units of Account

Just as U.S. dollars are subdivided into smaller units known as *cents* to facilitate smaller transactions, Bitcoin is divided into smaller units known as *milliBitcoins* (1/1000th of one Bitcoin). An even smaller unit is the *Satoshi (sat)*, which is equal to 1/100,000,000th of one Bitcoin).

Bitcoin Money Supply

A key consideration in the design of any currency is how many units of currency exist initially and whether—and under what conditions—that number can change over time. This concept is known as *money supply*.

The reason it's so important is that the value of money in any currency system is primarily determined by its scarcity. Something with an unlimited supply isn't worth very much. Bitcoin uses a *capped* money supply, meaning that it can never have more than a fixed number of currency units. The hard limit is 21 million Bitcoin. Once that limit is reached, there can never[13] be any more Bitcoin created. As of November, 2018, about 17.5 million Bitcoin are already in circulation.

How and when are Bitcoin "minted"?

Bitcoin come into existence when *miners* are paid for validating transactions. You can think of this like a waiter in a European restaurant tallying your bill. They first add together the cost of the items you ordered, and then they add a *service charge* for themselves. In the Bitcoin system this service charge is known as a *coinbase*, but instead of being based on a percentage of the bill, it's a fixed number of Bitcoin. In the beginning, the coinbase paid to miners was quite generous, but it gets cut in half every few years to moderate the rate of competition between miners. Currently, the coinbase paid to miners is 12.5 Bitcoin for each new block added to the blockchain.

Every Bitcoin in existence was created when it was paid to a miner somewhere for completing a block. Satoshi mined the first block in the chain himself, and then allowed others to join in the competitive game of mining. Early participants in Bitcoin mining made a whole lot of Bitcoin very easily.

In the beginning, a single personal computer could realistically complete a block on its own and collect the entire coinbase fee. These days, many computers owned by different people must band together in *mining pools* to even have a chance at being the first to complete a new block, and then they split the coinbase among the contributors of the computing resources that jointly solved the math problem required to add the new block to the chain.

There are two ways to obtain Bitcoin: the first is to mine them yourself, which today means buying a very high-performance computer and joining a mining pool. Unlike the early days when miners were rolling in Bitcoin, nowadays it's very competitive and the value of the Bitcoin you can realistically expect to earn from mining will only exceed the cost of

---

[13] It is always possible (with an agreement of the miners) for the Bitcoin software to be changed to allow a higher money supply limit. As of this writing, the cap was 21 million Bitcoin and most people in the Bitcoin mining community believed that it should not be changed.

Chapter 5:
Bitcoin – The First Cryptocurrency

electricity to run your mining rig if you're lucky enough to live in a place with relatively low electricity costs.

The second way to obtain Bitcoin is to buy some (or some fraction of one coin if your budget is small) from someone else who already has them. *Bitcoin Exchanges* are businesses that buy and sell Bitcoin in exchange for U.S. dollars or some other conventional currency.

How do miners get paid when the money supply is used up?
The Bitcoin money supply is capped at 21 million Bitcoin, yet the whole network clearly depends on (and cannot exist without) miners whose incentive is the coinbase they receive in newly minted Bitcoin.

This presents a conundrum: what happens when the money supply limit is reached, and no more Bitcoin can be minted? What incentive will there be for the miners to continue securing the network when this occurs? Satoshi thought of that, and designed *transaction fees* into the system. Today the primary incentive for mining is the coinbase miners receive for adding a block to the blockchain, eventually the coinbase will drop to zero and the only compensation miners will receive will be transaction fees.

The fee amount is set by supply and demand. In other words, there is no set fee, but at some point when the coinbase drops to zero, miners will have no reason to include transactions in new blocks unless they are offering a fee that warrants the miner's time and energy. The person sending a payment gets to set the size of their own transaction fee, but it's up to the miner to decide whether the fee is big enough to warrant their attention.

This is a brilliant design: In the beginning, *coinbase* payments allow the transaction fees to be low or zero. Everyone is happy and the popularity of the network can grow because one of its features is that the transaction fee, while technically present, can be zero in the beginning. Over time, the coinbase will continue to get smaller and miners won't validate transactions unless they contain a transaction fee. But this won't happen until the network is much more popular, at which point the market will presumably be better able to absorb transaction fees without major objection.

Do I need to open an account to keep my Bitcoin in?
Yes and no, mostly no. At any particular moment in time, every Bitcoin in existence is *owned* by a specific Bitcoin *address*. In one sense, a Bitcoin address is a type of account, and it is true that the only place you can keep any Bitcoin is within such an account. But this is not like the kind of

account you have to open with a banker after giving them all sorts of personal information. Think of it as something akin to a numbered Swiss bank account, where the owner of the account controls access to their money through a password, and the bank never asks for or knows the owner's legal identity.

Bitcoin addresses are a step beyond numbered Swiss bank accounts. You create your own Bitcoin addresses, and it's a trivial operation—so trivial that many Bitcoin users create a new address for every single transaction they conduct.

When you create a Bitcoin address, you specify a *private key*, which is similar to a password in a computer system. Most Bitcoin users control quite a few different addresses, and it would be next to impossible to remember all the different private keys. For this, a Bitcoin *wallet* is a list of addresses and private keys. If someone steals this wallet, it's just as if they stole a conventional wallet full of cash—you lose the money.

There are several different versions of *Bitcoin wallet* systems—some hardware-based and some software-based, and they both help people keep track of all their addresses and private keys in a secure way. They generally use encryption to keep the private keys safe, and the wallet is "unlocked" by some action the owner takes. That action could range from knowing a password in a software-based wallet to scanning one's fingerprint in a hardware-based wallet.

How Bitcoin payments work

The rules are very simple. Anybody can deposit any amount of Bitcoin *into* any Bitcoin address. You don't need permission from anyone (including the owner of the address), and it's a very simple operation to send Bitcoin already in an address you control to any other Bitcoin address.

But once Bitcoin has been "deposited" to an address, it's locked there until someone *who knows the private key* for that address authorizes a payment to be made to a different address. If you forget the private key, you lose the Bitcoin in that address. There are no exceptions, and by some estimates as many as 20% of all Bitcoin in existence have been lost this way. One poor soul had more than ten million U.S. dollars worth of Bitcoin and then accidentally threw away the hard drive that contained his private key wallet! Oops.

Chapter 5:
Bitcoin – The First Cryptocurrency

If there are accounts, how is it like Cash?

When you write a check against a conventional checking account, or make a PayPal payment on the Internet, the sender and recipient must both have an account, which is registered under their legal name and usually includes their national Tax ID (social security number in the case of U.S. residents). When a payment is made, a permanent audit trail is created linking those two accounts. While it is possible to own multiple PayPal or Checking accounts, each one must be registered and the audit trail reflects this.

With Bitcoin, anyone can create a new Bitcoin address at any time, for any reason, and there is no need to disclose your identity in the process. So while it's true on one hand that Bitcoin can only exist inside of an *address* which could be thought of as a kind of account, it's easy to create a brand new address for a single transaction.

If you want the equivalent of handing someone a hundred-dollar bill, you create a new address and put a hundred dollars worth of Bitcoin in that address. At that point you can use that address to send all of its Bitcoin to the recipient, or you might just as easily give the recipient the private key (password) for that address instead of sending a payment—as long as it only contains the funds they are due. Once they have the private key, they can spend the money in that address themselves. There is no registered "owner" of each address. Anyone who knows the private key for any address has the ability to spend the Bitcoin contained in that address.

Is it really anonymous?

No. It's pseudonymous, and the legal identity of a Bitcoin transaction participant can often be deduced with a little detective work.

Every payment in the Bitcoin system follows the form "Address X sends Y Bitcoins to address Z". The addresses are big numbers that don't appear to have any logical format—such as embedded dates or location codes— and the identity of the transaction participants is never recorded directly. This leads many people to incorrectly conclude that the system is completely anonymous and untraceable. That's simply not true.

Every transaction that has *ever* occurred in the Bitcoin network is recorded in the *public* blockchain. That means there is, in fact, an audit trail, and everyone can see it. This is best illustrated by example. Suppose that a person learns it's possible to buy illegal drugs on the dark web, paying in Bitcoin. So they create a new Bitcoin address and then buy $500 worth of Bitcoin (currently a fraction of one coin) from an exchange. They then use their private key to transmit the full amount to the drug dealer's Bitcoin address.

The only things that are recorded on the public blockchain are that someone bought $500 worth of Bitcoin from an exchange, put it in address X, and then transmitted it to address Y. The system is pseudonymous in the sense that the drug dealer who owns address Y (along with everyone else who cares to inspect the public blockchain) will be able to see address X as the source of the payment, but will have no idea who that person is.

Suppose for sake of this example that the drug dealer turns around and transmits the $500 worth of Bitcoin directly to another exchange, and converts it back into dollars. In this example, a sleuth looking at the public blockchain could easily deduce that someone used $500 U.S. dollars to buy Bitcoin from an exchange, and then they sent those Bitcoin to someone else who in turn sent them to another exchange and converted the Bitcoin back to dollars ... But they *still* have no idea who any of the participants are or the purpose of the transaction.

Now suppose that several months later, the police bust the drug dealer, and seize his computer after serving a search warrant. They find his Bitcoin wallet and get the list of addresses he's used to receive drug payments. In other words, they use good old-fashioned police work to discover address Y. It's very easy for anyone to look at the public blockchain and see where address Y received payments from. In this case they would discover address X as the source of a payment to address Y in the amount of the Bitcoin equivalent of $500. Once they know address X, they repeat the process and see what Bitcoin address sent the money to address X.

For the sake of keeping the example simple, assume the police were easily able to recognize the source of the payment to address X as an exchange. Then they subpoena the exchange and demand that it identify the person who bought the Bitcoin that was first sent to address X. This allows them to identify and prosecute the buyer of the drugs.

An accomplished criminal could convolute the audit trail so as to make it extremely difficult for all but the most tech-savvy law enforcement personnel to track him down. Similarly, the buyer might pay with Bitcoin he had mined rather than purchased to avoid the connection to an exchange that knew his identity. But the main point to understand here is that the Bitcoin ledger itself is completely public and everyone can see it for all time. It does not register the identities of the owners of the addresses, but these can often be deduced in other ways.

The Millennial Generation and Crypto Mining

So how did crypto mining become such a big hit with the millennial generation? Here's my hypothesis: Those math problems that miners have to do are best performed not by a computer's CPU, but by a very high performance GPU, or *Graphics Processing Unit*. Meaning, a high-end video card. For technical reasons I won't bother going into here, the circuitry in a video card is better suited to solving the busywork math problem than the computer's main CPU.

So to make any money mining cryptocurrency, you need a computer with at least one really serious high-performance video card. Better yet, more than one video card. Who already owns computers with fast CPUs and really high-end graphics cards? *Gamers*. The highest performance computer games require connecting together *four* top-of-the-line graphics cards to get lifelike virtual reality performance.

Becoming a Bitcoin miner is a very expensive undertaking that requires building a very sophisticated, purpose-built *mining rig* with several top-end video cards. But if you're a millennial gaming addict, you probably already have at least one such computer. Then someone comes along and tells you that there's this new thing called crypto mining where your super high-performance gaming computer can literally mint enough money to more than pay for itself when you're not using it for gaming? Talk about a no-brainer!

Not everyone in the millennial generation is interested in computer gaming, but almost everyone in that generation knows someone who is. When those folks started to mint their own money in their spare time, word got out fast. And that's my unofficial theory for how the millennial fascination with cryptocurrency began.

Cryptocurrency vs. Commodity, Representative and Fiat Money

We've seen how Bitcoin works and we understand that it's a currency system unto itself which achieves a degree of scarcity from the fact that its money supply is capped at 21 million Bitcoin. Ok, fine. But what does that make Bitcoin when we compare it to the three forms of money that exist in conventional currency systems? Is Bitcoin a type of *commodity money*, is it *representative money*, is it *fiat money*, or is it a new category entirely? To some extent we have to acknowledge that it's a new category, but even so, to make sense of it we still need to evaluate how it compares to the known forms of money.

Start with the easiest one: Bitcoin is *not* fiat currency. The definition of fiat currency is money that has zero or very low *intrinsic value* (it's just paper), and derives all of its value from the fact that government has decreed it to be *legal tender* for payment of public and private debt. No government in the world has decreed Bitcoin to be legal tender[14], so therefore by definition, Bitcoin is not fiat currency.

Bitcoin is not *representative* money because it cannot be redeemed for physical gold or silver, or anything else for that matter. The only assurance owners of Bitcoin have is that they can transmit that Bitcoin to another Bitcoin address so long as there is a miner willing to process the transaction. It's safe to say Bitcoin is not *representative money*.

Is Bitcoin *commodity money*? That one is more subjective. On one hand Bitcoin is nothing but bits on a computer network. Unlike gold, silver, or barley, you cannot use your Bitcoin for another purpose such as food or to make jewelry. The definition of *commodity money* centers on whether or not the commodity in question has *intrinsic value*, which is to say value unto itself, independent of its use in a money system.

The most common measure of *intrinsic value* centers on what else you could use the money for if it stopped being money. Clearly gold, silver, and barley all have *intrinsic value* because you can use them for food or jewelry. By this definition, Bitcoin has zero intrinsic value, because if the Bitcoin network were no longer used as money, the bits and bytes that make up a Bitcoin token would have no other use.

But another definition of *intrinsic value* centers on the cost of *producing* the commodity. Some have argued that by this definition, the electricity and computing resources that went into mining the Bitcoin represent intrinsic value, even though there is no way to convert the Bitcoin *back* into electricity or use it for any other purpose besides money in the Bitcoin network.

Yet another point of debate focuses on the concept of *scarcity*, which is the principal source of gold's intrinsic value. Bitcoin's money supply is capped

---

[14] This was true as of October, 2018 but I won't be surprised if it has changed by the time you read this. Already smaller governments like Malta are starting to talk about digital currency as the way of the future, and some of them are likely to embrace cryptocurrency initially as money. I predict they'll eventually favor government-issued digital currency over cryptocurrency.

Chapter 5:
Bitcoin – The First Cryptocurrency

at 21 million Bitcoin and there can never be more than that. In contrast, there's already far more than 21 million ounces of gold already mined. This leads some Bitcoin fans to the conclusion that based on scarcity alone, a Bitcoin is worth more than an ounce of gold.

The counter-argument is that gold is an *element* that exists in limited (scarce) supply on the planet. Bitcoin's 21 million coin money supply cap could be arbitrarily changed to 21 trillion Bitcoin by agreement of the miners to change the rules and update the software, and likewise other people could create hundreds or thousands of copycat cryptocurrencies which work just like Bitcoin but have their own money supply. With these considerations, the "scarcity" argument is effectively nullified.

An even more controversial question is whether Bitcoin (and other cryptocurrencies) represent something more or less valuable than fiat currency. If you want to incite a riot between cryptophiles and cryposkeptics, this is the topic to bring up!

In the eyes of a cryptophile, Bitcoin (and other cryptocurrencies) are *far superior* to fiat currency. Bitcoin is not only far more scarce than gold (because of the 21 million coin money supply cap), but more importantly (according to proponents), it's the way of the future. Bitcoin has the biggest and most reliable blockchain of any crypocurrency. It's the Cadillac of cryptocurrency and is infinitely more valuable than any fiat currency! To even make the comparison borders on fighting words to some cryptophiles.

But in the eyes of a cryptoskeptic, it's quite a lot simpler than all of that. Fiat currency is defined as currency which has no intrinsic value because it cannot be exchanged or redeemed for any hard asset, but still has fiat value because it carries a government decree saying it must be accepted as payment for all debts. Bitcoin, on the other hand, is currency which has no intrinsic value (still can't be redeemed or exchanged for any hard asset), but lacks any such government decree. By definition, it is therefore far *less* valuable than *any* fiat currency in existence today!

Needless to say, this is a sensitive subject for some people in the crypto community. One very important thing to understand is that *value* and *price* are *not* the same thing. The fact that Bitcoins have been bought and sold for prices as high as $19,666 U.S. dollars for a single coin is absolutely *not* evidence of Bitcoin's actual value, any more than the extraordinary prices paid for Tulip Bulbs in the 1630s *Dutch Tulip Mania*[15] were an indication of the flower's true value.

I've tried to be as balanced and unbiased as possible in describing both sides of the arguments thus far. Now I'll weigh in with my own opinion: Bitcoin's historic significance is that it delivered the first true implementation of *digital currency*, something that's certain to change the world. The superiority of digital currency tokens over paper banknotes cannot be overstated. Satoshi's *Bitcoin* is every bit as important to the advancement of humanity as the Wright Brothers' *Flyer*.

But what does that actually imply? Really, it means that we now have the technology to create a far superior version of either *representative* or *fiat* money. In both cases, the conventional versions of those systems rely on paper banknotes which have myriad shortcomings. Digital currency solves them all and delivers incredible advantages. *So the real invention here is that we have a far superior way of creating either fiat or representative money than we ever had before.*

To my thinking, claiming Bitcoin is commodity money because of the unrecoverable cost of electricity that went into mining it is ludicrous. Commodity money refers to *commodities that have alternative practical uses besides being used as money*, something Bitcoin can never do. So Bitcoin has no value as commodity money. It has no value as representative money because Bitcoins are not backed by or redeemable for any hard asset, *although digital currency could be used to create such a representative money system*. Bitcoin has no value as fiat currency because it does not *yet* have the endorsement of any sovereign government as legal tender.

So what value does Bitcoin really have? It's a less-than-fiat currency (because it's redeemable for nothing and has no legal tender status) *but it demonstrates technology so far superior to paper banknotes that the invention of digital currency itself is certain to change the course of history*. Ok, but even with that endorsement, where does that leave us with respect to the actual value of Bitcoin tokens?

The answer is that it depends entirely on whether there's any chance (even a small one) of the Crypto community's vision coming true, meaning Bitcoin eventually evolves to become a major currency system in the global economy. If that really and truly is what's going to happen, then the value of Bitcoins is much higher than the current record price of $19,666. *Much,*

---

[15] https://en.wikipedia.org/wiki/Tulip_mania

Chapter 5:
Bitcoin – The First Cryptocurrency

much higher. But in the far more likely case that Bitcoin is eventually outlawed after governments re-establish that only *they* decide who can issue money, then Bitcoin tokens are far less valuable—perhaps less than $1 per coin.

The reason I describe Bitcoin as *less-than-fiat* is because it lacks the *legal tender* decree of a sovereign government needed to meet the definition of *fiat* money. But what if that changed? What if small crypto-friendly countries start officially designating Bitcoin to be their *official* digital currency system, perhaps in parallel to their paper fiat money at first? Now that's an entirely realistic scenario, and if it were to happen Bitcoin would suddenly become the most *advanced* fiat currency on earth, because its digital tokens are so far superior to paper banknotes.

Even without a sovereign government's *legal tender* decree, Bitcoin is unlikely to ever go away completely—even if outlawed, there will be a black market. But in that scenario, Bitcoin tokens will almost certainly be worth far less than they are traded for today.

Beyond Blockchain: The Death of the Dollar and the Rise of Digital Currency

Chapter 6: Practical, Regulatory & Viability Challenges for CryptoCurrency

I've been an outspoken critic of the "investors" who participated (with reckless abandon in many cases) in the speculative mania in Bitcoin and other cryptocurrencies over the last few years. But I want to be crystal clear on this point: What I've criticized is the judgment of people who confused value with price, and failed to recognize the risks inherent to speculating in a currency system that could face serious (read: existential) legal challenges in the near future. My criticism is not of the quality of the digital currency technology itself, but rather I question the investment acumen of the speculators who expressed unbridled certainty that the price can only go higher.

To make sense of all this, we need to separate three distinct issues:

1. Whether or not a non-government sponsored cryptocurrency is a viable money system with respect to practical and regulatory considerations, such as whether governments will eventually outlaw its use
2. Technical evaluation of the software design of Bitcoin and blockchain, and a critique of its shortcomings.
3. Regardless of the above issues, whether the price action in cryptocurrency represents a speculative mania which risks a dramatic collapse.

The third point is easy, so let's cover that right now: In my opinion, yes, crypto prices have prompted an irrational speculative mania for the last several years. Think about what happened with Internet stocks in the late 1990s. Sure, the Internet is a really big deal, and has changed—and will continue to change—the world. They got that call *right*. Similarly, digital currency is just as big a deal, maybe even bigger. So on some level, the market is correct reacting to crypto with a big fat "Wow".

But just like the prices paid in 1999 for stocks of .com companies never made sense when many of the companies didn't have a viable business plan or even the prospect of ever making a profit, neither did paying $19,666 for a single Bitcoin in December 2017. Digital currency *is* going to change the world. But buying up Bitcoins on speculation now makes no more sense than buying up Wright Flyers would have made in 1904. There are plenty of reasons to think digital currency is the way of future, but few good reasons to think Bitcoin will be the predominant digital currency system.

Bitcoin is a really cool invention—don't get me wrong on that score. By the same token (pardon the pun), tulips are really beautiful flowers. Just as irrational behavior in the 1630s bid the prices of tulip bulbs up to astronomical levels in the *Dutch Tulip Mania,* history repeated itself with the cryptocurrency mania of the late 2010s. Comparing these two periods with respect to percentage price appreciation over time, the Bitcoin mania has already *eclipsed* the tulip phenomenon.

Paying almost $20,000 for a single digital token which is backed by—and convertible into—exactly *nothing*, and which was worth only pennies a few years earlier, was just plain crazy. A large group of novice investors made a classic mistake: confusing *value* and *price.* More specifically, they interpreted rapidly increasing price as evidence of rapidly increasing *value*, when there was no fundamental basis for higher valuation.

Issuing money has always been the exclusive purview of government

For thousands of years of monetary history, governments have controlled who issues the money. There have been several cases of governments delegating this authority to privately owned banks, but only under government charter. Libertarians have suggested for decades that the private sector should be allowed to create its own currencies to compete with government-issued money, but this has never been allowed.

Until now, that is. Since 2009, Bitcoin and the other cryptocurrencies have been *coining their own money*. Don't forget, Bitcoin is a bona fide *currency* system. It has its own money supply, it has its own rules for how new currency is issued (coinbase transactions in the *mining* process), and it is being used as a *store of value, unit of account,* and *medium of exchange* by hundreds of thousands of people worldwide. So without a doubt, cryptocurrency is (so far) doing something nobody else has ever gotten away with: *For the first time in history, someone other than a sovereign government or a bank authorized by government charter is coining money*

Chapter 6:
Practical, Regulatory & Viability Challenges for CryptoCurrency

and using it to transact domestic and international commerce all over the world.

Why have Bitcoin and other cryptocurrencies been able to do this when nobody else but governments and their bankers have been allowed to do so for centuries? Is it really the case that governments have changed their mind about reserving the authority to coin money exclusively to government and its appointees? I rather think not.

If Government was going to suddenly change its ways and allow the private sector to coin its own money, do you really think that the people they would first permit to do this would be a bunch of libertarian activists, hiding behind pseudonyms, who very clearly advertise that their primary mission is to use technology to make it difficult, if not impossible, for governments to do things like monitoring international payments for suspicious activity? Keep in mind, these are things that government considers to be an essential part of its role in fighting terrorism.

Assuming that governments haven't changed their mind, I can only think of two remaining possibilities to explain what's going on here:

1. Government may hate the idea, but there's absolutely nothing they can do to stop it, and that's the brilliance of what Satoshi invented.
2. Government is simply so slow, inefficient, and technology-illiterate that most senior policymakers have yet to truly get their heads around what Bitcoin actually is, and why it poses such a serious threat to the *status quo*.

I'll debunk the popular myth that government is powerless to shut down Bitcoin and other cryptocurrencies in short order. Meanwhile, my very strong opinion is that #2 above summarizes what's happening.

Consider some recent quotes from the central bankers—the senior government officials who are supposed to be in charge of such matters:

> *"The FSB's initial assessment is that crypto-assets do not pose risks to global financial stability at this time ... Their small size, and the fact that* **they are not substitutes for currency** *and with very limited use for real economy and financial transactions, has meant the linkages to the rest of the financial system are limited."*
> -Mark Carney, FSB Chair and BOE Governor

Mr. Carney is correct that crypto doesn't pose a stability threat to the global economy, and he's also correct when (in other statements not quoted here) he's criticized the price appreciation in cryptocurrencies as a *speculative mania*. But notice how quick he is to insist that crypto is "not a substitute for currency", clearly showing that he doesn't recognize that Bitcoin and the other cryptos *are* bona fide currency systems.

Here's another real beauty:

> *"Whether you call it crypto assets, crypto tokens—definitely not cryptocurrencies—let that be a clear message as far as I'm concerned, I don't think any of these cryptos satisfy the three roles money plays in an economy."*
> -Klaas Knot, President of the Dutch central bank

Again, the pattern is clear: The central bankers insist that Bitcoin and the other cryptos are *not currencies*. Mr. Knot goes on to explain that they don't satisfy the *tripartite definition* discussed in Chapter Two. Upon what logical arguments do Carney and Knot base these declarations? So far as I can tell, the answer is simply the belief that nobody but central bankers are *allowed* to *coin money*, so surely it can't be true that someone else is doing it. That's not permitted!

Mr. Carney and Mr. Knot, take note: The crypto crowd has been *coining their own money* for a full decade now, and by the way, *it happened on your watch*. These cryptocurrencies most assuredly *are* currencies, and certainly *do* meet the tripartite definition of money. For you guys to smugly declare that they are not something they really *are* is ludicrous. What you actually mean to say is that non-government entities organized by libertarians with an agenda to undermine the government are *not supposed to be allowed to coin their own money*.

I've searched far and wide for any sign of Knot or Carney substantiating their statements and explaining why Bitcoin is "definitely not a currency", or why it allegedly fails to satisfy the tripartite definition. I can find none, and the facts lead persuasively to the exact opposite conclusion: Bitcoin is *money*. The one and only thing it lacks is the blessing of government.

Furthermore, while it may be true that Bitcoin was the stuff of computer hackers and libertarian activists in its early days, it has decidedly gone mainstream. All of the major Wall Street investment banks have already opened cryptocurrency trading and custodianship operations, or have announced intentions to do so.

Chapter 6:
Practical, Regulatory & Viability Challenges for CryptoCurrency

Someday, Mr. Carney and Mr. Knot and the rest of the central banking elite are going to *wake up* and become far more proactive in taking action to stop crypto in its tracks.

Myth: Government cannot outlaw Crypto

A widely held belief in the crypto community is that government is powerless to outlaw or shut down cryptocurrencies like Bitcoin. After all, that's exactly what Bitcoin was *designed for*—to be impervious to government tampering.

There's an element of truth to this argument. Bitcoin is a network that operates on top of the public Internet. Short of shutting down the entire Internet, it would be extremely difficult for government to throw a switch and shut down Bitcoin. Furthermore, Bitcoin's software engineers could easily harden its defenses further by using other encryption technologies to hide the Bitcoin protocols and make it very difficult for law enforcement to even detect the presence of Bitcoin-related message traffic. So there's plenty of truth to the argument that no obvious mechanism exists for government to "pull the plug" on the Bitcoin *network*.

That's missing the point entirely. Government could very easily *outlaw the use* of Bitcoin, and most current users would stop using it. Legitimate businesses advertising prominently on their websites that they accept Bitcoin payments would cease doing so. Law-abiding citizens who don't want to risk getting caught would stop using Bitcoin regardless of whether the network was still operating or not.

More to the point, governments could outlaw the exchange of Bitcoins and other cryptocurrency tokens *for government-issued fiat currency*. The government's strong control over the conventional banking system makes it easy to pass regulations prohibiting any bank from facilitating any transaction that could result in Bitcoin being converted into dollars, or dollars into Bitcoin. With that sort of restriction, for all intents and purposes you've shut down the Bitcoin currency system for the vast majority of its current users.

Bitcoin cannot and will not be outlawed overnight

Keep in mind that the cryptocurrency trend has already gone global. Bitcoin is owned and actively traded by people all over the planet. A consequence is that when various nations begin to outlaw it, opportunities will be created for others. Think of it as similar to the tax havens that have existed around the world for many decades.

If Bitcoin were outlawed in the United States, it would be difficult to convert dollars to Bitcoin and vice versa, but it would still be relatively easy for those willing to break the law to continue holding and even transacting commerce with the Bitcoin *they already own*.

Under those circumstances, it wouldn't take long at all for small, hungry nations to recognize the lucrative opportunity to become *crypto havens*. Can't use dollars to buy more Bitcoin due to a new American law? Send a PayPal payment denominated in dollars to a dealer in a crypto haven on some remote island nobody ever heard of, where they can exchange it first into their own local currency, and then legally use the proceeds to purchase Bitcoin, which is then sent back (after a commission is deducted, of course) to a Bitcoin address you provided with the PayPal payment. Need to go the other direction and convert Bitcoin to dollars? Send the Bitcoin to some guy in Kazakhstan who (after taking a similar commission) will send you some dollars using Western Union or any number of other payment systems in common use.

At first the newly formed crypto havens would easily facilitate everyone's needs, just as tax havens faced very little resistance for the first few years of their popularity. But it wouldn't take long before the U.S. threatened to cut countries off from PayPal and Western Union, or at least began monitoring their transactions. Eventually the U.S. and Europe might threaten harsher sanctions on countries that acted as crypto havens, just as they've made similar threats to tax havens.

So it *is* a myth that governments are powerless to shut down Bitcoin, however doing so would be a long and complex process. Various degrees of black and grey markets would continue to exist indefinitely, and it's unlikely that government could ever "shut down" Bitcoin completely. Law-abiding citizens might give up on Bitcoin, but professional criminals will always find a way to operate black markets, and cryptocurrency will serve their needs for a long time to come.

The longer that cryptocurrency goes unregulated, the more difficult it will be to outlaw it. In particular, the more voting citizens that invest in cryptoassets, the more politically difficult it will be. The value of Bitcoins as measured in U.S. dollars would crash on the announcement that Bitcoin was banned—no one's going like that, and votes will be lost.

For this reason, I predict that there will be plenty of hints from government that outlawing crypto is under consideration well before it ever happens.

Chapter 6:
Practical, Regulatory & Viability Challenges for CryptoCurrency

The more they can say that warnings were provided, the more they can defuse the objections of investors who lose their money.

Conclusions

I can find no evidence whatsoever to suggest that central bankers or any other senior government officials are coming around to the view that maybe it's ok to allow the private sector to coin their own money. I'm not even aware of any evidence to suggest that central bankers fully understand that cryptocurrencies are bona fide money systems.

Law enforcement has figured out that cryptocurrencies can make illegal activities much harder to track. But so far government appears to be completely ignorant to the much *larger* threat that cryptocurrency poses: offering people something superior to government-issued money.

The picture is crystal-clear in my mind: The reason that cryptocurrencies have gotten away with coining their own money is simply that governments are so bureaucratic, inefficient, and technology-illiterate that even a full decade after the invention of Bitcoin, senior policy makers are still basically clueless. They don't understand what cryptocurrency really is, and they definitely don't understand the threat it poses to the monopoly they enjoy over *issuing money*—and being able to decree that we all must use their recklessly managed currency systems, whether we like it or not.

There are two really big "aha moments" coming that central bankers have yet to experience:

1. The realization that cryptocurrencies really are bona fide money systems that pose a serious risk to the status quo.
2. That *nobody stands more to gain than government itself* from the invention of digital currency.

It will be interesting to see which of these they wake up to first. The former may prompt them to aggressively work to outlaw cryptocurrency, while the latter will lead them to embrace the innovations of distributed ledger and double spend-proof digital cash.

Here's an analogy: Pretend someone invented breakthrough technology for voting in elections. This new technology advance completely eliminates voter fraud and makes sure every citizen gets exactly one vote and there's no way for anyone to monkey with the system. Now without a doubt, society should welcome that invention because it offers the opportunity to correct the horrible injustice of voter fraud and rigged elections. There's just no plausible way to think of it as anything but a really wonderful invention.

But now suppose that the guy who invented this new technology uses it to stage his own elections! Whoa, hold on—inventing a fairer way of voting was a wonderful contribution to society, but it doesn't entitle the inventor to run his own elections and appoint government officials on his own!

The analogy here is that Satoshi invented something so dramatically superior to paper banknotes that he actually got away with launching his own currency system to compete with government-issued money, something that's never been allowed before. The question now is how long it will be allowed to continue.

The point to really embrace here is that the importance of digital currency to the future of society simply cannot be overstated. But does that mean governments will let the guys who invented it launch their own private-issue money system to compete with government money? I think not, but I could be wrong. They've already gotten away with it for far longer than I would have thought possible.

What's *certain* is that the invention of digital currency makes continued use of paper banknotes just plain crazy. We now have a much better way. So the question becomes, will the guys who invented a far better alternative to banknotes continue to get away with launching their own currency system to compete with government money, or will the government eventually wake up and say "Hey, wait a minute – we want your invention, but only the government is allowed to use it!" I think the latter is far more likely.

As a libertarian I sincerely hope the Crypto guys somehow achieve the impossible and that their cryptocurrencies evolve to compete with and win out over government-issued money. But I *sincerely hope* for lots of things, including world peace. When I apply the filter of knowing what's likely to be *realistic*, I still think that *without a doubt* digital currency is the way of the future, but sadly privately issued digital money will probably be outlawed as soon as governments figure out that they can issue their own digital currency and perpetuate their monopoly over issuing money. I sincerely hope the crypto community proves me wrong.

Chapter 7: Technical Challenges for CryptoCurrency

I'll be the first to admit that criticizing blockchain for technical imperfections such as the inefficiency of the *proof-of-work* algorithm is like to criticizing the Wright Brothers for failing to use a jet engine. Sure, there's plenty to question about the technical design of Bitcoin and blockchain, but that comes as no surprise. We're still very early in this story, and it should be expected that the very first versions of any new technology will leave room for improvement.

Satoshi figured out how to make double spend-proof digital cash work. That was a *breakthrough* accomplishment. That the first version has serious performance and scalability issues doesn't impact on evaluating the historical significance of the invention. Time and incremental cycles of innovation and improvement will cure these issues, as they always do.

In my opinion, some aspects of Bitcoin and particularly blockchain are still only "proof-of-concept quality". I'm not saying they're bad; but the future will bring improvements that will be far superior, such as finding a more efficient way to thwart Sybil attacks than the current *proof-of-work* approach.

If we were talking about *hardware*, I'd have really serious reservations about putting any money at all into something that was clearly never meant to last beyond the proof-of-concept phase. But when we're talking about *software*, it's another story.

I'll stick with the example of the *proof-of-work* shortcomings of blockchain. The performance and scalability limitations we're talking about pose a very serious problem, and reason to think twice about whether Bitcoin has any future at all. But already, something known as the *lightning network* is being implemented. It doesn't solve all the problems posed by *proof-of-work,* but it goes a long way towards providing a workaround.

Bitcoin is adding new features all the time and the Bitcoins that were minted before these features existed are *legitimately increasing in value* as the sophistication of the network improves. So unlike the objections I've voiced earlier, the criticisms I'll make here I expect can and *will* be solved by future updates to the Bitcoin software system.

Understanding Proof-of-Work

Here's a thought experiment. Forget completely about digital currency for a moment, and pretend the following story was true … an eccentric billionaire is out to prove that people will do just about anything to make a buck. So this crazy guy conjures up a contest to see who can waste the most electricity and computing resources doing something completely pointless—something that serves no benefit to society. What's more, he lays out some really silly prize money. *Every ten minutes, twenty-four hours a day, seven days a week, he gives away a quarter-million U.S. dollars to whoever is able to waste more electricity and computing resources than anyone else in the entire world!*

The contest is organized by handing out a ridiculously complex math problem every ten minutes. Solving the math problem doesn't help to cure cancer or advance any field of science. It's just a gigantic experiment to see what lengths people around the world will go to in order to win a quarter-million dollar prize. And the billionaire knows how to *leverage greed.* He's only giving out *one* prize every ten minutes, but thousands of people will compete, collectively wasting hundreds of times more total electricity and computing resources.

The result is that people all over the world change their lives, shutter their businesses that were serving their local communities, and spend all their time and computer horsepower trying to solve one of these pointless math problems before anyone else. It becomes a societal mania.

Crypto mining really isn't far from this scenario. By the way, the part about the prize being a full quarter-million U.S. dollars every ten minutes was only true very briefly in December 2017 when Bitcoin's price peaked at almost $20,000 USD. But wait, you say, that's different! The work the miners are doing is absolutely necessary to secure the Bitcoin network.

Yes and no, mostly no. Recall that calculating the answer to the big cryptographic math problem isn't actually necessary *to validate transactions* being added to the blockchain. The sole purpose of the busywork math problem is purely a disincentive to prevent unscrupulous miners from taking over the network. It has no part in the actual process of validating transactions.

Chapter 7:
Technical Challenges for CryptoCurrency

99.999%+ of the work the miners do is competing with one another to see who can solve this arbitrary math problem the fastest. The winner gets the prize of 12.5 Bitcoin for successfully adding a block to the blockchain. All of the other miners all over the world (who lost the contest) consumed a huge amount of electricity and computing resources and nothing useful came of it. They lost the contest and got paid nothing. Only one miner out of thousands in the network gets paid for each 10-minute contest.

Now don't get me wrong. Satoshi's ingenuity in using proof-of-work to make double spend-proof digital cash work in a completely de-centralized network was nothing short of genius. Nobody else had figured out a way to make it work, and many other very smart people had been trying for decades. It truly was a brilliant insight.

If someone could figure out an even better way to thwart Sybil attacks, the opportunity exists to reduce the massive overhead (electricity and computing power needed to run the network) by well over 99%. And they will. I believe in human ingenuity. Someday, someone will break through the proof-of-work barrier and figure out how to make a truly decentralized distributed ledger work without the need for proof-of-work.

Plenty of smart people are already on the case. One particular effort getting a lot of attention is *proof-of-stake*. The idea is that to be a miner, you have to cryptographically prove that you already own enough Bitcoin that it makes no sense for you to do something that would compromise the value of your existing holdings.

Proof-of-stake has its share of critics already—and I certainly don't claim to know a better solution. But when I look at how proof-of-work is used in blockchain, it's like pointing very expensive searchlights (powered by the electric grid) at solar panels for the sake of generating "green" electricity. People actually do that in some countries where the electric grid power is subsidized and tax credits are offered to people who generate energy from solar power. But obviously, surely there has to be a better way.

When someone eventually solves the proof-of-work issues and comes up with a much better way to make a decentralized distributed ledger work reliably, will it mean that Bitcoin and its blockchain ledger are obsolete and soon to be forgotten? Almost certainly not. A far more likely outcome is that the Bitcoin currency will continue and adopt any new, more efficient distributed ledger infrastructure.

Crypto "Mining": Bug or Feature?

Ask someone who put their gaming computer to work mining Bitcoin a few years ago, and became a millionaire before the age of twenty-five as a result, what they think of the general concept of *mining* in a cryptocurrency—and they're likely to tell you that it's the best part. To be sure, *for them* it was the *best* part.

Take a step back and consider the big picture. The very expensive process of mining can only occur if the miners are willing to endure the rigors of the proof-of-work math contest, and that's precisely why the coinbase is needed. Those 12.5 Bitcoins are the incentive to keep the network secure. But nothing in life is ever free. Who is actually paying the cost of this very generous perk handed out every ten minutes?

Each coinbase transaction is funded by increasing the total money supply, and that directly equates to diluting the value of every Bitcoin already in existence. Put another way, the entire Bitcoin community is underwriting that 12.5 BTC payout every ten minutes. Most holders of Bitcoin don't notice it directly, but the need to pay the miners so well is costing everyone else money, and it's not a trivial amount.

Now, suppose that next week or next month, some genius figures out a way to make blockchain just as secure with a vastly more efficient algorithm that is just as effective at thwarting Sybil attacks. Suddenly, the amount of electricity and computer power needed to mine a block and add it to the blockchain is 0.00001% of what it was before.

Is there still any good reason to reward the miners with 12.5 Bitcoins for doing something that now requires far less electricity and computing horsepower? No, of course not. What's more, it becomes possible to eliminate the whole concept of mining completely, so that nobody's Bitcoins are being diluted in value every ten minutes.

A hypothetical new cryptocurrency that was decentralized and just as secure as Bitcoin, but which had no miners and didn't devalue every ten minutes, would be far superior to the current design. But I'm willing to bet most of the *miners* would disagree. Mining Bitcoin has made some people very wealthy, and the ability to earn more coins by dedicating your computer as a mining rig is almost a rite of passage in the crypto community.

When someone figures out a way to eliminate *mining* completely (which really would be better), there will be a popular revolt among miners—and it's essential to understand that the miners are in control. They are the ones running the current version of the Bitcoin software, which is programmed to use proof-of-work to thwart Sybil attacks. Imagine they all got a notice saying "Hey guys, great news, somebody figured out how to design a better mousetrap, so now we're going to phase out both proof-of-work and mining. Oh, and by the way, that means your primary income stream will be cut off. Sorry. You can download the new version of the software here …"

The miners are not going to be happy.

Bitcoin might very well be upgraded to use a new, more efficient algorithm, but eliminating mining from Bitcoin entirely would never fly because of the vested interests of the existing miners. And that's despite the fact that a mining-free decentralized cryptocurrency really would be superior.

My guess is that Bitcoin devotees would say that Satoshi already thought of all this. Bitcoin is designed to systematically reduce the coinbase so that it eventually becomes zero when the money supply cap of 21 million Bitcoin is reached. They would say that diluting everyone else's holdings with the coinbase was a brilliant way to get us through the stage where proof-of-work had been the only known way to make blockchain work. The original plan had been to replace the coinbase with transaction fees (paid to miners), so replacing proof-of-work with something better only means that those fees can now be lower! So what's the problem?

Those are excellent arguments, and it's easy to see why Bitcoin is likely to always have *mining* as part of its architecture even after technological advancements make it possible for mining to be eliminated. Eventually, new competing cryptocurrencies that don't include mining will be introduced. But I'll concede that their advantage over Bitcoin, especially after the coinbase in Bitcoin is eliminated and the money supply cap is reached, would be minimal.

There's one more point I want to touch on now just briefly. If you are a government working to develop a global-scale digital currency system, you don't need mining in your architecture. Permissioned distributed ledgers already offer a way for a government-issued digital currency system to be designed without any need for mining whatsoever. For now I just wanted to plant the seed in the back of your mind that it's a matter of perspective whether mining is a feature or a shortcoming of blockchain-based cryptocurrencies. For the sake of the holders of already-issued currency, it would be great to eliminate the concept completely. But the culture that has evolved around cryptocurrency isn't going to like that one bit.

Beyond Blockchain: The Death of the Dollar and the Rise of Digital Currency

Chapter 8: Nobody Stands More to Gain than Government

If the U.S. Government had been paying closer attention, it would have realized by now that it could secure its monopoly over the global financial system for several more decades by being first to market with a national (or even supranational) digital currency. Doing so would beat Russia and China to market, and prevent them from displacing the dollar as global reserve currency with a digital currency of their own design.

Three important points to understand here are:

1. The most important difference between conventional currency and digital currency is that in a digital currency system, technology can be used to change the amount of power that government has over the populace.

2. One possibility is to use technology to create a digital currency that *reduces* government's power to monitor, regulate, and control the financial affairs of private citizens (cryptocurrency).

3. But it's equally possible to design a digital currency system that uses technology to *increase* the power of government to do the same things (government-issued digital currency).

Here and now at the end of 2018, it feels like the whole world is very quickly getting in touch with points #1 and #2, whilst almost everyone is completely missing point #3! Why is this? Because the people with a vested interest in promoting digital currency technology are its inventors—the cypherpunks who are committed to #2 *with religious conviction*.

Central banks haven't proposed a digital currency of their own issue (save for Nicolas Maduro's *Petro*[16]) due to ignorance of the fact that nobody stands more to gain from digital currency technology than the central banks themselves. They've yet to even figure out what the crypto crowd is

---

[16] Venezuela claims to have already delivered a government-issued cryptocurrency called the *Petro*, but most experts regard it as a publicity stunt on the part of Nicolas Maduro which has little or no credibility. As of this writing there has been no serious (read: credible) government announcement of any central bank-sponsored digital currency. *Yet.*

actually doing, never mind to realize that they themselves stand far more to gain from digital currency than anyone else—including the original inventors of cryptocurrency.

This is starting to change, but only slowly so far. In early October, 2018 the government of Malta announced that it was taking the official policy stance that cryptocurrency is the future and that Malta wants to be known as an early leader in the digital currency age. Note that the Maltese government isn't yet distinguishing cryptocurrency from digital currency, and that they still have a little more homework to do. But the point is, they "get" the basic idea—digital currency is the way of the future. They want to be part of it.

Malta's announcement looked more like marketing than substance to my critical eye, but that's not the point. They see the big picture. Sadly Malta is in a very small minority at the moment. The global monetary system is still controlled by such intellectual heavyweights as Mark Carney and Klaas Knot. Would they ever admit that the tiny nation of Malta is actually way ahead of them?

If the mainstream central bankers could get their heads out of their own posteriors for long enough, they would realize that cryptocurrencies not only meet the *tripartite definition* of money, but they are superior to government-issued fiat currency in many ways. Are the central bankers thinking about how to embrace technology to advance their own agendas and (in the case of the U.S. Federal Reserve) to protect their strangle-hold monopoly on reserve currency status? No, and what's more, they seem completely oblivious to the gift horse of digital currency technology which has been staring them in the face for nearly a full decade.

Without a doubt, the one entity that stands the very most to gain from digital currency technology is the U.S. Government. A "digital dollar" that leads the charge toward a global digital currency standard would effectively thwart the threats which the dollar will otherwise face from countries like Russia and China. But nobody in the U.S. Government appears to be terribly concerned about Sergei Glaziev's de-dollarization campaign.

Meanwhile the chorus of voices around the world calling for less dollar hegemony and an alternative to SWIFT for international trade settlement is growing louder and louder. At first it was just the BRICS countries. Iran and Venezuela just became charter members, and that should surprise nobody. But Germany? And then a month later the entire European Union? Now that's a whole new trend!

Chapter 8:
Nobody Stands More to Gain than Government

Does any of this cause the U.S. Government to take pause and reconsider the prudence of unilaterally withholding access to the SWIFT system from nations like Iran and Venezuela? No, they're going to do as they please without regard to how many nations around the world express grave concerns over *weaponizing* the world's global reserve currency as a coercive foreign policy tool. The U.S. is dead set on playing hardball with Iran and other nations which haven't even been sanctioned by the U.N., and restricting access to the global reserve currency is one of their favorite tools of influence. *They're the United States, they have the most power, and they're going to continue to do as they please.* Russia has already issued two clear warnings that the U.S. is risking its own reserve currency status by taking these extreme policy actions, but these warnings have fallen on deaf ears among American policymakers.

Russia and China appear to be paying much closer attention to the formative digital currency revolution. In my not-so-humble opinion, the U.S. Government would do well to focus *less* energy on worrying about whether China is a currency manipulator, or if Russia hacked the 2016 Presidential elections, and a whole lot *more* on the question of whether China and Russia are conspiring to build a supranational global digital currency system designed to upstage the U.S. dollar and replace it as global reserve currency. I've seen far more credible evidence of *that* than any supporting the election hacking narrative.

Who benefits from Government-issued Digital Currency?

Digital currency would benefit governments in so many ways that it's hard to know where to start. Not all of the benefits are complimentary. For example, it's true on one hand that digital currency would be of tremendous benefit to the United States government, *if the U.S. Government leads the world in its adoption.* The reason is that it would allow the U.S. Government to significantly advance its own agenda and much more closely monitor international money flows in the fight against terrorism.

On the other hand, one of the primary appeals of digital currency to the Chinese and Russian governments is the very real chance of taking the title of global reserve currency away from the dollar. So all things considered, is a world-wide digital currency a benefit or a threat to the U.S. Government? The answer is a resounding *both.* Just like a new weapon system, it's either a big advantage or a big threat, depending on who figures it out first and knows what to do with it.

Globalists seeking a single world currency

For years there have been calls for a single world currency, and a number of different arguments have been presented for why one should be desired. A supranational digital currency system would be far more suitable for this purpose than a conventional currency system. Functional advancements in the form of instantaneously cleared international payments (no bounced checks), improved security, and enhanced monetary policy options would all help a digital currency achieve global single-currency status much more easily than a conventional currency system.

One advantage technology offers in this realm is to balance the playing field by limiting any one nation's authority over the system. In contrast, to promote an existing supranational currency such as the Euro and propose it as a global currency would be difficult because it would give the European Central Bank disproportionate authority over the system. Just as it's possible to use distributed ledger to eliminate central authority in the Bitcoin system, it's also possible to design a digital currency system which is global in scope, but allows national central banks access to monetary policy tools which are effective only within their own jurisdiction. This is a major advantage over conventional currency systems. It also overcomes one of the biggest objections to having a single global currency system in the first place.

Everyone who wants to outlaw cash

Central bankers and elite members of academia such as Harvard University Professor Ken Rogoff have long argued that cash should be banned for the betterment of society. Their arguments usually focus on the extent to which cash transactions enable organized criminals and terrorists to finance their operations. By outlawing cash either entirely or for all but the smallest transactions, such as buying a newspaper or cup of coffee, it's been argued that terrorists, arms dealers and mafia bosses could be stopped in their tracks. The rationale is that the existing banking system already offers law enforcement the ability to identify suspicious non-cash transactions and track down the parties involved, and the power to seize bank accounts where probable cause can be shown to suspect criminal activity.

I think the story line about terrorists and arms dealers is designed for public consumption and that their true motives have a lot more to do with tax enforcement and increasing the government's ability to do all the things Satoshi believed it shouldn't be allowed to do. But the libertarian

Chapter 8:
Nobody Stands More to Gain than Government

philosophy Satoshi and I share on such matters really isn't relevant. The point is, a lot of powerful people in government would like to see cash outlawed, and a government-issued digital currency system offers the perfect opportunity to achieve that goal. And it needn't work like Bitcoin. It could just as easily be designed to make it much easier for government to track every single financial event.

In the case of central bankers, their desire to ban cash is motivated primarily by their desire to use negative interest rates as a monetary policy tool. Negative interest rates create a very strong incentive to *spend money right now* rather than saving it. While many of us think it's crazy for government to discourage the public from saving for a rainy day, policymakers view this as a way to "jump start the economy" by urging everyone to start spending money—especially after a recession.

But there's a catch: negative interest rates—particularly if they are substantially negative—encourages *cash hoarding* which, if it were to occur *en masse* across society, could risk a run on the entire Fractional Reserve Banking system. If people recognize that the banks are paying *negative* interest rates on deposits (meaning savers have to pay a fee to keep their money in the bank), they might just withdraw all their money and put it in a safe deposit box or under a mattress.

The central bankers can't risk allowing that to happen, because it threatens the entire system. Making it illegal for anyone to hold more than a small amount of cash solves the problem by forcing people to accept negative interest rates on deposits—when withdrawing all their money and storing the cash in a safe is no longer an option.

De-Dollarization and SWIFT

I've already explained in earlier chapters why many countries would like to reduce dependency on the U.S. dollar and have an alternative to the SWIFT payment network that isn't beholden to the U.S. government. A global-scale government-issued currency system introduced by any country other than the United States would satisfy these desires.

Governments that want more power to monitor, regulate, and control money

Cryptocurrency is one edge of a double-edged sword. Digital currency systems could easily be engineered with the exact *opposite* goals of Bitcoin, embracing a design which enables government to monitor, regulate, and control every single payment that occurs anywhere on earth. Proponents of such a design would argue that it would make it possible for government to wipe out terrorism and organized crime for once and for all by taking away their ability to fund their illicit operations.

I'm sympathetic to Satoshi's view that giving government Orwellian power and authority poses a risk to society that might outweigh the benefits. But Satoshi and I are in the minority. We live in a world where the trend is away from individual liberty and toward collectivism. I don't happen to agree, but I'm a realist, and I know that in this day and age, it's only a matter of time before Government figures out that digital currency can be designed with the exact opposite goals that Satoshi envisioned for Bitcoin. More importantly, I recognize that *when they do, most of the population will support giving government more authority over the financial system in the name of fighting terrorism.*

Central bankers don't even know what they're missing!

Digital currency technology could be used to engineer entirely new monetary policy tools that go far beyond what central bankers are used to in conventional monetary systems. I'm going to save the details for later, after we've covered the concepts of conventional central bank policy tools. For now, suffice it to say that digital currency could offer central bankers far greater control over the monetary system than was ever possible before. They just haven't figured that out yet.

To get serious about Digital Currency requires first understanding Conventional Currency!

Hopefully I've persuaded you that governments stand more to gain from digital currency technology than anyone else. But I don't think cryptocurrency as it exists today will interest governments much. Bitcoin was very intentionally designed with a *minimalist architecture*. It has a fixed money supply, and by design it offers no ability for a central bank or other oversight agency to manage the currency the way conventional currency systems are administered. Remember once again, the cypherpunk designers of Bitcoin are strongly of the opinion that central banks are the problem, and they wanted to design a currency system that was free from their influence.

For these reasons, I don't think any major government would seriously consider adopting any of the existing cryptocurrency designs as the basis of a government-backed digital currency[17]. Regardless of what would be

---

[17] I don't count Nicolas Maduro's state-sponsored *Petro* cryptocurrency as a serious undertaking. In my view it's nothing more than a publicity stunt on Maduro's part.

Chapter 8:
Nobody Stands More to Gain than Government

best for society, the fact is that the people who are in charge at the moment (the central bankers) are very strongly of the opinion that currency systems must be designed to allow central banks to use *monetary policy tools* to oversee and regulate a currency system. While this may be anathema to the values of the cypherpunks, it's a core value of the central bankers, and right now they are the ones with all the power and authority.

Central bankers who have evaluated cryptocurrency have made some very foolish mistakes. They evaluate something like Bitcoin, which was *designed* to make currency management through monetary policy impossible, and they arrive at the conclusion that digital currency would never be suitable as a national or supranational currency system because it lacks all the monetary policy bells and whistles they need! Well *Duh*, if you intentionally design something *not* to have those features, it should come as no surprise when those features are absent.

The fallacy of their logic is the conclusion that something isn't possible merely because someone else with opposite values *didn't want it*. They should instead recognize that technology offers the ability to go far beyond what was possible with conventional currency systems. And that works both ways—technology can be used to intentionally eliminate monetary policy tools, which was the cypherpunks' goal, or it can just as effectively be used to enhance conventional monetary policy tools. That's what the central bankers should focus their attention on.

But we really can't have a serious discussion about a central bank-friendly digital currency design without first understanding currency from the perspective of the status quo. This is a complex subject, but I'll be keeping this as simple as possible so that you can easily understand what a digital currency system would need to offer in order to appeal to central bankers as a replacement for any major currency system, as well as the special considerations unique to the U.S. dollar as the world's global reserve currency.

Beyond Blockchain: The Death of the Dollar and the Rise of Digital Currency

Chapter 9:
Fractional Reserve Banking

"It is well enough that people of the nation do not understand our banking and monetary system, for if they did, I believe there would be a revolution before tomorrow morning."
- Henry Ford, Founder, Ford Motor Corporation

I've included this quote from Henry Ford, one of the most respected American businessmen of all time, to make the point that it's not just fringe bloggers and conspiracy theorists who question the prudence of the *fractional reserve banking* (FRB) system. FRB was invented centuries ago, and has been the basis of most countries' monetary systems for as long as anyone can remember. Notwithstanding critics who argue that the entire system is a gigantic government-sponsored confidence scheme, the fact remains that it's been used successfully for centuries.

In order to consider how government-issued digital currency might someday replace conventional currency, it's essential to first understand that conventional currency issued by government only represents a small part of most currency systems' money supply. The lion's share of all money in existence around the world wasn't created by the world's governments, but rather, it was created by the commercial banking system. Therefore if we are to consider replacing government-issued conventional currency with government-issued digital currency, it begs the question whether the commercial banking system would still create most of the money, and if so, how this "bank money" would fit into the design of the digital currency system.

If that last paragraph wasn't enough to boggle your mind, consider that all of the following statements are true:

- The total amount of money that the government has issued is much less than the total amount of money on deposit in bank accounts. (Ask yourself how this could be possible, in the sense of where the money came from to deposit in the banks in the first place, if that amount of money never existed to start with!)
- This means it's impossible for all of the money in bank accounts to be withdrawn, because there isn't enough money in circulation to

satisfy all the withdrawal requests simultaneously. Most money is literally stuck in the banking system.

- Virtually every dollar is created when it's *loaned into existence* by the commercial banking system. Yet commercial banks have no license or authority to issue money themselves.

- Every time a loan is repaid, money is destroyed and the money supply shrinks. This means that if all borrowers were to simultaneously repay all their loans (seemingly, an act of financial responsibility), the money supply would collapse and a massive financial crisis would result.

- Nobody owns the money deposited in their own bank accounts.

If you feel thoroughly, completely confused by all of this, you're not alone. So put your seatbelt on, because if Henry Ford was right—learning how it all works might just inspire you to start a revolution.

Visualizing Money Creation

The easiest way to understand this complex system is to simplify it. Pretend for a moment that there is only $100 of money in existence, and just one person named George owns every penny of it.

Now suppose that George deposits his $100, which is all the money that exists in the entire world, with First National Bank. At this point George is still worth $100. He has his money in the bank to keep it safe, rather than in his back pocket, but he's still worth $100. First National Bank has the actual cash (an asset valued at $100), but they also have a matching liability of $100 owed to George, so the bank hasn't gained any net worth from this transaction so far.

Chapter 9:
Fractional Reserve Banking

Now Mary applies for and is granted a loan for $90 which she will use to buy a new dress from Contemporary Clothing, Inc. First National Bank loans Mary $90 of the $100 George deposited. So now First National only has $10 in cash left over. Mary has the other $90, which she has agreed to repay in twelve monthly installments, which will include both principal and interest. The latter is income for the bank.

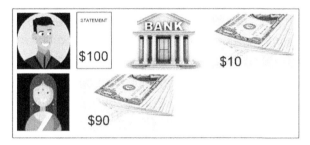

To be clear, the total amount of currency in existence is still just $100. Mary has $90 of it, and First National has the other $10. But here's how commercial banks are able to effectively *loan money into existence:* Look at this closely—George still has $100 of asset value, which happens to be *on deposit* at First National for safe keeping. Meanwhile First National has $10 of total cash on hand, and Mary has $90.

Hey wait! That's $200 total in the money supply—$190 between George and Mary, plus another $10 of bank reserves at First National. But how could that be? Just a minute ago, there was only $100 in the whole world. The answer is that each time a bank makes a loan, they are creating new money. The bank *doesn't* have a license to coin or "print" new money, and the grand total amount of currency in existence is still just $100. But the total money *supply* including "bank deposits" is now $190. The money *supply* has almost doubled, but no new dollar bills have been printed. If we add bank reserves of $10 at First National, the total amount of currency plus bank deposits is now $200.

And the story doesn't end there. What happens when Mary buys that dress for $90? Contemporary Clothing, Inc. would presumably deposit the $90 into the banking system. They might then pay $50 to the vendor they bought the dress from, but once again, the vendor will most likely deposit the money back into the banking system. One way or another, that $90 finds its way into deposits in someone's bank account.

What does the banking system do next? You guessed it—they loan out 90% of it, or $81, to someone else who uses it to pay someone else, who again deposits the proceeds of that loan in the banking system. Then 90%

of that amount, or $72.90 gets loaned back out to someone else. Already we have a money *supply* of $100 + $90 + $81 + $72.90 = $343.90. So at least four different people now have bank accounts that seem to give them the legal right to withdraw in total between them $343.90 in cash, but there is still only $100 of cash in existence. And First National only has $10 of it!

So what happens when George walks into First National and tries to withdraw $50 in cash, something he's been assured that he has the legal right to do any time he chooses? The bank doesn't have the money and couldn't possibly honor the withdrawal. How can this be?

This simplified example where just one guy owned all the money isn't realistic. Now pretend that this story has ten guys like George who each had $100 and they all deposited their $100 with First National Bank. The bank then made $90 loans to a total of ten people like Mary. Now First National has accepted a total of $1,000 in deposits and made a total of $900 in loans. They still have $100 in the vault.

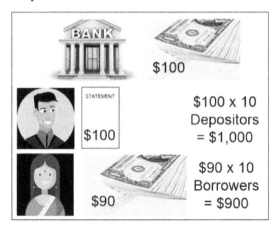

In this more realistic scenario, when George comes in to withdraw $50 in cash, there's no problem, because First National has $100 in the vault—twice the amount needed.

Okay ... what if George and two of the other guys who deposited $100 to start with all come into First National, and all three of them want to withdraw $50 each? Again, First National doesn't have enough money, and can't satisfy the withdrawal demands.

In this situation, just three out of ten depositors (30%) came looking to withdraw cash from First National Bank. All of them were only looking to withdraw half of their original deposit. So the total withdrawal demand is only 15% of First National's total deposits. How would a real-life bank

Chapter 9: Fractional Reserve Banking

respond to a situation where customers came in to withdraw just 15% of the total amount of money on deposit with the bank?

The bank probably won't be able to satisfy those withdrawal demands without requesting emergency intervention from the central bank—because they simply don't have the money.

It sounds impossible. Surely it can't be true that real-life commercial banks are unable to honor requests that would call for the withdrawal of just 15% of their total deposits? *It really is true.* But in actual practice, there are many, many more than ten guys like George, and the scenario in which 30% of them all show up wanting to withdraw 50% of their money at the same time is never likely to occur. The bankers and their regulators know from analyzing historical statistics that just 10% is a sufficient *reserve ratio* to cover the withdrawal demands likely to occur under normal circumstances. *The only reason the system works at all is that most people leave almost all of their money in the bank most of the time.* The scenario in which people suddenly want to collectively withdraw more than 10% of the deposits in the bank *almost* never happens.

Now, I know what you might be thinking. Something doesn't add up here. This description doesn't make any sense, because the whole reason people keep money in banks is to keep it safe. If it's really true that commercial banks not only don't have enough money to let everyone withdraw all their deposits, but they literally don't even have enough money to let everyone withdraw just *fifteen percent* of their deposits, then they might understandably feel inclined to withdraw all of their money from the bank while they still can! *Now you understand the quote from Henry Ford.*

Didn't they "fix this problem" after the Great Depression?

Yes and no. The scenario where depositors suddenly want to withdraw more than the bank has cash to hand out is known as a *bank run*. All it takes is for depositors to demand the cash withdrawal of about 10% of the total amount on deposit, and the bank has a serious problem. The *reserves* they keep on hand to satisfy withdrawals are insufficient. Prior to the creation of the *Federal Deposit Insurance Corporation*[18] (FDIC) in 1933, bank runs were common because as soon as even a minor problem arose, people would become fearful that the bank was about to go bankrupt, so they would all rush to withdraw all their money. This would overwhelm the

---

[18] This section applies specifically to the United States banking system. This information may be different in other jurisdictions.

system and in many cases *caused* the very outcome that had been feared—the total bankruptcy of the bank.

The FDIC was created to solve this problem. FDIC insurance guarantees most deposits in commercial banks, currently up to $250,000 per account[19]. The limit had been $100,000 since 1980, and was increased in October 2008 to allay fears that might have led to a run on the entire banking system at the beginning of the Great Financial Crisis.

The primary purpose of this insurance is to reassure the public that they needn't fear the bankruptcy of an insolvent bank, because FDIC insurance is always there no matter what happens to the bank. The principal reason FDIC was created was to prevent bank runs from occurring in the first place, by creating sufficient public trust that people would not be prone to rushing to withdraw all their money at the first sign of trouble.

What most people don't realize is that FDIC insurance was created and designed only to protect the public against the insolvency of any *single bank*. While FDIC insurance supposedly "protects" most bank accounts in the country, the reality is that FDIC doesn't have anything close to the assets needed to protect the public if a run were to occur against the entire banking *system*. Even if they did, there is nowhere close to enough physical currency in circulation to allow such a system-wide cash withdrawal of deposits. *The money literally doesn't exist.*

Consequences of FRB

While some cynics have suggested that the entire system was conceived to create a perpetual monopoly for the banking industry, FRB has been the basis of commercial banking and most countries' monetary systems for several hundred years. And while Henry Ford's words certainly underscore that most people in society don't fully understand how the system works, bank runs very seldom occur and the FRB system has prevailed.

An immutable truth is that *most of the money has to stay inside the banking system, all of the time.* In one sense, the commercial banking system can create new money supply, as new money is *loaned into existence*. But the banking system can't create money that could ever be taken out of the banking system all at once. Small amounts are fine, but the entire system depends on most people being inclined to leave most of

---

[19] This is an intentional simplification. In actuality the $250k limit applies to an *ownership category*, which could comprise more than one account, and more complex rules govern the situation where one person owns several accounts at the same bank. But this definition will suffice for the purposes of this chapter.

their money in the banking system most of the time. Anything else is literally impossible.

The money created by FRB makes up most of the money in the money supply. A consequence of this is that when the government wants to stimulate or slow down the economy, its principal *monetary policy tools* focus on influencing the rate of lending in the commercial banking system.

"Gold Backing" under FRB

A very common misconception is that back when we still had a *gold standard*, every single U.S. dollar was "backed" by gold bullion in a vault. This simply wasn't true. Instead, only every dollar of *base money*—a phrase used to describe the money created by the central bank—was backed by gold bullion. But *base money* only represented a small percentage of the overall money supply. Most of the money in the system was *bank money* created by the commercial banking system when each dollar was *loaned into existence*.

It's easy to see how widespread misconceptions about money and its gold backing occurred. Was it really true that under the gold standard, each and every dollar bill was backed by gold bullion? Yes, absolutely. But does that mean that everyone could rest assured that every dollar of wealth they had in the bank was backed by and convertible into gold? No way, not even close. Because while every dollar bill was backed by gold, there weren't nearly enough physical dollar bills in circulation to allow everyone to withdraw all their savings from the banking system. If you counted all the money that everyone could claim, *including the money the commercial banking system created during the gold standard era*, there was never anywhere close to enough gold to back everyone's savings.

FRB and Digital Currency

Now consider how digital currency systems—both cryptocurrencies and future government-issued digital currencies—might relate to FRB.

Cryptocurrency and FRB

The inventors of cryptocurrency are definitely not fans of FRB. Like many other critics, they think that the very notion the amount of money on deposit in banks can exceed the amount of money that actually exists is crazy. Their goal in designing Bitcoin (and later, other cryptocurrencies) was to create an alternative to the status quo that was more reliable, and which allowed central bankers far less control over how the system works.

Does this mean that Bitcoin is immune from FRB? Nope. Assume for sake of argument that a few years from now, Bitcoin reaches its design money supply limit of 21 million Bitcoins in circulation. The Bitcoin software will take care of making sure that no more Bitcoins are created after that. But that won't stop Bitcoin from being *fractionalized*, and it's entirely possible that Bitcoin-denominated bank accounts could allow the creation of another 50 million Bitcoins. But how can this be? After all, isn't every Bitcoin a digital token that is managed by the Bitcoin software in the Bitcoin network? How could there ever be more than 21 million of them if the software is designed intentionally to prevent it?

There can only be 21 million Bitcoin of *base money*. But if someone starts offering bank accounts denominated in Bitcoin, when you deposit 100 Bitcoin to such an account, it's just like when George deposited his $100 to First National Bank. The bank can be expected to turn around and lend those Bitcoins back out to someone else.

But wait! That's not what Satoshi wanted. The whole idea was to move away from FRB because Satoshi thought the system was crazy. Perhaps, but the commercial banking system can *fractionalize* any currency. How would they entice anyone to deposit Bitcoin in the first place? By offering a small amount of *interest* paid in Bitcoin, and then turning around and charging borrowers like Mary a higher rate of interest. The bank earns a gross profit equal to the rate of interest Mary pays, less the rate of interest they have to pay to George to entice him to keep his Bitcoins on deposit with the bank rather than just using a Bitcoin wallet.

I know what you might be thinking ... Nobody who truly *understands* the motivations for Bitcoin's design would ever deposit their Bitcoins into a fractionalized banking system, where the system is unable to allow all the depositors to withdraw all their deposits at once. Are you sure of that? An article[20] from May of 2017 describes how Japanese Bitcoin exchange *Coincheck* has begun offering interest-bearing Bitcoin depository accounts, and has begun lending Bitcoin at interest to borrowers. While the article doesn't come out and explicitly say, "We are applying fractional reserve banking, which Satoshi despised, to your Bitcoin", they are clear in explaining that this will mean you lose your Bitcoin if *Coincheck* were to go bankrupt. This is fractional reserve banking applied to depositing and lending of Bitcoin, plain and simple.

---

[20] https://www.nasdaq.com/article/japan-to-receive-its-first-interest-paying-bitcoin-deposit-accounts-cm787551

Chapter 9:
Fractional Reserve Banking

My point is simply to emphasize that Satoshi's dislike of FRB and his efforts to design Bitcoin to offer an alternative to FRB can't stop banks from fractionalizing Bitcoin itself, something which is already happening today.

Government-issued digital currency and FRB

Now consider how a government-issued digital currency might work with FRB. For those who hold FRB in great disdain, I'm going to ask you to trust me that for right or for wrong, FRB is very much at the center of how the central banking establishment thinks money systems *ought* to work. So while some readers might be hoping to find ways digital currency could be designed to undermine or circumvent FRB, I'm going to focus on how digital currency could be designed to *improve* FRB and enhance central bankers' ability to manage the currency system.

Any digital currency could be fractionalized, including Bitcoin. But what if a digital currency system were *designed to be fractionalized*? More specifically, what if we were to examine some of the problems central bankers face managing FRB currency systems, and think about how a digital currency system could be designed to relieve some of those problems?

The aftermath from the 2008 Great Financial Crisis (GFC) provides a perfect example to consider how a government-issued digital currency system might have expanded central bankers' options. When the GFC began, central bankers first tried lowering short-term *policy interest rates* to stimulate lending in the commercial banking system.[21] But it wasn't enough. By March of 2009 they had to resort to an extreme measure: *quantitative easing*, meaning that the Federal Reserve would take the unprecedented action of creating trillions of dollars of new *base money* and use it to buy U.S. Treasury Bonds on the open market.

The rationale was that by taking all that supply of treasury bonds off the market, prices of those bonds would be forced higher, and that would directly result in the yield (interest rate) returned by investing in those bonds to go much lower. The whole idea was to force *long-term* interest rates lower in addition to already-low short-term interest rates. The goal was to stimulate low-cost lending within the commercial banking system.

Fed chairman Ben Bernanke's plan was for the Fed to force the yield on U.S. Treasury bonds low enough that most of the banks holding them wouldn't want them anymore, because they no longer produced

---

[21] The reasons that lower interest rates stimulate lending will be explained in Chapters 10 and 11.

satisfactory investment returns. Bernanke hoped that to replace the income they were no longer getting from treasury bonds, the commercial banking system would start lending aggressively, at relatively low interest rates, and that all the new commercial bank lending to businesses and consumers would jump-start the economy.

The banks were selling their treasury bonds to the Fed, and the money they received for those bonds increased their capital, giving them the opportunity to use the money-multiplying effect of FRB to make lots of loans. Bernanke reasoned that for every dollar of new *base money* he created with *quantitative easing*, the commercial banking system would be able to lend several dollars of new "bank money" into existence—jump-starting the economy.

But that's not what happened. The problem was that the Fed could create new base money with quantitative easing, and they could put it in the hands of the commercial banking system by buying up all the U.S. Treasury Bonds in sight. *But they couldn't control what the commercial banking system actually did with the newly created base money.* The banks made some trading profits selling their Treasury bonds to the Fed at inflated prices, and the resulting reduction in long-term interest rates helped financial asset markets stage a brisk recovery—quantitative easing was a great success. For Wall Street, that is.

Main Street? Not so much.

Despite the infusion of new reserves, the banks never engaged in the degree of lending Bernanke anticipated.

Now suppose we'd had a government-issued digital currency system. What if the Fed had used *quantitative easing* to create a special new category of base money which by law could only be used as reserves to make new loans against, but not for any other purpose? Remember, in a digital currency system, it's possible for each and every unit of currency to be tracked through a distributed ledger system. With conventional money, the Fed can get the money into the banking system's hands, but it can't control what the bankers do with the money. In a digital currency system it would be trivial to impose such controls.

A new category of base money that could only be used to back more loans to needy consumers and businesses might be perceived as having lower value than ordinary dollars, because the recipient banks would have to accept restrictions on the use of this money. But so what? That would just mean the Fed would have to pay a higher price and create a larger surplus of special economy-stimulating base money. Once it had served its purpose and the Fed was satisfied with the growth in lending, the Fed could remove the restrictions on those special dollars with the click of a mouse, lifting their use restrictions and turning them back into regular dollars that could be used for any purpose.

Alternatively, the Fed could issue the special restricted-use base money with a promise that it would revert to unrestricted currency on a specific date—say, three years after it was first issued. That would alleviate the problem of banks demanding a steep discount on the bonds for accepting the restricted-use dollars, because the duration of the restriction would be known in advance.

What's more, this is but just one tiny example. The real point here is that digital currency opens a whole new realm of possibilities. When the Personal Computer was first introduced, its own inventors were often stumped when asked what it should be used for. The most common answer given at the time (and yes, I do remember the introduction of personal computers in the 1970s) was that you might use it to balance your checkbook.

The real value of the PC was that it opened the door for thousands of creative minds to dream up all sorts of uses that the original developers of the computers themselves never could have thought of in a million years.

I remember the introduction of the Tandy TRS-80. It was instantly clear to me that a general-purpose programmable computer that anyone could afford was going to change the world. And I was only twelve years old at the time. But I had no idea as to the full scope of change PCs would bring about in society. The corollary is that neither I nor anyone else knows the full scope of how digital currency will change the mainstream government-issued money systems of the future. One purpose of this book is to inspire smart people to start thinking about it.

My example describing how quantitative easing could have created a special category of base money was only about as creative as the "balance your checkbook" pitch the Radio Shack salesmen were pushing to get people to buy TRS-80s back in 1977. Where are the ideas for Photoshop and Microsoft Excel and web browsers going to come from?

At least that answer is easy—it's you, dear reader. I wrote this book to inspire others to start thinking about the possibilities.

Beyond Blockchain: The Death of the Dollar and the Rise of Digital Currency

Chapter 10:
Money Supply

Perhaps the most important concept to understand in any currency system is that the quantity of money in that system determines its value. The reason gold is so valuable is that it's a very rare element, and mining more of it out of the ground is very expensive. If a gigantic gold meteor were to strike the earth so that suddenly millions of extra tons became readily available, the gold already in existence would drop in value because it would no longer be as scarce.

Even when the currency system in question is fiat money, which gets all of its value from government decree that it's legal tender, the quantity of that fiat money is still the most important factor in determining its value. If we're talking about a national currency system, the value of each unit of currency is the total wealth of that nation divided by the number of units of currency in circulation. Double the amount of money in circulation, and by definition its value is cut in half.

But as the previous chapter explained, the money created by governments in modern fiat currency systems is known as *base money*, or *narrow money,* and represents only a small percentage of the total money supply. Most of the overall money supply is loaned into existence by the commercial banking system. That money is known as *broad money*, or *bank money*.

Money supply and the economy

There is a very strong historical correlation between the growth and contraction of the money supply, and the performance of the economy on whole. When the money supply is growing rapidly, more money is coming into existence, primarily as a result of bank lending. The people borrowing that money spend it to buy products and services, and that creates more demand for labor and raw materials. The result is that prices go up and unemployment goes down. In short, happy times for the economy usually occur during periods of money supply expansion.

Conversely, when money supply is contracting, less total money is available in the system to buy products and services. This can occur as a result of consumers becoming uncomfortable with borrowing more money (slowing the rate of money supply expansion), or in more severe cases when borrowers are unable to repay their loans. In the latter example, lenders are forced to write off bad loans. When they do so, money is extinguished, and the money supply contracts.

The economy fluctuates in periodic cycles known as the *business cycle,* which typically last four to seven years. In the expansion phase, people feel confident and are quick to borrow money. That borrowed money fuels growth in the economy, causing price inflation and less unemployment. Everyone feels good. But eventually the economy gets ahead of itself, and that price inflation makes it difficult for many people to afford basic essentials. In some cases they may even default on their loans, and this causes the cycle to reverse. As the money supply contracts, less and less money is available, and unemployment increases as a result. The newly unemployed can't pay their bills, and more loan defaults result, reinforcing the process. Eventually the cycle runs its course and starts anew with a fresh period of economic expansion and money supply growth.

Central bank management of the money supply

Libertarians and free-market capitalists are quick to insist that the business cycle is a natural phenomenon that governments should stay out of and not try to manage, but this is a minority viewpoint. The central banking establishment is very much of the opinion that their primary mission is and should be to *manage the economy* by stimulating money supply growth when necessary to get the economy going, and to discourage money supply growth to slow the economy if it starts to get ahead of itself.

Measuring the money supply

So how big is the money supply at any given moment in time? There is no single answer, because there are several different categories of money contained in the money supply. However, a system of measures has been devised which categorizes money and measures the supply of each category.

The high-level categories are:

Narrow Money: The money created by the government, or more specifically, by the government's *central bank*. This measure is also known as **MB,** and it includes both the physical currency in circulation and central bank depository accounts.

Broad Money: The money which is *loaned into existence* by the commercial banking system. This is further sub-divided into several

Chapter 10: Money Supply

categories M1 thru M3 (described below) in government-published statistics.

The high-level categories above are further subdivided into more specific categories known as the **M**'s, ranging from narrowest to broadest measures of money, as shown below.

M0 is the currency (notes and coins) actually in circulation.

MB is the total central bank-created money supply, or *narrow money*. This includes M0 plus *Federal Reserve Deposits*, special accounts that banks can use to place money on deposit with the central bank itself.

M1 includes both money in circulation (M0) and money on deposit in *demand deposit accounts*, meaning checking and NOW accounts. M1 does not include *savings accounts* or *time deposits* (certificates of deposit).

M2 is M1 plus savings accounts and time-deposit accounts (certificates of deposit, or CDs) under $100,000 in face value.

M3 is M2 plus large time deposits (CDs over $100,000), large institutional money market accounts, repurchase agreements, and other large liquid assets. However, the U.S. Federal Reserve stopped publishing the M3 statistic in 2006.

MZM stands for *Money at Zero Maturity*, and removes time deposits from M3. The idea is to measure the size of the money supply available for immediate use (not subject to a time deposit restriction).

Private-sector credit expansion is the primary governor of the money supply

In the conventional banking system, the actual currency in circulation (M0) represents less than 30% of the total U.S. money supply. The rest is "bank money" created by the commercial banking system. The total size of the money supply is determined almost entirely by the commercial banking system through the process of lending.

The effects of credit expansion on the economy are profound. A massive credit expansion will always cause widespread economic good times *at first*. But good times usually lead to excessive exuberance and over-confidence, and consumers and businesses tend to take advantage of easy money policy to borrow and spend beyond their means. This can lead to horrific busts when these debts become unserviceable, and the necessary reaction of tightening credit in response to such events can lead to outright economic depressions.

How Securitization corrupted credit markets

Prior to about 1980, most bank lending worked as described in Chapter Nine (fractional reserve banking): People deposited their money in banks, and the banks kept about 10% of it on hand to accommodate the minority of depositors withdrawing some of their deposits in cash. The rest was loaned out to borrowers. This version of how bank lending works was called *portfolio lending*, meaning that the banks were using the capital they received from depositors to build a *portfolio* of loan assets that would generate interest income for the bank for many years to come. If something went wrong and some of the borrowers were unable to repay their loans, the bank was exposed to that credit risk.

If the borrowers honored the loan terms and made their payments as agreed, the bank was making a gross profit equal to the interest received from borrowers less the interest that had to be paid out to depositors. But as soon as someone defaulted on a loan and stopped making payments, the bank itself was on the hook. For this reason banks were very careful to demand solid collateral they could repossess, if necessary, to avoid taking a big loss on a bad loan. Similarly, they required large down-payments on financed purchases to assure that even after the collateral was sold off in an auction under difficult market conditions, the proceeds would still be adequate to pay off the remaining loan principal.

The banks weren't stupid, and didn't loan money out unless the odds of getting it back were extremely high.

Banking was good solid business, and most banks were very profitable. Many investors were envious of the profits banks earned on their portfolio loans. And that led some innovative bankers to recognize an opportunity that would change everything. They realized that the bank's process of *originating* loans to put the bank's own capital to work could be expanded so that instead of just loaning out its own money, banks could make loans and *sell them off to other investors*.

A trend that would become known as *securitization* was born. Banks would make loans as before, but they changed the fine print on the loan agreements to allow the bank to *assign* the loan to another financial entity. Usually the originating bank would continue to receive and process the payments, so from the borrower's perspective the change was almost invisible—they'd borrowed money from First National Bank, and they sent their monthly payments to First National Bank. The fact that their loan had been sold to XYZ Pension Fund and that First National Bank was now just servicing the payments received on behalf of XYZ Pension Fund was hidden behind the scenes. Most borrowers didn't realize that banks which previously kept all their loans in their own *portfolio* were selling them off to third parties.

The really big change came when bankers figured out that instead of just selling a group of loans to another bank or a pension fund, they could *securitize* them, meaning that they would make a whole bunch of loans, then assemble a group of loans with similar credit profiles, and combine them together in something like a shell corporation which was known as a *special purpose vehicle*, or SPV. This allowed a bundle of mortgage or auto loans, or even credit card debt, to be repackaged as *bonds* that could be sold to institutional investors all over the world through the corporate bond market.

At first glance, this all makes perfect sense and there's no reason for undue concern. The people buying the bonds were professional investors who understood the creditworthiness and historical performance parameters of the borrowers, and so they understood the risk they were taking.

But the consequence of this was that suddenly, many *times* more capital was available for bankers to lend out. No longer were they just looking for a place to deploy the bank's own capital. They had a huge market of pension funds and other institutional investors eager to buy these bonds. They suddenly had a lot more money to lend than ever before.

More borrowers would be able to borrow and more investors would be able to profit from the interest income. There's certainly nothing wrong with that. But now consider the *systemic effects* of this new trend. There was a whole new source of much more capital, so banks were lending more than ever before. *And the money supply started growing very rapidly as a result*.

Have you ever asked yourself why the 1980s were known as the "go-go eighties"? Was there some profound invention or macroeconomic driver that brought an end to the *stagflation* that defined the 1970s? I'm not alone in my view that *securitization* of lending was a primary economic driver. The whole credit equation changed. Banks were much more willing to lend because it was no longer just the banks' own capital they had available to lend out.

In the beginning, all of this was probably innocent enough. But eventually the bankers figured something out: if the credit risk was going to be *someone else's problem*, they could make more money by relaxing their lending standards, and making loans they previously would never have made under *portfolio lending*. After all, it was the bond buyer's job to evaluate the credit risk, and the buyers were professional investors. Why wouldn't the bank be more aggressive in making more loans—even loans to borrowers with questionable credit history? The bank's risk was limited to the period of time from when the loan was first made until it was sold to another institution, often a matter of only several weeks. Why not go ahead and start loaning money to questionable borrowers, and let the bond buyers take the credit risk?

The *subprime lending* business was born.

This led to even more dubious practices on the part of the bankers. Many banks started offering variable-rate loans with *teaser rates*—artificially low interest rates for the first six to twelve months on a mortgage that would then "reset" to a market-determined rate after the initial period. These *teaser rates* were promoted as an innovative way to help new homebuyers cushion the financial impact of buying a home during a period which often required a number of subsequent purchases in the first year such as furniture and appliances.

The low teaser rate would help keep mortgage payments affordable during this "crunch period". Or that was the sales pitch anyway. Pardon my cynicism, but it's pretty clear to me that the real purpose of *teaser rates* was to make sure the odds of borrowers defaulting *during the period the lending bank was still on the hook for the default risk* would be extremely low. Once the loan had been sold off through a bond issuance to a pension fund or other institution ... well, then it wasn't the lending bank's problem anymore, was it?

This trend accelerated and grew throughout the 1980s and 1990s, and eventually culminated in the 2007 housing bubble. By that time bankers had figured out they could sell almost any mortgage, no matter how dubious the creditworthiness of the borrower. All they had to do was get one of the major bond rating agencies to give the bond an investment-grade rating, and there would be buyers for the bonds. The bankers knew full well that many of the loans would never be repaid.

The originators of the loans were using terminology like *Liar Loans* and *Ninja Loans,* which stood for "No income, no job, no assets". They were literally adopting new industry terminology poking fun at the absurdity of loaning money to insolvent borrowers. But the trend marched on just the same. Ninja or otherwise, if they could get an investment grade rating, they could sell the bonds. They had no reason to care what happened after that.

The result was the 2008 Great Financial Crisis, which had horrific consequences for millions of people. So many families were losing their homes to foreclosure that government systems couldn't even keep up with the process. Courts were setting aside centuries of precedent and scheduling single hearings for dozens of foreclosures at a time. You know the rest of the story, it was an absolute mess.

What does all of this have to do with digital currency? Private credit expansion is incredibly important. When it goes astray, as occurred with subprime mortgages, the consequences to society can be astronomical. But what if all money were digital, including the money in the commercial banking system? What if government regulators had much more precise instrumentation showing them exactly what was going on in the private credit system?

What if people just as smart as the cypherpunk inventors of cryptocurrency set their minds to designing a system where reckless lending practices were immediately visible to regulators and central bankers, because the entire monetary system was designed to use technology to enhance both the instrumentation and the monetary policy tools central bankers have at their disposal?

True, once government is in charge, the digital currency systems of the future won't match Satoshi's libertarian vision. But I know the brightest minds in the crypto community are capable of designing a government-issued digital currency system that could help prevent things like the subprime fiasco from recurring.

Fitting digital currency into the system

Suppose that we're designing a new government-issued digital currency system to replace an existing national currency system. How should digital money fit into the equation?

A government-issued digital currency system could replace the actual currency in circulation (M0, the notes and coins issued by the Treasury) with a government-sponsored digital currency that works similar to a cryptocurrency like Bitcoin. In this scenario the *central bank money* would be replaced by digital currency that uses public-private key security to move monetary value around between *addresses* just like Bitcoin does today. Then the commercial banking system would do what it's always done; offer checking accounts, savings accounts, time deposits and so forth. Just like the current conventional currency system, the banking system would account for the money on deposit using its own systems of record.

When you deposit a digital coin with a bank, the bank would *owe* you an equivalent digital coin. But your deposit at the bank wouldn't be stored in the digital currency system—it would be stored in the bank's accounting system, the same way the current system works. The digital coins you deposited would be lent out to other customers, and the total amount of digital coin deposits in the banking system would exceed the number of digital coin tokens that exist in the digital currency system, just as today's bank deposits exceed the amount of currency issued by the government. This would allow banks to continue offering loans and the other services they currently offer, and that society relies on them to provide.

But hold on … Is that really the best way to modernize the monetary system using digital currency technology? Take pause and consider why the system even works this way to start with. If prominent Americans like Henry Ford think the system is so crazy that there would be a revolution if everyone fully understood how it really works, should we be trying to figure out how to make digital currency work in that *same* system? Or *would it be better to rethink the system itself*, and figure out how to use digital currency to build a *better* system?

What if the whole system were redesigned with cognizance of how central bankers want to be able to manage the economy, as opposed to figuring out primitive ways to cajole a system that evolved over centuries without much forethought? My contention is that a digital currency system could be designed to be so far superior to conventional monetary systems that the issuing government and its citizens would derive a significant financial advantage over the rest of the world, and the currency system would have a far better chance of displacing the U.S. dollar as the world's global reserve currency.

Securitization led to horrific unintended consequences for society, and it shows *just one example* of where digital technology could be used to design something much better. But the opportunity isn't by any means limited to securitized mortgages. *The entire FRB system could be completely re-engineered using digital currency technology.*

Critics of FRB, including the cypherpunk inventors of cryptocurrency, might suggest that FRB is the whole problem and that it should be abolished completely. While there may be some merit to their arguments, I very strongly doubt that the whole system would ever be thrown out completely, because society has become dependent on *bank loans*. We use borrowed money to buy homes and automobiles, and credit cards and home equity lines of credit have expanded in use over the last few decades.

Assume for sake of this discussion that bank lending is here to stay, and that society needs bank loans and other forms of credit. A widely accepted standard is that the private-sector commercial banking system should do the lending. Lending involves risk and reward, and that risk should be taken by the private sector, not by government. The ability of the commercial banking industry to increase the money supply by making loans is something we need to preserve.

But does it make sense to just assume the new system should work just like the old one? Where the money supply expansion occurs on the books of commercial banks, using the same fractional reserve mechanisms to regulate and control its growth.

Should we replace M0 with digital currency and let the banking system continue to do business the way it always has, or would it make more sense to make all money—both central bank money and commercial bank money—digital, so that digital currency technology could be used to clean up the old ways of doing business?

Monetary policy is imprecise, primitive, and often ineffective

The tools available to central bankers are anything but precise. They monkey around with interest rates under their direct control which have no direct impact on consumer or business lending, but which *indirectly* create financial incentives for bankers to be more or less aggressive in their lending policies. The overall system was never designed to work as effectively as possible. Rather, the business of bank lending and consumer lending developed out of necessity, and then central bankers started to figure out after-the-fact how to influence the process to have some semblance of control over the economy on whole.

At risk of sounding like a broken record, I can't help but wonder what could be possible if the entire system were carefully redesigned so that the currency system is fully digital—not just the base money, but all of the commercial bank money as well. And what if the whole thing were designed to give central bankers more precise instrumentation to understand credit flows as they occur in real-time (as opposed to after-the-fact analysis)? And what if the new system offered central bankers an entirely new suite of monetary policy tools such as more direct and precise mechanisms to incentivize or dis-incentivize private sector lending, as opposed to today's system where they struggle to influence the system through very imprecise, indirect "levers" of control?

In short, what if people just as smart and tech-savvy as the cypherpunks had the opposite goal, and decided to put their heads together and design a new global digital currency system which allowed the status quo central bank power structure to continue, but made it several orders of magnitude more effective? *How would the citizens of the countries using that new monetary system fare relative to the rest of the world still struggling along under conventional monetary systems?*

Chapter 11:
Central Banks & Monetary Policy

> *"A private central bank issuing the public currency is a greater menace to the liberties of the people than a standing army. We must not let our rulers load us with perpetual debt."*
> –Thomas Jefferson, while serving as U.S. Secretary of State

The phrase *central bank* refers to the government institution which is responsible for managing a country's monetary affairs. In the case of the *European Central Bank*, it's not just a country but the entire European Union's *Euro* currency system. In the case of the *Federal Reserve*, the United States' central bank, it's organized as a group of several private corporations. But despite this bizarre legal structure, for all intents and purposes the Federal Reserve operates as a part of the U.S. Federal Government. The President of the United States appoints its chairman, and it is accountable to Congress. The Fed was created by and draws its authority from the *Federal Reserve Act of 1913*.

The very question of whether the United States should even have a central bank has been an extremely controversial issue throughout American history. Thomas Jefferson worked very hard to prevent the creation of a central bank, and was instrumental in causing the demise of America's first two central banks. That's right, the *Federal Reserve* isn't the United States' first or only central bank, but the *fourth*, and the first three all had scandalous histories.

The first U.S. central bank opened in 1782, before the Constitution was even signed. It was called *The Bank of North America*, because its founders hoped at the time that Canada would soon join the rebel colonies and form a union occupying the entire North American continent. But by the end of 1783, the nation's first Central Bank experiment was over, following allegations of fraud and graft.

The next U.S. central bank would be the First Bank of the United States, proposed to congress in 1790 by Alexander Hamilton, and vehemently opposed by Thomas Jefferson, then Secretary of State. Congress granted the First Bank of the United States a twenty year charter in 1791. Those twenty years were punctuated by more allegations of fraud and malfeasance, and the charter was never renewed. The First Bank of the United States closed on January 24, 1811.

Thomas Jefferson, the most outspoken opponent of having a U.S. central bank, retired from politics in 1814, and it didn't take long before the Second Bank of the United States (the third such attempt, remember) was proposed in 1816. This bank became the subject of immense public debate, this time with President Andrew Jackson leading the charge against the bank in Jefferson's stead. The Second Bank of the United States lasted until 1836, when it finally closed its doors and its founders were prosecuted for fraud and graft.

After three strikes in a row for central banking in the United States, President Andrew Jackson had won the battle begun by Thomas Jefferson. All three of the nation's central bank experiments had been organized as private banks owned by private investors, but granted special charters by the government, effectively granting them a license to control the nation's money. In all three cases, the story ended with widespread allegations of fraud and abuse against the central banks' organizers and senior bankers. The idea of allowing a privately owned bank to control the nation's money was finally dead.

But it was resurrected seventy-seven years later with the passage of the *Federal Reserve Act* in 1913, which once again chartered a privately owned bank to run the country's monetary system. The Fed has been our central bank ever since. Today's Fed has its share of critics, but no one as influential or outspoken as Thomas Jefferson and Andrew Jackson were in their day. The Federal Reserve is owned by all of the commercial banks in the country, which are each required to own stock in one of the twelve regional Federal Reserve Banks.

What does the central bank actually do?

The Federal Reserve and its twelve regional Federal Reserve Banks have a long list of important but relatively mundane responsibilities. These range from compiling economic statistics and publishing reports, to regulating some aspects of commercial banks and operating the federal payment system, which allows commercial banks to place money on deposit with the Federal Reserve and to borrow from the Fed under certain circumstances.

While all these functions are important, the real action occurs in the *Federal Open Market Committee*, or FOMC, which sets monetary policy

Chapter 11:
Central Banks & Monetary Policy

and decides what *Open Market Operations*—meaning buying and selling securities on the open market—the Fed should engage in. This function of setting the nation's monetary policy and deciding whether, when and how to use the Fed's unlimited spending authority to buy and sell securities (usually treasury bonds) is the reason that many scholars agree that the Chairman of the Federal Reserve is the second most powerful person on earth, behind the President of the United States. Many geopolitical experts agree that Janet Yellen's service as Fed Chair made her the most powerful woman in world history.

Most central banks around the world issue the national currency, in addition to setting monetary policy. The United States is unusual in that it has a separate *Treasury Department* which issues the currency, but the Federal Reserve is the principal policy-setting entity.

The Fed's many functions are an interesting subject, but they're beyond the scope of this book. The balance of this chapter will therefore focus on *Monetary Policy*—the power the Fed has to manage the economy by setting policy which influences (among other things) the size of the money supply.

Dual Mandate

Since 1977, the Federal Reserve has operated under a *dual mandate* from Congress to "promote effectively the goals of maximum employment, stable prices, and moderate long term interest rates". The part about "stable prices" was added in 1977, after several years of runaway inflation caused great damage to the economy.

Maintaining "stable prices" is another way of saying that the central bank's job is to ensure that the currency system serves as a reliable *store of value*, one of the requirements set forth in the *tripartite definition of money*. In other words, the Fed's job is to make sure that money retains its value and inflation doesn't get out of hand. But that said, the Fed has interpreted this to pertain to relatively short time horizons. As noted in Chapter Two, the U.S. dollar has lost more than 97% of its purchasing power since the Fed took over managing the currency in 1913, but this isn't considered a failure by the central banking community because it occurred slowly and gradually over a long period of time.

Monetary Policy

Monetary policy is the process through which the central bank manages the currency system to achieve its goals of maximum employment and price stability. Monetary policy is usually divided into the broad categories of *conventional monetary policy*, the tools central bankers use routinely, and *unconventional monetary policy*, special tools and techniques employed when conventional policy proves insufficient to achieve goals.

Conventional Monetary Policy

The central bank can directly change the amount of *narrow money* (M0 or MB) in the money supply. But since M0 represents less than 30% of U.S. M3, it should be clear that the most effective way to stimulate or curb growth in the economy is for the central bank to influence the rate of commercial bank lending, which is the principal source of growth in *broad money* and makes up most of the money supply.

The way to increase sales of anything is to put it *on* sale—to reduce the price. Conversely the way to slow the pace of sales is to increase the price. When the "something" in question is money itself, the "price" of that money is the interest rate at which it can be borrowed. So most monetary policy involves the central bank doing things to *influence* the rate of interest charged when taking out loans. Bring the interest rate down, and more lending will occur, causing the money supply to increase and (usually) helping to accelerate the pace of economic growth. Raise the interest rate

Chapter 11:
Central Banks & Monetary Policy

and lending will slow down, reducing the rate of expansion or even bringing about contraction of the money supply. This usually has the effect of *taking away the punch bowl*—causing the rate of economic growth to slow down.

What can central bankers do to influence the rate of interest commercial banks offer to borrowers? They have three principal tools: *policy rates, open market operations,* and *reserve requirements.*

Policy Rates

Interest rates charged to borrowers are set by the commercial banking system, through the process of free-market price discovery. In other words, banks compete on supply and demand for lending business, and the central bank doesn't have the ability to dictate what interest rates should be charged. But the central bank *does* have the ability to directly set interest rates charged to the banks themselves. These are known as *policy rates* because they are set as a matter of central bank policy.

In the case of the U.S. Federal Reserve, the primary policy rates are the *fed funds rate* and the *discount rate*. These two interest rates are closely related; they both determine the cost the banks pay for short-term (usually overnight) loans, which they use frequently to finance their own operations. When banks lend their excess reserves to one another, the *fed funds rate* is used. When banks borrow from the central bank, the *discount rate* is used. The Federal Open Market Committee (FOMC) sets both of these interest rates as a matter of policy.

The theory of operation is that changing the banking system's own cost of borrowing is likely to cause the bankers to pass those costs or savings on to their customers. Think of it like a system where taxi cab fares are determined by supply and demand. The government can't directly set the fares, but they can change the price the taxi drivers pay for gasoline by adjusting tax rates. It's an indirect mechanism, but lower gas costs will generally result in more competition and lower taxi fares.

These *policy rates* are usually the first line of defense (or offense, as the case may be) when the Fed wants to influence markets. The FOMC meets about once every six weeks, and the finance industry follows their official FOMC policy statements like groupies at a rock concert waiting for an autograph. Changes in policy rates are the most obvious indication of a change in central bank policy or intentions, and are followed very closely by investors and economists.

Policy rate *easing* and *tightening* cycles

Policy rates can be changed by the FOMC at any time in either direction, but in practice the FOMC usually hints publicly at its intentions before taking action to change policy rates. This usually occurs in gradual increments, typically involving a series of rate cuts or hikes which are made one-quarter percent (twenty-five basis points) at a time.

When the FOMC decides it needs to stimulate the economy through policy rates (an *easing* cycle), it will typically make a series of quarter-point interest rate cuts, no more than once every six weeks. Conversely, when the FOMC wants to reverse direction with a *tightening cycle*, this generally occurs with a series of quarter-point rate hikes, again no more than once every six weeks. Each cycle usually includes at least four and sometimes as many as twelve or more consecutive cuts or hikes to gradually achieve the FOMC's objective.

This process is very imprecise, and the mechanism of transmission to the economy is difficult to predict. Easing and tightening cycles are usually ineffective at first, but eventually take hold and often overshoot their objectives, forcing a reversal of FOMC policy.

The most insightful explanation I've ever heard for how central bank tightening cycles work came from a commentary written by Eric Janszen, a former tech entrepreneur turned macroeconomic analyst. Paraphrasing Janszen's description from memory, here's how it works: Suppose you are the central bank, and worried that the economy has started to get ahead of itself, bringing rise to concern about inflation risk. You want to very gradually slow the economy down, but in a way so you don't accidentally crash the economy.

Now imagine you're standing in front of a bookshelf. A very heavy concrete cinder block rests on a shelf well above your head. This represents the economy running a little hotter than you think it should. So you wrap an elastic bungee cord around the cinder block, and then put the ends between your teeth. Then, very slowly, you step back from the bookshelf, just one quarter inch at a time.

After the first step back, nothing happens. You wait six weeks and take another step back. Still nothing. Another six weeks, another step back. Still nothing. The process continues for many months, and there's no apparent change in the economy. But you diligently follow the process as your central bank mentors taught you. Finally, as the bungee cord grows very tight, you take just one more fateful quarter-inch step back.

Chapter 11:
Central Banks & Monetary Policy

After you wake up with a concussion in the hospital, you schedule a press conference and announce that there was absolutely no way to see the recession coming, and you're going to respond immediately by beginning an easing cycle!

All joking aside, the process really *is* very imprecise. However, these tightening and easing cycles in policy rates are still the central bank's *most* effective and commonly used tool to regulate the economy and manage the currency system to avoid inflation or deflation. *These are the best tools they have.* Isn't it time for society to look towards technology to design a better mousetrap?

Open market operations

Policy rates determine the interest paid on overnight loans made to banks. They have a *transmission effect* that carries over to other interest rates, but generally only influence the rates charged on other relatively short-term loans.

When central bankers want to influence longer-term interest rates, they need a different tool. Most long-term lending rates are determined by adding a profit margin to the yield offered by government treasury bonds. That means that the way to influence long-term interest rates is to cause a change in the yield of government treasury bonds.

Open market operations refers to buying or selling securities (usually government bonds) on the open market. All financial markets work on supply and demand. If a big buyer, such as a pension fund, starts buying any particular security such as a stock or bond, the price of that security will go up as a result. Similarly, when the central bank starts buying government bonds, the price will go up. When the central bank starts selling, the prices go down. The *yield*, or effective rate of interest generated from owning a government bond varies inversely with its price. Push the price higher, and the yield goes down. Push the price lower, and the yield goes up.

When the central banks want higher longer-term interest rates, they sell treasury bonds on the open market to push the price down, and the yield up. When they want lower long-term interest rates, they do the opposite and buy treasury bonds on the open market.

But this process is incredibly inefficient. Hedge funds and other professional traders take advantage of this process using a technique known as *front-running.* When pension funds and other institutional investors decide to buy or sell any security in size, they are incredibly secretive about their intentions. They know that if word gets out that they plan to buy millions of shares of stock in a hot technology company, smaller more agile traders will immediately buy before they do, then wait for the price to rise knowing there will be a buyer to sell to.

It's like jumping in line at a delicatessen to buy all the best selection of cold cuts. Then when good ol' Mrs. Jones shows up for her weekly purchase of a half-pound of pastrami, the deli will be sold out. At that point you pretend to be a nice guy and offer to sell Mrs. Jones the pastrami you just bought, but at a price 20% higher. If that sounds to you like a despicable way to take advantage of an elderly woman, then you're probably not a Wall Street banker. They do it all the time, but the stakes are much higher and the product is treasury bonds, not pastrami.

The central bank is a government entity that can't operate in secret. When the FOMC starts to buy treasury bonds, everyone on Wall Street knows that it's very likely to be the beginning of a trend. All the hedge funds and proprietary trading desks *front-run* the Fed by buying treasury bonds, then turn around and sell them back to the Fed a few months later when the Fed's goal of pushing prices up has been achieved. The profit these speculators make from front-running the central bank is an expense burden shared by the rest of society. There's no good way around this in the current system, because it's easy for the bankers to know the Fed's intentions, and to anticipate their next moves.

Reserve Requirements

The final conventional policy tool available to central bankers is to change the reserve requirement—the percentage of deposits that the banks must keep on hand in case any of those pesky depositors show up and want some or all of their money back. By decreasing reserve requirements, the central bank can stimulate lending because the banks are now at liberty to make more loans against the same amount of reserves.

This is dangerous business. If the criticisms of fractional reserve banking weren't enough already, lowering the reserve ratio is really asking for trouble. It means the banks will have even less capital on hand to deal with the situation where depositors want to exercise their legal right to withdraw their funds. For this reason, changes to reserve requirements are seldom used in routine application of monetary policy.

Chapter 11:
Central Banks & Monetary Policy

Unconventional Monetary Policy

Conventional monetary policy centers on the central bank influencing interest rates to encourage or discourage growth of the money supply through commercial bank lending. The primary tool for stimulating economic growth is to lower interest rates. This begs an obvious question: *what happens when interest rates fall to zero and there's no room for them to go lower?*

This situation is known as the *zero bound*. Once short-term interest rates are lowered to zero, there's no way to lower them further. This situation is also known as a *liquidity trap,* because the central bank's primary tool to stimulate liquidity in financial markets is lowering interest rates—which becomes impossible when they are already at zero.

Or it *used* to be considered impossible. Prior to the Great Financial Crisis, *negative interest rates*—the situation where depositors must pay a fee for the privilege of putting their savings in a bank so that the bank can turn around and lend the money out to someone else at a positive interest rate—was considered to be such a ludicrous idea that it would be out of the question. Until 2014, that is, when the European Central Bank added *negative interest rates* to the list of other unconventional monetary policy tools available to central bankers.

As should already be clear, unconventional monetary policy refers to what central bankers do when they're *desperate*—when nothing else is working and they have to find more creative ways to achieve their goals. Before the ECB added negative interest rates to the menu in 2014, the list of unconventional monetary policy tools was usually described as *forward guidance* and *quantitative easing*.

Forward Guidance

When the Fed speaks, people listen. In fact, that's a huge understatement. When the Fed signals a monetary policy decision *may* be on the horizon, financial markets often react dramatically. Prices of everything from the stock market to interest rate derivatives jump in one direction or another in reaction to even the *hint* that a tightening or easing cycle may be under consideration by the FOMC.

Financial institutions have even gone to the extreme of hiring body language experts to carefully watch the Fed chairman approach the podium at FOMC press conferences, hoping that some unconscious gesture will give away what he plans to announce, allowing speculative traders to front-run those who must wait just ten more seconds to hear what he actually has to say. That's obviously an extreme example, but Wall Street really does pay *that much attention* to the Fed's policy statements.

The Fed knows this, and takes advantage of it. Simply put, *forward guidance* means using press conferences to *signal* what the FOMC members are thinking and what they foresee. A chart released with FOMC policy statements known as the *dot plot* graphically depicts each FOMC member's best guess as to where short-term interest rates will be at various times in the future. Even small changes in the dot plot can cause big swings in financial market prices as investors reconcile their own expectations with those of the policy makers who actually have the power to influence them.

Forward guidance has been used very extensively by the Fed throughout the Great Financial Crisis and its aftermath to signal the Fed's policy intentions and set expectations with investors. It allowed them to effectively say, *"Not only have we lowered rates to zero, but we promise to keep them at zero for quite a while"*.

Quantitative Easing

Quantitative Easing (QE) is a controversial policy tool in which the central bank expands its balance sheet by creating more *base money* (MB) and using the newly created money to buy government treasury bonds through *open market operations*. The difference between QE and conventional open market operations is that QE involves expanding the monetary base to create money that never existed before to fund the open market operations. Generally speaking, QE occurs on a much larger scale than open market operations conducted as a part of conventional monetary policy.

Contrary to popular misconception, QE is not "money printing" in the sense that the central bank is not printing new banknotes (dollar bills) or otherwise putting the newly created money directly into public circulation. QE *does* involve conjuring *base money* into existence which didn't exist previously—something only the central bank can do. That money is then used to buy government treasury bonds, mostly from commercial banks.

Critics have argued that QE helps the banks, but not the rest of society, and there's a lot of merit to those criticisms. But let's start with former Fed Chair Ben Bernanke's explanation of how QE works and what he intended to achieve when the Fed started using this controversial policy tool under his leadership.

Chapter 11:
Central Banks & Monetary Policy

According to Ben Bernanke, the whole idea is that when ten-year treasury bonds were yielding 5% or 6%, they were offering commercial banks a pretty comfortable and very safe yield. They could earn a return on their capital considerably higher than inflation, and which involved taking almost no risk—something very appealing to the bankers in 2009 when financial markets were in a state of melt-down. Bernanke reasoned that by taking much of the supply of treasury bonds off the market (because the Fed bought them all up), the prices of those bonds would rise, and that equates to lowering the *yield*, or effective rate of interest they generate.

The idea was supposed to be that bankers hungry for yield that was no longer available from super-safe treasury bonds would start lending more aggressively, because the higher rates of interest they could generate from lending to consumers and businesses would appeal more than the artificially suppressed yield on treasury bonds. This was supposed to incentivize more lending, and Bernanke hoped that would jump-start the economy.

Critics thought that if the Bernanke Fed was going to conjure new money supply out of thin air, it should go to Main Street, not Wall Street. But Bernanke argued that the well-known *money-multiplier* effect of fractional reserve banking would mean that every dollar of monetary base (MB) created by quantitative easing would lead to several dollars of new lending (M3). He believed that, in the end, his approach would help Main Street more (because of the money multiplier effect) than so-called "helicopter money", meaning central banks issuing new currency and giving it directly to consumers to stimulate the economy.

Who was right? That's a subjective matter of opinion. Ben Bernanke most certainly succeeded in lowering long-term interest rates to unprecedented low levels. That had an enormous effect on asset prices. Stock markets soared, and previously depressed home prices started to recover. The so-called *wealth effect* caused people who own stocks either directly or through pension and retirement funds to benefit. Many critics still argue that most of the benefit went to Wall Street rather than Main Street.

The main point to observe about QE (and monetary policy in general) is that it's another very imprecise science. Central bankers don't have *direct* control over the things they wish to manage. Instead, they seek to *influence* how markets price things by using policy tools working through indirect and imprecise mechanisms. What more would you expect from a system which has evolved over several centuries, and which was never designed to give central bankers tools that efficiently achieve their objectives?

Monetary Policy in Context

To the best of my knowledge, central bankers do not employ divining rods, voodoo dolls, or witch doctors in the course of administering monetary policy. That's the good news. But the tools they do use are very primitive and the entire system is long-overdue for an overhaul.

If the whole point of all these monetary policy tools is to manage and oversee the process of money supply growth and contraction in the commercial bank lending process, wouldn't it make more sense to devise instrumentation to accurately monitor that process, and add controls and incentives to more directly encourage commercial banks to engage in lending most needed by society?

What if all of the money—including the "bank money" in M3—were digital currency, meaning that every transaction, every loan, every loan payment, and every other nuance of the commercial lending process were recorded on a secure distributed ledger? What if commercial banks were required to record metadata about every loan transaction, such as the ratio of loan principal to collateral value, and the credit rating of the borrower—all on that distributed ledger? For competitive reasons lenders would resist making that information public, but this problem could easily be solved using public-private key encryption, keeping the trade-secret information out of public view while still giving central bankers access to robust real-time monitoring tools.

Instead of using a single discount rate applicable to all transactions, the fed could offer several *tiered* discount rates. Incentives could be defined so that when lenders make loans in sectors of the economy policymakers deem most important to society, the banks earn points that allow them to borrow more money at the lowest discount rates. Bankers who choose to ignore the incentive offer would still pay the higher discount rate. This would allow central bankers to incentivize lending in a much more targeted and far more effective way.

What if quantitative easing created a special category of digital currency token that came with temporary restrictions requiring the money to be used (at least initially) for the purposes the central bank intended when it created that money, so that central bank liquidity injections meant to stimulate lending to businesses and consumers couldn't be redirected for speculation in the stock market?

Chapter 11:
Central Banks & Monetary Policy

We live in a world where the most powerful policymakers on the planet oversee the global economy by using tools about as sophisticated as a horse and buggy. *Whether or not* technology will be used to re-engineer the entire system to create something far superior isn't even a question in my mind. What I wonder about is *who* will be first to seize this opportunity, *how long will it take* before it happens, and what amount of advantage they will gain over the rest of the world.

Beyond Blockchain: The Death of the Dollar and the Rise of Digital Currency

Chapter 12:
Sovereign Debt

The phrase *sovereign debt* refers to the debt national governments owe to investors, both foreign and domestic. In other words, *government bonds*. This seems clear enough: governments borrow money to finance deficit spending and to meet other financing needs. The government effectively borrows money by selling bonds (a promise to repay the money borrowed, plus interest, by a certain date). Investors buy these bonds, effectively loaning money to the government.

But *sovereign debt* plays a special role in the monetary system that many people don't understand. Just to be clear, sovereign debt generally is a very involved topic, and entire books have been written about it. A complete examination of sovereign debt is well beyond the scope of this book—this chapter is just to acquaint you with some basic aspects of government bonds you need to understand to make sense of my vision of the future of digital currency—in which a *digital sovereign bond market* will eventually play a very important role.

The "Risk-Free" Asset

The *yield* on government bonds is known in finance circles as the *risk-free rate*, meaning the rate of return (interest) from investing in something completely risk-free. That sentence alone should raise some eyebrows. *Risk-free?* Is it somehow impossible for the government to default on its debt obligations and leave investors hanging? Well, that seems to be the sales pitch. The conventional wisdom goes something like this: Government bonds offer the full faith and backing of the federal government, and since any good patriotic citizen knows this is the most wonderful, amazing country on earth, nothing can go wrong. Cue the patriotic music …

In reality, history teaches us that governments have a long history of defaulting on their sovereign debt. Moreover, they have the power of law to change the rules so they can simply *restructure* their own debt in a way that results in not paying back all the money as originally agreed—and then still claim they never defaulted. Governments that borrow and spend recklessly are usually forced eventually to either default (not pay back the debt), or else use monetary policy to cause very high rates of inflation, which dilutes the amount of purchasing power value that must be repaid to service the debt. Either way, the investor who made the "risk-free" loan to the government gets screwed.

At the end of World War II, when the United States was a net creditor nation and had without question the strongest economy on the face of the earth, it was easy to understand why the words *Full faith and backing of the United States Government* caused investors to perceive U.S. Treasury bonds as being as safe as gold. But not only is the United States no longer a net creditor nation; it's now the biggest debtor nation *in the history of the world*. So there's plenty of reason to question just how free from risk the so-called *risk-free rate* really is. But right or wrong, it's accepted practice in finance to consider government bonds to be risk-free.

The role of government bonds as an interest rate benchmark

Most loans and other products whose prices are expressed as an interest rate are priced by adding a profit *margin* to a *benchmark rate* which determines the overall cost of borrowing money, regardless of risk. By way of example, suppose that a young woman wants a thirty-year mortgage to buy a new home. How does the bank decide what interest rate to offer? They start by *qualifying* her based on credit history and other measures which gauge how much she can afford the house. From there they classify her as either a *prime borrower*, *subprime borrower*, or any one of a number of pre-defined risk categories the bank uses.

Each category has a defined *risk margin*—the amount of interest the bank will charge above and beyond the *risk-free rate* to compensate for the risk they are taking with the loan. If we're talking about a thirty-year mortgage, the bank will use the thirty-year government Treasury bond yield as the risk-free rate, and then add the risk margin. The sum of those two figures is the interest rate they'll offer. If it's a five-year car loan, they'll determine the risk-free rate from the yield on five-year treasury paper.

Sovereign bonds aren't just used to finance government borrowing. They're the benchmarks from which almost all other interest rates are determined. That means when government bond yields go up, it's not just the government's cost of borrowing that increases. Every other interest rate in that country's economy rises in sympathy.

Chapter 12: Sovereign Debt

The role of sovereign bonds as a foreign diplomacy tool

Major treaties and "deals" between nations often involve one nation buying a large number of the other nation's sovereign bonds in exchange for some other concession. Suppose for example that a small developing nation is struggling financially, but has rich oil reserves. The U.S. government might agree to loan them fifty billion U.S. dollars by buying their treasury bonds, if they first agree to give U.S. oil companies a twenty-year lease on their oilfield assets. In this example, the U.S. government isn't buying the $50bn in bonds because they want to diversify their investment portfolio; the motivation is to strike some other sort of deal.

This comes in many forms. The motivations are almost always political rather than financial. And when a country threatens to default on bonds that another nation holds in size, military retaliation isn't out of the question. There's usually more to the story than first meets the eye when one nation decides to buy another nation's sovereign bonds.

The role of sovereign bonds as a central bank reserve asset

The phrase *central bank reserve asset* is a fancy way of describing the savings account of a central bank. It's the money that countries set aside for a rainy day when they might need it to cope with a crisis.

It might seem that any country would favor its own sovereign bonds as a reserve asset. But that would defeat the whole purpose. The reason central banks keep reserve assets is so that they have "emergency money" to defend their own currency in the event of a crisis. In such a crisis, their own bonds probably wouldn't be marketable. So they need a reliable store of value they'll be able to sell easily, even during a financial crisis.

Suppose for example that the Thai baht (Thailand's currency) is collapsing as a result of an emerging market credit crisis spreading throughout Asia. This exact event happened in the late '90s. Suppose the value of the baht is collapsing on International foreign exchange markets. If this is allowed to continue, everyone holding Thai baht including Thailand's own citizens and businesses might panic and sell all of their remaining baht for fear of being left with completely worthless currency. The Thai central bank can't allow that to happen, because it would have devastating effects on the entire country's future.

If the Thai central bank's reserves were all held in their own sovereign bonds, it would be very difficult to sell those bonds, because the rest of the world would be skeptical of the value of sovereign debt issued by any country facing such a currency crisis. The Thai central bank would urgently need to raise cash to *buy its own currency on the open market for the purpose of supporting the exchange rate and not allowing it to collapse.* In central banking parlance, this is known as *defending the currency.* In order to be able to do that, they need to keep reserve assets which can be sold no matter what. They need to keep their reserves invested in some asset whose value won't be questioned even in middle of the worst crisis imaginable.

Central banks used to hold gold bullion for this purpose. Gold has consistently proven itself as a reliable *store of value* for thousands of years, so no matter what goes wrong, gold can be sold to raise money to allow the central bank to defend its own currency.

But there's a problem with gold: it doesn't pay interest. And bankers like the idea of holding reserves in assets that produce regular income, such as treasury bonds issued by *other* nations—particularly financially secure nations. In theory any sovereign bond issued by a creditworthy nation would suffice for the purpose, and central banks sometimes own several different nations' sovereign bonds as reserve assets. Remember, it's sometimes necessary for *diplomatic* reasons to buy another nation's sovereign debt, and these bonds may be used as central bank reserve assets.

The most important factors central bankers consider when choosing reserve assets focus on how easily the asset could be sold to raise cash needed to defend the central bank's own currency. Furthermore, to defend their own currency, they need to raise cash in a currency that has a liquid foreign exchange market against their own currency. So for the Thai government, holding reserve assets denominated in Swiss Francs wouldn't do them much good—they'd need to raise U.S. dollars to defend their own currency in a crisis.

Conclusion

Sovereign bonds are used for special purposes in the financial system, in particular the role they play as a central bank reserve asset. The reasons this is going to be so important to the digital currency story will be made clear in coming chapters.

Chapter 13:
Reserve Currency Status

The phrase *reserve currency* refers to the dominant currency in the global financial system. While it's technically possible for multiple currencies to serve in this role simultaneously, for most of monetary history the title of *global reserve currency* has been held by one currency at a time. The exceptions are transition phases when one reserve currency is falling out of favor and another is taking over.

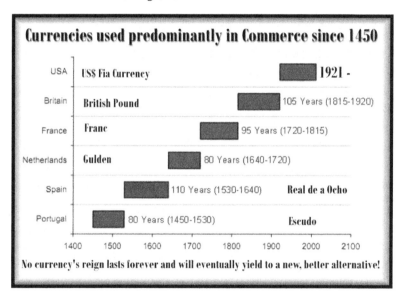

Figure 5: History of Reserve Currencies since 1450

Specifically, when a money system serves as *reserve currency*, this means two things:

1. Most international trade will be settled in that currency.
2. Central bank reserve assets other than gold bullion will usually be denominated in that currency.

Prior to World War I, the British *Pound Sterling* served for more than a century as the global reserve currency. The period from World War I to 1944 is an example of a transition period, when more than one currency served as reserve currency. The Pound Sterling was falling from favor, and the U.S. Dollar was gaining popularity. But prior to 1944, there was no officially agreed-upon reserve currency. Some central banks preferred U.S. dollars; others preferred to hold British pounds.

After World War II, the U.S. dollar was made the world's global reserve currency by international treaty at the *Bretton Woods* conference in 1944. The Bretton Woods system depended on the U.S. dollar's convertibility into gold. That system ended when President Nixon suspended gold convertibility in 1971, but the dollar has remained the de-facto global reserve currency ever since.

International trade settlement

Before the age of computers, it was absolutely essential to choose a standard currency for international trade settlement. Imagine what a logistic nightmare it would have been to pay for imported goods and services in the currency of the exporting nation. Countries would have to keep French Francs on hand to pay for the wine imported from France, have plenty of German Marks to pay for luxury German automobiles, keep Japanese Yen on hand in the era when Japan dominated low-cost offshore manufacturing, and so forth.

Obtaining all that foreign currency would be incredibly cumbersome. For these reasons, it's always been customary to choose a single, standard trade settlement currency. The logical choice is to use the same currency favored for central bank reserves.

Since 1944, almost all international trade has been settled in U.S. dollars. There's no law or treaty requiring this, and some transactions have always been settled in local national currencies. But for most international trade, everything gets priced in dollars and settled in dollars. For most of the world, this means that fluctuations in the exchange rate between the local currency and the dollar represent an unavoidable business risk. Many large non-U.S. corporations keep bank accounts denominated in dollars for this reason.

The necessity for a standard international trade currency has decreased in the computer age. International foreign exchange transactions occur at the click of a mouse. But that said, most trade is still settled in dollars as a matter of convention and convenience.

Central bank reserve assets

While it's true that the global reserve currency is used to settle most international trade, *reserve currency* really refers more to the currency which central bankers around the world favor to hold their *reserve assets*. A currency crisis could arise at any time without warning, and it's very likely that other parts of the global financial system would be affected too, meaning that there's good reason to assume global market conditions might be unstable when reserve assets are needed most. When it comes to selecting reserve assets, the name of the game is *safety and liquidity*. In other words, something that can be sold no matter what else is going on at the time, including major wars and other geopolitical crises.

Government bonds usually offer a yield that exceeds the rate of inflation, and can be bought and sold without the logistic complications of delivering and storing gold bullion. So *sovereign bonds* have become the favored central bank reserve asset.

There's no law or treaty dictating what asset central banks must choose as their reserve asset, but something known as *network effect*[22] almost acts as an unwritten law. Network effect means that any central bank is probably best off holding the same assets all the other central banks favor. If you have to sell them in a hurry, your fellow central bankers in other countries are likely to be ready buyers.

Network effect not only causes U.S. Treasury bonds (USTs) to be favored; it also has the effect of causing other assets to be eschewed. For example, gold bullion is still the most reliable store of value in existence, but you'll more easily find buyers for a billion dollars worth of USTs than a billion dollars worth of gold, especially if you need to sell in a hurry.

The result is that U.S. Treasury Bonds have become the de-facto central bank reserve asset of choice. This is slowly changing as more and more countries voice frustration over the way the United States takes advantage of the power it derives from being the reserve currency issuer. But for the most part, U.S. Treasury securities are still second only to gold in terms of their perceived reliability as a *store of value*. And unlike gold, U.S. Treasuries pay interest and trade in liquid markets.

Why the U.S. Dollar still holds the title

Although more and more countries around the world have become frustrated with America's monopoly over the global financial system, the fact remains that there simply is no viable alternative to the U.S. Treasury Bond market when it comes to choosing interest-bearing central bank reserve assets. No bond market in the world begins to match the *depth*

---

[22] https://en.wikipedia.org/wiki/Network_effect

and *liquidity* characteristics of the UST market. You can sell a whole lot of USTs all at once, and you can always expect to find a ready buyer. Furthermore, even if you are selling a very large number of USTs, it's unlikely you'll cause the market price to drop by very much. No other sovereign bond market can compete.

There's yet another aspect of *network effect* that comes into play, pertaining to the currency the reserve asset is denominated in rather than the depth and liquidity of the market for the reserve asset itself. A central bank might need to sell reserve assets to defend its own currency in a crisis, which means buying their own currency on the open market. Well guess what? Because the dollar is the dominant international currency, there's far more liquidity in the *foreign exchange* market for exchange of dollars for other currencies. Consequently, when a foreign central bank needs to sell reserve assets to raise cash, it's specifically U.S. dollar cash they need to raise. If they held reserve assets denominated in another currency, they would take on exchange rate risk because they'd still need to convert the other currency to Dollars before they'd be ready to defend their own currency in the open market.

Of course, this is a self-fulfilling prophecy; if the German Bund market were bigger than the U.S. Treasury market, and everyone agreed that the Euro was the dominant global currency, then it would be Euros that would be needed in a crisis and therefore German Bunds (denominated in Euros) would be preferable to U.S. Treasuries. But in today's world, everything is based on the U.S. dollar, so therefore central bank reserve assets need to be denominated in U.S. dollars. For all intents and purposes, that makes USTs the reserve asset of choice.

Russia and China in particular have been very outspoken in saying that the world should "ditch the dollar" and stop giving the United States a monopoly over the system. They've even used the phrase *financial terrorism* to describe U.S. policy. So far, most of the rhetoric from Russia and China has focused on *trade settlement* in other currencies, not on moving away from USTs as a central bank reserve asset. But it's the *reserve asset* use of dollar-denominated U.S. Treasuries that gives the U.S. dollar its hegemony over the rest of the global financial system. So if this is the case, why aren't Russia and China focusing on central bank reserves rather than trade settlement?

The answer is simply that there's no viable alternative to USTs. The Chinese government has been widely accused of less-than-accurate accounting practices, and the Chinese currency is still closed, meaning the

Chinese government doesn't allow unrestricted conversion of Yuan owned by Chinese into other currencies. Meanwhile, Russia defaulted on its sovereign debt in 1998 and the Ruble has collapsed in value against other currencies just in the past few years. These are hardly selling points to persuade the rest of the world to redenominate their central bank reserves in Russian or Chinese sovereign debt.

While it's essential to understand that there *simply is no viable alternative* to USTs as central bank reserve assets, *a growing number of national governments are strongly motivated to figure out how to create one*. Digital currency is likely to play a key role in that process, and a *digital sovereign bond market* integrated with a government-issued global digital currency system could redefine the global balance of power completely.

Advantages enjoyed by the reserve currency issuer

The issuer of the global reserve currency derives many advantages from this status. Perhaps the most obvious benefit is that, unlike every other country, American consumers and American businesses don't have to plan their affairs around the constant need to convert their national currencies to and from U.S. dollars. To the rest of the world, this is an accepted fact—and it's not free, either. In smaller emerging economies in particular, it's not uncommon for the cost of essential goods and services to double in the local currency even as their prices in U.S. dollars remain constant. This factor alone causes considerable volatility and uncertainty in those nations' economies.

The really profound benefits the U.S. derives from its status as reserve currency issuer are less obvious. Reserve status creates an enormous *artificial demand for both dollars and U.S. Treasury Bonds* world-wide. If the whole world settles most international trade in U.S. dollars—including transactions to which the U.S. is not even a party—that means everyone needs plenty of dollars on hand to facilitate that trade. And as the global economy grows over time, the number of dollars needed to support it grows accordingly.

Meanwhile, because USTs are the favored central bank reserve asset, there's also an enormous international demand for USTs. Have you ever wondered how the U.S. Government gets away with borrowing and spending so much more money than it takes in from taxes? Is the politicians' mantra that "Deficits don't matter" at odds with common sense? After all, if normal people go into excessive debt, it matters a whole lot. But as crazy as it might sound, the U.S. has amassed a $21.5 trillion national debt, and continues to deficit-spend as if borrowing and spending beyond one's means has no adverse consequence whatsoever. *How do they keep getting away with this?*

Artificial demand for U.S. Treasury paper is created by central banks around the world needing more USTs as their economies grow. So it really is true, *at least in the short term*, that deficit spending doesn't cause any *immediate* adverse consequence for the U.S. economy.

If any *other* (non-reserve issuer) country tried to get away with borrowing and spending the way the U.S. does, it would pay a very heavy price in the form of a much higher cost of borrowing for both its government and private sector, since private sector interest rates derive from government bond yields. But the U.S. gets away with it because even when the U.S. Government spends well beyond what it takes in from tax income, the treasury bonds that must be issued to fund the deficit are quickly sold to central bankers who cherish them as reserve assets. So long as there's plenty of demand for USTs from central banks, the U.S. can issue more bonds (which means borrow more money) without paying the price of higher interest rates.

Ultimately, *deficits really do matter*, and one of the oldest adages in finance still holds true: *there's no free lunch, and someday the piper has to be paid.* The U.S. Government was able to *get away with it* almost without any immediate adverse consequence whatsoever when the global economy was growing at a pace that caused the global demand for U.S. Treasury paper to grow at an even faster rate than the U.S. Government was borrowing and spending beyond its means. All that extra debt was scooped up by central banks that value USTs as second only to gold for their store of value, and therefore needed them as reserve assets.

Now the world is changing. More and more countries are questioning the wisdom of favoring the dollar as the center of the global economy. When the day comes that the artificial International demand for U.S. Treasury paper dries up, *budget deficits will suddenly matter again, and they'll matter a whole lot.*

When the cycle starts to work in reverse, and central banks are divesting their UST holdings in favor of other reserve assets, the adverse consequences for the American economy will be profound. It's fair to assume that quite a few governments would love to replace their dollar and UST holdings with an equally suitable non-U.S. alternative. The problem is simply that none exists. *Yet.*

Chapter 13: Reserve Currency Status

Consider what could happen if a global digital currency system *with a built-in digital sovereign bond market that not only matches but exceeds the depth and liquidity of the UST market* were introduced. If Russia or China introduced that digital currency/sovereign bond market system, they might completely upstage the dollar. On the other hand, if the U.S. were to beat them to the punch and introduce a Digital Dollar with integrated digital sovereign bond market, the U.S. could easily lock in the hegemony it now enjoys for another fifty years. *The stakes couldn't be higher.*

Just as reserve currency status causes enormous artificial demand for U.S. sovereign debt, the currency itself enjoys the same effect. Demand for dollars around the globe means that dollars tend to appreciate against other currencies. Americans pay lower prices for imported goods and services. What would American life be like if we no longer had Wal-Marts filled with cheap imported goods from China?

There can be an adverse effect here: American businesses that sell primarily to foreign buyers are damaged by too strong a dollar, because it makes their products unaffordable to foreigners. But the U.S. Government knows this, and can take action to intentionally weaken the dollar to protect U.S. exporters. The primary mechanism for doing this is to lower the interest rate paid on U.S. Treasury paper. By making USTs less attractive to foreign investors, there's less demand for dollars to buy those USTs. This translates to a lower cost of borrowing for the U.S. Government, lower taxes for American taxpayers, and lower interest rates for consumers and businesses in the U.S. It's a win-win all the way around. And all these benefits are made possible by the artificial demand for both dollars and USTs created by reserve currency status.

My opinion is that very few U.S. politicians understand how any of this works. We're prone to concluding that we lead the world economy because as Americans, we're just so much better than the rest of the world. What if we've just been getting a free ride from the benefits of reserve currency issuer status? *And what if there is a clear and present danger right here, right now, that a lot of governments want to remove the dollar as global reserve currency?* Are we taking these risks as seriously as we should? Do our politicians understand them? I think not.

Triffin's Dilemma

Economist Robert Triffin wrote quite a bit about reserve currencies back in the 1960s. That was more than fifty years ago, but what's become known as *Triffin's Dilemma*[23] or *Triffin's Paradox* is probably more relevant today than when Triffin first wrote about it. The essence of Triffin's Dilemma is that the reserve currency issuer faces a conflict of interest between domestic and international objectives with regard to its currency, because the need to meet international demand for the currency requires running a persistent current account deficit, but this is at odds with prudent domestic policy.

Plain English translation: the reserve currency issuer almost *has to* constantly run a trade deficit—buying more imports than exports it sells—in order to supply the world with all the extra dollars needed for international trade settlement. Furthermore, the demand for its sovereign bonds allows the reserve currency issuer to borrow and spend beyond its means without any *immediate* adverse consequence, and governments can never seem to resist doing so.

No, there's never a free lunch and there most certainly is an immense long-term adverse consequence.

Here's an even more direct simplification.

1. **Q**: How do you choose the reserve currency to start with?
   A: You pick the currency that is the *strongest credit*. At the end of World War II, with most of the world laying in ruin, there was no question that the U.S. was the strongest credit on earth.

2. **Q**: What is the *consequence* of becoming global reserve currency?
   A: The issuing government gets what is effectively a license to borrow and spend beyond its means *without immediate adverse consequence*. The reserve-issuing government can get away with decades of reckless deficit spending without suffering the usual penalty of a skyrocketing cost of borrowing.

3. **Q**: What is the *result* of the reserve issuer having this license to be reckless?
   A: It takes many decades to play out, but governments generally cannot resist taking advantage of this license, so they borrow and spend as if deficits truly don't matter at all, and they keep doing so until *eventually*, they reach the point where they're no longer the *best credit* and they're so over-indebted that their currency is no longer even suitable to continue as global reserve currency.

---

[23] https://en.wikipedia.org/wiki/Triffin_dilemma

Chapter 13:
Reserve Currency Status

4. **Q**: What happens then?
   A: The rest of the world figures out how to replace the reserve currency with something else more suitable. The former reserve issuer is then confronted with the harsh reality that benefits they'd taken for granted for decades suddenly vanish.

I believe that #3 has played out far enough to move on to the next step, but the world is currently stuck at implementing #4. Because *there's no apparent alternative* to the U.S. dollar *yet*.

What happens to currencies that lose reserve currency status? The last time that happened was when the British Pound Sterling lost the title. The currency system continued to exist and still exists today, but have a look at the below chart showing the decline in the real value of the pound in the years following the dollar's accession to the reserve currency throne. The transition from the pound to the dollar occurred between 1921 and 1944:

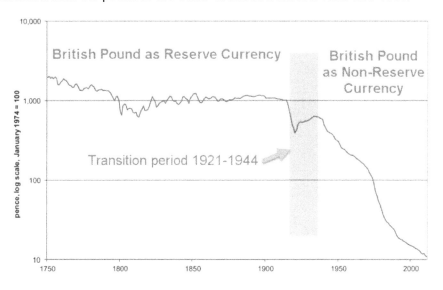

Figure 6: Loss in Real Value of the Pound Sterling, 1750-2011. Source: U.K. Parliament, FFTT

The U.S. has far more to lose than most Americans and American politicians realize when the world's central bankers collectively decide another currency system offers a superior alternative to the dollar. Russia has been an outspoken critic of the dollar's reserve currency status for several years. In 2018, first Germany and then the entire European Union began to side with Russia. This is a trend that should be of grave concern to all American citizens.

Beyond Blockchain: The Death of the Dollar and the Rise of Digital Currency

There's little doubt in my mind that the conventional U.S. Dollar will be replaced by a digital currency that will become the new global reserve currency. The only question is whether the U.S. Government or one or more foreign governments will be behind the new digital global reserve currency.

Chapter 14:
History of the U.S. Dollar

The word *Dollar*[24] has an interesting history dating back to 1520, and is the name of more than twenty currencies today. You can follow the link if you're curious; I'm going to focus on the more recent history of the U.S. dollar, particularly its role in the International Monetary System.

After the *Continental Dollar*[25] fiasco which resulted in a near-total collapse of purchasing power, the *gold and silver clause* was added to the new U.S. Constitution. The idea was supposed to be that we'd learned our lesson about fiat money and the framers hoped the gold and silver clause would prevent us from repeating our mistakes.

Colonial currencies had been backed by Spanish dollars, a popular silver coin of the day. Accordingly, the U.S. dollar was initially defined as a silver coin having the same weight of silver as the Spanish dollar, 371.25 grains of pure silver.

I'm going to keep this brief too so that we can focus on more recent history that contributes directly to the current situation.

Gold standard, Silver standard, or both?

Initially the value of the U.S. dollar was defined by the equivalent weight in silver specie. The precise amount of silver changed several times over the years. There were also periods when the definition was solely based on silver, and others when a gold-to-silver ratio was defined by law to fix the dollar's value to both gold and silver specie. This was known as a *bi-metallic standard*.

After civil war spending made it difficult for the U.S. Government to honor redemption of dollars for specie, pure fiat paper dollars known as *Greenbacks* were authorized and entered circulation in 1862. Once again, we'd returned to a fiat money system (at least temporarily), despite the lessons learned with the Continental Dollar fiasco. Silver was demonetized in 1873, and the U.S. Government eventually resumed redeeming dollars for gold. This would last until the Great Depression.

---

[24] https://en.wikipedia.org/wiki/Dollar
[25] https://en.wikipedia.org/wiki/Early_American_currency#Continental_currency

All privately owned gold bullion in the United States was nationalized by the Gold Reserve Act of January 1934. Americans would be allowed to own gold in jewelry and government-issued coins only; all citizens owning gold bullion were ordered to sell it to the Government at the official price of $20.67 per ounce. As soon as the privately held gold bullion had been collected, the dollar was promptly devalued from $20.67 to $35 per ounce of gold bullion. This was deemed a necessary emergency measure to cope with the effects of the Great Depression.

The United States Government has changed the definition of the dollar more times than I was accurately able to count researching this book. The one consistent theme I observe through the dollar's early history is that whenever circumstances became dire, the rules were changed and the promises made to the people assuring them that dollars could always be redeemed for gold or silver were usually not honored.

Bretton Woods System: A whole different kind of Gold Standard

After World War II, it was clear that the prior system in which the British *pound sterling* had served as global reserve currency needed an overhaul.

The *Bretton Woods*[26] conference was held at the Mount Washington Hotel in Bretton Woods, New Hampshire, during the first three weeks of July, 1944. The purpose of the conference was to define a new post-war financial order. With most of the Western world laying in ruin, the United States was in a far superior economic condition to most. The choice was clear: The U.S. dollar would sit at the center of this new financial world order.

The system conceived was a form of *gold convertibility* standard, similar to that described in Chapter Two. But this was a special breed of gold standard. The United States dollar would serve as the *anchor currency* for the rest of the International Monetary System. The U.S. Government would guarantee the convertibility of U.S. dollars to gold at the guaranteed fixed exchange rate of $35 per ounce. This would make the U.S. dollar literally "as good as gold" to holders who had the guaranteed right (until the U.S. defaulted on the deal in 1971) to trade their dollars in for gold any time they liked.

But there was a catch, and it was a big one! This right of conversion from dollars into gold would be honored for foreign *governments* only. It wasn't available to foreign commercial banks, companies, or individuals. And not

---

[26] https://en.wikipedia.org/wiki/Bretton_Woods_Conference

only did the deal *not* extend to the United States' own citizens, but they weren't even allowed to own gold bullion at all. The rules enacted in 1934 prohibiting ownership of gold bullion by private individuals in the United States still remained in effect.

This created a completely different kind of "gold convertibility standard". On one hand, the value of the dollar was still fixed (for domestic purposes) to silver, not gold. Most coins in the American currency system contained silver through 1965, so in the sense of American *citizens* having a right of conversion to precious metal it was a silver standard, not a gold standard, and it ended in 1965. This is why some texts describe 1965 rather than 1971 or 1976 as the year the United States moved from representative to fiat currency.

But for *international purposes*, the primary metal standard of interest was the *gold convertibility* standard guaranteed by the Bretton Woods treaty. But this guarantee only applied to foreign governments, not to individuals and firms. Therefore, even after silver coins were removed from circulation in 1965, the dollar still had a precious metal convertibility provision that applied to foreign governments who held dollars.

The next major provision of the 1944 Bretton Woods treaty was that all the other member nations would fix the exchange rates of their currencies to the U.S. dollar. The idea was to create an indirect global gold convertibility standard. All of the currencies of the world would once again be *considered* to have *gold backing* because those countries central banks always had the *guaranteed* legal option to redeem their dollar holdings for gold bullion any time they wanted. By fixing their own currencies' exchange rate to dollars, the intended effect was to persuade everyone that it didn't really matter how much gold (if any at all) these other countries actually had in their vaults, since the all-powerful United States had plenty, and the Bretton Woods treaty guaranteed all the governments of the world could convert dollars for gold at any time.

The Nixon Shock & Collapse of Bretton Woods

The Bretton Woods system worked beautifully for the first twenty years. The world could sleep at night knowing their money was as good as gold. After all, the United States was the most powerful nation on earth, and the treaty *guaranteed* that no matter what, all the other governments of the world could exchange their dollars for gold any time they liked, no questions asked! Who could ask for better than that?

But then something unexpected happened in the late 1960s: France *exercised* its "guaranteed" right to exchange dollars for gold. A lot of them. Those pesky Frenchmen! Why couldn't they understand that a confidence scheme like Bretton Woods only works until someone calls the bluff?

The U.S. had recklessly spent beyond its means on the Vietnam War, without raising taxes to fund those expenditures. The French government realized that the American Government's largesse left the U.S. dollar worth less in terms of real purchasing power than the gold it was still "guaranteed" to represent. So they took the only sane action available to them, and exercised the right promised to them by the Bretton Woods treaty and said, "We'll take our gold, please!"

President Nixon responded with a television address,[27] in which he angrily blamed "the international money speculators" who "attacked the dollar". But Dick Nixon had your back. He vowed to protect the American people by "defending the dollar" by directing the Treasury Secretary to "suspend temporarily" the convertibility of the dollar into gold.

This event would become known as the *Nixon Shock*. The abject absurdity of President Nixon's words couldn't be understated. First of all, nobody even had the option to convert dollars for gold other than foreign *governments* who were party to the Bretton Woods treaty. And the whole point of the treaty had been to *guarantee* their right to do so. Had the "international money speculators" the President spoke of actually existed, they wouldn't have posed a threat—because the convertibility clause only applied to foreign governments.

What really happened was that as soon as someone asked the United States to actually *honor* its primary obligation under Bretton Woods, President Nixon responded by defaulting unilaterally on the treaty system that formed the basis of the entire International Monetary System. With the benefit of this explanation of what really occurred, I encourage you to watch the video of President Nixon's address. It's a real testament to how governments restate the facts to suit their own agendas.

But one way or another, the Bretton Woods system was over. The United States broke its promise, and kept its gold rather than honoring the French governments' request. President Nixon's "temporary" suspension of gold convertibility remains in effect to this day, forty-seven years later.

---

[27] https://www.youtube.com/watch?v=iRzr1QU6K1o

Chapter 14: History of the U.S. Dollar

For all practical intents and purposes, Bretton Woods gold convertibility ended on August 15th, 1971. But at first, the law of the land continued to define the dollar as convertible to gold by central banks. After all, the suspension was just 'temporary', according to President Nixon's now-famous address. But by 1976 with inflation rapidly devaluing the dollar much further, it was clear that the official policy could never again be honored. The law was quietly changed in 1976, deleting the official exchange rate. This was the moment that the world was truly on a fiat money standard, and there was no room left to deny it. But that had already been clear to everyone who really understood what was going on. You'll find different sources citing 1965, 1971, and 1976 as the year the world moved to fiat currency—scholars are prone to nitpicking semantics, so they argue. One thing is clear: Dick Nixon unilaterally took the whole world off the gold convertibility standard, and we've lived in a pure fiat currency world ever since.

1970s runaway inflation

As soon as Nixon made his August 1971 announcement, not only was it clear that the dollar's true value was not as advertised, but also clear the U.S. knew it was in deep trouble. The result was entirely predictable: the Great Inflation of the 1970s began, and the effect on the economy was devastating. The economy wouldn't fully recover until the debt securitization trend of the early 1980s expanded the money supply.

Petrodollar system

U.S. Secretary of State Henry Kissinger knew that America had a serious problem. The Bretton Woods system had put the dollar at the center of the entire global monetary system. While I've been quick to criticize *today's* American politicians for not understanding the true importance of the dollar's reserve currency status, Kissinger was no dummy. He knew that the United States was screwed if the dollar lost the title. But after the Nixon Shock, not only was the dollar no longer convertible to gold, the whole world knew there was *plenty* of reason to "ditch the dollar", and Kissinger knew it.

Kissinger wasted no time. He got on a plane and headed to Saudi Arabia, where he met with the royal family. Several accounts indicate that Kissinger pitched a "protection scheme" that would have made any mafia boss proud. He made the Saudis *an offer they couldn't refuse.*

Kissinger pointed out that the royal family had it awfully good, sitting on top of oil reserves worth more than the gross national product of half the world.

And it would be a "real shame" if that situation changed. He offered the Saudi Royal Family the backing of the United States Military any time they needed it to put down a coup. *On one condition*: they had to promise to price all of their oil exports in U.S. dollars, regardless of the buyer. All oil deals get settled in dollars, and if they don't, well, *yous guys might just find you needed that protection we offered yous after all*. Oh, and just one more thing: the Saudis could keep the profits they made on the oil—it was theirs to keep, *provided they invested all those profits in U.S. Treasury bonds.*

It was a brilliant scheme. In effect, the dollar's monopoly over reserve currency status was extended indefinitely, despite the Nixon Shock fiasco. Oil is the biggest international trade market in existence by a wide margin—everybody needs oil. And if the price is always in dollars, everybody needs dollars. And if they all need dollars to pay for oil, well, heck, they might as well just keep using dollars as the global reserve currency for everything else, too. Meanwhile the Saudis would be buying enough USTs to keep the Triffin effect going in full force, allowing U.S. deficit spending to continue despite the Great Inflation having been *caused* by reckless deficit spending.

I should admit that my telling of the story is based on reading several accounts written by authors who probably share my own cynicism about the dubious ethics of big government conduct. Maybe what really happened wasn't quite as reminiscent of Mafia protection schemes and coercive tactics; I don't know—I was just a little kid at the time. But one way or another, oil would be priced in dollars and oil profits reinvested in USTs for many decades to come. King Dollar retained its throne.

Until recently, that is. The dynamics of global oil trade have changed a lot in the last ten years. The U.S. now produces more of its own oil than Saudi Arabia produces in total, and the percentage of Saudi oil exports which go to the U.S. are a small fraction of what they once were. In short, the U.S. is no longer Saudi Arabia's biggest customer. The two countries still enjoy a close diplomatic relationship, but the extraordinary leverage America once held over Saudi Arabia doesn't exist anymore.

The Petrodollar system is already under attack. If it fails and oil transactions are no longer priced and settled exclusively in dollars, that by itself poses a serious existential risk to the dollar's monopoly on global reserve currency status. There's never been a more ripe time than *right now* for someone to come along with a superior currency system to challenge the dollar's title as reserve currency. Digital currency technology offers the means to achieve that superiority.

Chapter 15: Sergei Glaziev's De-Dollarization Campaign

Most politicians worldwide are completely ignorant to the true significance of *reserve currency* status and its consequences and implications, but there are a few exceptions. I've already mentioned France's Valéry Giscard d'Estaing and America's Henry Kissinger, who both had a keen understanding of exactly how reserve currency status works and what was at stake. Russia's exception to the rule is Sergei Glaziev (sometimes transliterated to Sergey Glazyev).

Born in Ukraine in 1961, Glaziev holds three degrees in economics including a Ph.D., and he understands *exactly* what's at stake here. Glaziev is a somewhat controversial but very active political figure in Russia. He led the nationalist *Rodina* political party and ran for President of Russia in 2004. In early 2018 he was officially appointed as economic advisor to President Vladimir Putin, a role he had served informally for years.

While d'Estaing was furious about American *exorbitant privilege* in the 1960s, there wasn't much he could do about it. But Glaziev is much more aggressive. His *de-dollarization* campaign aims to lobby governments around the world to ditch the dollar and use other currencies instead. Glaziev understands quite clearly how much advantage America derives from reserve currency status, and he's on a mission to change it. His efforts to date have focused primarily on trade settlement rather than central bank reserve assets, presumably because he knows there is presently no viable alternative to U.S. Treasury bonds.

Glaziev doesn't mince words in his public statements. He has directly accused the U.S. Government of "financial terrorism", and urged other governments to abandon the dollar for international trade and to work to create alternatives to SWIFT and other essential infrastructure systems supporting the global economy.

For example in an English interview with Chinese TV channel CCTV4,[28] Glaziev is quite outspoken in saying that Russia and China should use their own currencies for international trade, after describing the dollar as "toxic". Glaziev goes on to describe American sanctions against Russia as acts of "financial terrorism", and then calls the American financial system a "threat to Eurasian development". He says that Russia and China must create their own financial architecture independent from the dollar, saying "in order to avoid a secret war which is now organized by the United States, we have to create our own zone of economic development … we must protect our markets from financial terrorism".

Those are some pretty strong words coming from a man who serves as an economic advisor to Vladimir Putin.

Am I just behaving like a wild-eyed conspiracy theorist when I speculate that perhaps Mr. Glaziev already understands the principal contention of this book, i.e. that the best way to give dollar hegemony a run for its money is to design a digital currency system for that purpose? Ok, if you think I am, ask yourself why an economic advisor to the Russian president gave this keynote address[29] to the Blockchain leadership summit in Zurich, Switzerland in March, 2018? And why does he describe Blockchain as a "very important tool to fight corruption and fraud"? Remember, by his definition, *corruption* could refer to the dollar-centric International Monetary System.

I can't find any videos of Mr. Glaziev giving keynote speeches to technology conferences focused on other subjects, but it seems that both Russia and China have taken a keen interest in digital currency technology. On October 9, 2018, Li Liangsong, a researcher for the Peoples Bank of China proposed a yuan-linked digital coin[30] in a Chinese financial op-ed.

Separately, Vladimir Putin met recently with Vitalik Buterin, creator of the *Ethereum* cryptocurrency. The Russian head of state doesn't grant appointments to just anyone. I can't help but wonder whether using the Ethereum platform to build a government-sponsored digital currency system was a topic of conversation.

---

[28] https://glazev.ru/articles/165-interv-ju/59460-glaz-ev-interv-ju-kitayskomu-telekanalu-tv4-englis. Please note that the web page linked here is in Russian, but the video itself is in English. Just click the play button.
[29] https://www.youtube.com/watch?v=erW7w_IB_Is
[30] https://cointelegraph.com/news/china-should-consider-launching-its-own-stablecoin-central-bank-expert-says-in-op-ed

Chapter 15:
Sergei Glaziev's De-Dollarization Campaign

Mr. Glaziev seems like a very candid, straight-talking man, and I'd love to ask him directly whether Russia is pursuing a digital currency strategy, and whether they are collaborating with the People's Bank of China on such matters. I've sent Mr. Glaziev several invitations to be interviewed on my weekly MacroVoices podcast,[31] but have yet to receive a reply.

China's Yuan-denominated Crude Oil contract

Crude oil is the world's biggest, most active commodity market. Crude trades primarily through *commodity futures markets*. For many years, there have been two primary benchmark futures contracts which determine the price of crude oil in the global marketplace. *West-Texas Intermediate Crude* (WTIC) is the American crude oil contract. It trades on the *New York Mercantile Exchange*, and is settled via physical delivery in Cushing, Oklahoma. The *Brent Crude* contract is the global (non-American) benchmark oil contract. It's based on North Sea (Brent) crude oil prices, and trades primarily on the *Intercontinental Exchange* (ICE). Both contracts are priced and settled in U.S. dollars, consistent with the Petrodollar standard.

But there's a new kid on the block. Starting in mid-2018, China has introduced its own crude oil futures contract, trading on the *Shanghai Futures Exchange*, and *settled in Chinese Yuan rather than U.S. dollars*. And it's no secret that a principal motivation for introducing this contract was to create a non-dollar-denominated oil market. Trading volume has been brisk, considering the fact that it's a new entrant to the global marketplace and many skeptics questioned whether it would ever gain traction with investors.

Curiously, China's marketing for this contract has emphasized "gold backing" as a feature. On close inspection, it turns out that there is no direct pricing of oil in gold or even any guarantee that proceeds from oil trades could be used to secure a specific quantity of gold. All this "gold backing" really amounts to is that if you sell oil for Chinese Yuan on the Shanghai exchange, you have the option to use the Yuan proceeds to buy gold on that same exchange at prevailing market prices, and then take delivery of the gold.

While the gold "backing" of the new oil contract appears to be more marketing than substance, it's telling to me that China feels inclined to promote the very *idea* of oil being traded for gold rather than dollars. It's almost as if the Marketing Department said "Ok, we know the world is

---
[31] http://www.macrovoices.com/

going to be skeptical of the practical value of a contract that lets them sell their oil for Yuan, a closed currency system, so let's go out of our way to illustrate how they could use the contract to achieve a gold-for-oil transaction if they wanted to". I find the fact that China is even suggesting that international investors start thinking about gold rather than dollars as payment to be quite telling.

At first, it was just the BRICS countries...

Mr. Glaziev's *de-dollarization* campaign has been ongoing in one form or another for several years now, but until very recently it was confined to Russia, China, and other nations who have in the past been outspoken critics of U.S. foreign policy. To my thinking, Germany's August, 2018 call for a replacement for SWIFT which is free from U.S. influence marks an important symbolic milestone. It's well known that France, the U.K., and other long-term U.S. allies have long had their share of frustration with America's tendency to act unilaterally in matters of international diplomacy.

Now even long-time U.S. allies in the West like Germany are saying publicly that dollar hegemony is a *problem that needs to be solved*. In October, 2018, several famous people in the world of finance including hedge fund manager Ray Dalio and J.P. Morgan strategist Marco Kolanovic publicly expressed concern that U.S. policy is jeopardizing the dollar's reserve currency status. But U.S. senior policymakers aren't taking these objections as seriously as they should. The world is changing, and is more ready than ever for a viable alternative to the U.S. Dollar.

Chapter 16:
SWIFT

The *Society for Worldwide Interbank Financial Telecommunication*[32] (SWIFT) is effectively the world's *international wire transfer network*. SWIFT is a consortium founded in 1973 and organized under the laws of Belgium. It is owned by its member financial institutions all around the world, and in theory is not beholden to any specific government. But in practice, the U.S. Government has been successful in pressuring SWIFT to break off relations with nations the U.S. imposes sanctions against.

In the case of Iran, SWIFT initially denied any wrongdoing when it continued doing business with Iranian banks after U.S. Sanctions had been imposed. But when the U.S. Senate Banking Committee approved sanctions against SWIFT itself, the coercion tactic worked; SWIFT caved to U.S. demands and severed ties with Iranian banks.

The debate got much more heated in the wake of the May 2018 announcement in which U.S. President Donald Trump unilaterally backed away from the Iran nuclear deal. In August 2018, German foreign minister Heiko Maas publicly called for the creation of an alternative to SWIFT that isn't subject to U.S. intervention. Writing in the German daily Handelsblatt, Maas said, *"Europe should not allow the US to act over our heads and at our expense. For that reason it's essential that we strengthen European autonomy by establishing payment channels that are independent of the US, creating a European Monetary Fund and building up an independent SWIFT system".*

One month later, on September 24th, 2018, the European Union announced its intention to create a *Special-purpose Vehicle* (SPV) for the express purpose of allowing European companies to continue legal dealings with Iran without the threat of U.S. interference. Following a meeting at the U.N. between Iran, the E.U., France, Germany, United Kingdom, Russia and China, E.U. foreign policy chief Federica Mogherini made a side-by-side press announcement with Iranian foreign minister Mohammad Javad Zarif. Mogherini said the agreement reached *"will mean that EU member states will set up a legal entity to facilitate legitimate*

---

[32] https://en.wikipedia.org/wiki/Society_for_Worldwide_Interbank_Financial_Telecommunication

financial transactions with Iran, and this will allow European companies to continue trade with Iran".

Figure 7 Iranian Foreign Minister Mohammad Javad Zarif and European Union foreign policy chief Federica Mogherini announcing Europe's intention to bypass SWIFT and enable lawful commerce between European corporations and Iran in defiance of unilateral sanctions imposed by the U.S.

Stop and think about the historic significance of this. At the United Nations in New York City, the European Union announced that it would take action to make it easier for European corporations to ignore U.S. sanctions by creating a temporary mechanism to transact payments without using the SWIFT system which is now seen as controlled by the U.S. government, despite its supposedly independent status.

Official representatives of the E.U. and other major Western governments are openly accusing the U.S. of wrongdoing, and emphasizing the need for a global financial system independent of U.S. abuse. *The world is losing its patience with the U.S. acting unilaterally, and is already taking decisive action to insulate itself from unreasonable U.S. influence.* Yet American policymakers ignore these warnings. Today's American politicians simply don't understand how much the U.S. has to lose if the dollar loses its reserve currency status. Sergei Glaziev understands this all too well.

This isn't the first time that the U.S. Government has enraged European lawmakers. SWIFT came under pressure for breaching its members' privacy in contradiction of SWIFT's own rules in late 2006, after it was revealed that the U.S. Treasury, Central Intelligence Agency, and other U.S. Government agencies had been given full access to the SWIFT transaction history database for the purpose of searching for terrorist financing transactions. Strong objections from European constituents complained that their privacy had been breached in violation of SWIFT's published data privacy policies.

These objections led to SWIFT redesigning its systems into a segregated architecture, where transactions directly involving the United States are kept in one database, and other transactions not involving U.S. banks directly are kept in a segregated database (meant to be safe from the prying eyes of the U.S. Government) which is located in Europe.

Whistleblower Edward Snowden has alleged that notwithstanding the new segregated database architecture, the U.S. National Security Agency (NSA) routinely spies on *all* SWIFT international payment transactions without having obtained any search warrant to do so.

SWIFT is a communication network, not a payment system

Contrary to popular misconception, SWIFT is not actually a *payment system per se*. SWIFT is a secure messaging network. Its principal purpose is to allow bankers to send secure messages to other bankers in a standard format that is conducive to authorizing payment transactions. The SWIFT system does not *settle* or *clear* any payments. It only delivers messages between bankers in a secure network that bankers trust to be immune to hacking and other similar forms of interference.

This is best illustrated by example. Suppose that a company in France wishes to send an international wire transfer to settle an invoice for 100,000 Euros, payable to a vendor in Brazil. After receiving her customer's authorization, the banker in Paris sends a SWIFT message to the banker in Sao Paulo. The essence of the message is, "I hereby authorize you to make a payment to XYZ Manufacturing Company in your country, in the amount of 100,000 Euros, and you are authorized to *debit my bank's correspondent settlement account* to fund this transaction".

All that SWIFT does is to deliver the message securely, so that the banker in Brazil can rest assured that it really came from the banker in Paris, and that the content of the message wasn't tampered with. But SWIFT does not and cannot settle any payments. The only way the transaction can be completed is if both banks had already pre-agreed to set up *correspondent accounts* with one another, for the purpose of settling international payments using their own independent systems and procedures.

An important consequence of this is that it's *not necessarily possible for any bank in the SWIFT network to send a payment to any other bank in the network*. The only banks that can effect international payments are those that have pre-arranged their own system for clearing and settling those payments. Not all banks have *correspondent relationships* with all other banks around the world. Generally speaking, for any pair of countries, only a few banks will have set up such procedures for clearing and settling international payments.

This complicates all international payments. Going back to our example, suppose that our French businesswoman now wants to send a payment to another vendor in Mexico. But when she calls her banker, she's told that her bank has no correspondent relationship with any Mexican banks. The procedure is that she must now call her vendor in Mexico and ask him to call his banker, and ask who their correspondent bank in France is. Once she identifies the French bank that has a correspondent relationship with her vendor's Mexican bank, her banker can initiate the transaction. But another middleman is involved—the other French bank. Similarly the vendor in Mexico may be working with a bank that has no French correspondents either, in which case intermediaries are needed on both sides of the transaction. All of this is very cumbersome and time-consuming, and adds overhead expense to the cost of doing international business.

Consider what could be possible using *digital cash* technology. Bitcoin is already being used for some international commerce because it can transmit money value through the network instantly without the need for intermediaries, correspondents, or secure payment authorization networks like SWIFT.

Now imagine what Russia and China could achieve if they introduced an international digital currency system that allowed instantaneous settlement of international payments the same way that Bitcoin does. If this were part of a government-sponsored digital currency, it would likely be much more widely accepted and adopted than Bitcoin has been thus far. And it would be superior to SWIFT because it would be available to all banks and businesses worldwide, it would clear and settle payments instantaneously, and no middlemen or independent clearing procedures would be required.

Russia Welcomes Foreign Banks to SWIFT Alternative Network

On October 19, 2018, just as this book was going to press, Moscow announced that its *System for Transfer of Financial Messages*, a Russian-made alternative to SWIFT, was fully implemented in Russia and that foreign banks were now welcome to join the network. The implication was that Russia had completed its plans (begun in 2014) to create a system functionally equivalent to SWIFT but operated by Russia and therefore immune to U.S. interference.

Moscow's announcement implied that the system was fully operational and that foreign partner banks would 'soon' be joining the network. Needless to say, government press releases of this nature are always suspect and often prone to exaggeration. Because the news was released as this book was finishing its editing cycle, it was not possible to research the veracity of Moscow's claims.

I think it worthwhile to mention that I've been studying de-dollarization and the dollar's role at the center of the global financial system for more than a decade, but more relevant news has come out just during the few months this book was being written than had occurred over the past several years. *Things are heating up, and the pace is accelerating.*

Conclusions

SWIFT is just a secure message delivery system, nothing more. The technology to clear and settle international payments instantaneously didn't exist when SWIFT was designed, and that's why SWIFT requires the cumbersome and inefficient use of correspondent accounts and intermediary banks. Russian's new system presumably works the same way and is quite unlikely to offer any substantive improvement aside from being immune to U.S. influence.

A global digital currency system using digital cash technology to achieve instantaneous clearing and settlement of international payments would have an immense competitive advantage over SWIFT and/or Russia's new alternative to SWIFT. Combine this with the current geopolitical climate, which has the whole world hungry for an alternative to SWIFT not under the influence of the U.S. Government, and you have another very good argument for a global-scale digital currency system.

Beyond Blockchain: The Death of the Dollar and the Rise of Digital Currency

Chapter 17:
Crypto Revisited

Phew! *Finally*, it's time to return to the central topic of this book: digital currency. As we've seen, the world's conventional monetary system leaves plenty of room for improvement. *Whether* or not we'll eventually advance to a global-scale digital currency system isn't even a serious question. Digital currency offers so many advantages over conventional currency that it's nearly impossible that it will never happen. The real question is *how* it will happen, *which* digital currency system(s) will prevail, and who the winners and losers will be on the international stage as the transition occurs.

The vision of the crypto community is that cryptocurrencies will lead the charge and come to dominate the global financial system. Obviously there are lots of people in the crypto community with lots of different viewpoints. But to summarize the prevailing consensus view among them, it goes something like this: centralized, government controlled money is the problem, and cryptocurrency is the solution. Cryptocurrency offers an *alternative* to the government-controlled monetary system. The world will recognize that cryptocurrency is superior, and government-issued money will eventually be abandoned in favor of decentralized cryptocurrency.

Many crypto advocates see the fractional reserve banking system as corrupt and the source of great social injustice. Their hope is that big banking institutions, central bankers, and government Treasury departments, will all fade into obsolescence as cryptocurrency takes over as the standard payment system for global commerce.

I love the idea of scrapping the old system and moving on to something better—don't get me wrong on that. But to have a serious discussion about whether cryptocurrency (as it exists today) is ready to replace all the functions of the conventional system, you needed a full understanding of that system before the conversation even makes sense—we've done that in the previous chapters.

Here's a rhetorical question: *If we're going to throw out fractional reserve banking, how is anyone going to get a mortgage to buy a house?* Today's mortgages are only possible when banks can expand the money supply by *loaning new money into existence.* And to do that, they must first have capital on hand from other depositors. Since most cryptocurrency advocates don't favor fractionalizing cryptocurrency in a fractional reserve banking system, it's not at all clear where a mortgage loan would come from in the crypto-dominated world they envision.

Are the crypto guys really saying that society doesn't need to have mortgages and other forms of loans to finance large purchases? *Or would it be more accurate to say that the crypto crowd has yet to really stop and fully assess what it would take to completely replace the conventional system?* I think it's the latter.

I chose this example with mortgages because if you stop and think about it, there's a very good answer to my question that plays quite nicely into the crypto community's vision. Recall the discussion of *securitization* from Chapter Ten. Banks had been making mortgages through the fractional reserve banking system's ability to create new money supply by *loaning money into existence* under the *portfolio lending* regime. But then they figured out it was more lucrative to monetize their loan origination talents by selling bonds, which effectively packaged the loan assets created by fractional reserve banking into a more marketable financial instrument.

Do you see the opportunity here for a new model of crypto loan? The new loans could be capitalized with investor-supplied capital (in the form of digital currency tokens sourced by selling mortgage bonds), and that capital could be loaned out to create a new kind of mortgage, without the need for fractional reserve banking. That might be the basis of a whole new kind of lending using digital currency. For those who believe that central bankers should have a role in managing the economy, there are several ways to create incentives and levers to allow that kind of lending to be encouraged in targeted ways.

So my point is *not* that it's impossible for cryptocurrency be developed to the point where it could replace parts or all of the conventional monetary system. Quite to the contrary, now that you understand the basics of how the conventional system works, we'll consider how cryptocurrency might evolve.

Revolutionizing the global monetary system: Is Crypto up to the task?

Let's start the analysis with the crypto community's favored scenario: where privately developed cryptocurrencies with no government backing

Chapter 17:
Crypto Revisited

offer an alternative so superior to government-issued money that the cryptocurrency takes over as the basis of the global monetary system.

The crypto community has the *technological talent* to make this happen. I had a very successful career in software, and I pride myself in my ability to recognize really talented software designers. The folks who invented cryptocurrency are just way past smart—even to real genius level; there can be no question about that.

But an *illusion* is causing too much confidence in the viability of their vision. For ten years they've made great advances, and some indications are that government is unable to stop them—their cryptocurrencies will inevitably continue to gain market traction.

The illusion is that, in my opinion, government is not *powerless* to stop them, but merely *clueless* as to what's really going on. That's why there have been no serious initiatives to outlaw cryptocurrency on a broad scale. Not because governments decided they're okay with what the crypto community is trying to achieve, but simply because government is so slow, bureaucratic and stupid that they've yet to really *figure out* what the crypto community is trying to achieve.

My prediction is that when they do figure it out, the picture won't be pretty for cryptocurrencies.

Remember, outlawing crypto in practical terms would be easy; all they have to do is ban the exchange of crypto tokens for fiat currency, so that no one except criminals who are willing to use illegal black markets can convert crypto tokens into dollars or other fiat currencies.

The other dimension of this illusion is the huge following of crypto-loving citizens who have become supporters in recent years. Part of this story involved a period when the guys who got in early on Bitcoin mining were becoming millionaires in their mid-20s by doing almost nothing but having fancy gaming computers. It should come as no surprise that this created a cult following for crypto.

But putting this in proper perspective, what really happened was a *speculative mania* created the illusion that crypto token appreciation is an unlimited wealth machine. And that only lasted for a short time. That party is over now—as I predicted on my *MacroVoices podcast*[33] when Bitcoin was still well above $15,000 USD per Bitcoin. I said it was a speculative bubble that was sure to pop and prices would crash. And that's exactly

---

[33] http://www.macrovoices.com/

what happened. Suddenly the magical allure of crypto is fading for those entranced by the illusion that the price could only keep going up, and that making money hand over fist by speculating in crypto tokens is easy.

A realistic "Crypto Wins" scenario?

As I've said repeatedly, I absolutely do think that digital currency technology will be used to redesign the entire global monetary system. But this isn't a technology question; it's a matter of power and influence. *How will this occur, and who will be in charge?* If there is a path forward where an existing cryptocurrency evolves to become a major world currency, it would be most likely to occur through evolution and a merger with a government initiative.

The most logical source of a global-scale digital currency system would be a joint effort between the Russian and Chinese governments after they conclude the best way to achieve their goal of a dollar-challenging global-scale digital currency would be to start with one of the existing cryptocurrency systems and modifying and extending it to suit their needs.

Bitcoin would probably *not* be their first choice. In many ways, *Ethereum* would most likely be the best pick. Well guess what? Ethereum is the brainchild of Vitalik Buterin, a Russian-Canadian software developer just twenty-four years old. And guess who he had a personal meeting with last year? Russian President Vladimir Putin.

Not just anybody gets a personal meeting with Putin. There must have been something on the Russian government's mind that led to this turn of events. Were they feeling Buterin out to see if he was ready to join the effort to design a state-backed Russo-Chinese digital currency? Were they evaluating whether they could use his Ethereum platform as a base? I can assure you they didn't meet just because he's a charming young lad who happens to be of Russian descent.

For the current generation of cryptocurrencies to change the world, it will have to involve joining forces with a major government sponsor. And yes, that will require changing priorities and giving up some of Satoshi's libertarian vision of a money system. For *now* the brightest minds in the world of digital currency are focused on *beating them* rather than *joining them*. And in many ways, that's ok. The change from conventional to digital currency will be revolutionary, and government probably would have taken forever to bring it about on their own. The crypto revolution is showing the world that digital currency is possible and has myriad advantages over

Chapter 17: Crypto Revisited

conventional money. And we as a society very much need that to happen. So I'm delighted the crypto revolution has evolved as it has thus far.

The crazy price speculation in late 2017 never made sense, and I'm sorry that a lot of late-comers to the crypto markets lost their shirts. But novice investors confusing *value* with *price* and getting caught up in a speculative mania of epic proportions has nothing to do with the viability of digital currency.

Can crypto ever take over the world economy with *private-issue* money? I sincerely doubt it, but I'd be delighted to be proven wrong.

I'm reminded of the anti-war movement of the late 1960s. Activists sincerely believed an all-out *revolution* was needed. Overthrow the government and install a new one. That never happened, nor should it have. But the world most assuredly did change. Awareness of race inequality and of the social and economic cost of pointless wars increased significantly, even though there was never an actual revolution.

I think of the *cryptocurrency revolutionaries* the same way. Just like the anti-war activists, society *urgently needs these young voices speaking their minds—it will change society for the better and help us advance to a global digital currency-based economy.*

But just like the '60s, I don't think an actual revolution will occur, or that private-issue crypto will conquer the global economy. Instead I think the crypto revolution will be the catalyst that forces governments to take notice of the opportunity digital currency offers them. I just hope the crypto movement awakens the general public to the risk of an Orwellian outcome so that when governments finally embrace digital currency, *we the people* are ready to insist that the rights of the citizens are protected in the design process.

What it would take for the crypto community to prove me wrong

What would it take for crypto to prove me wrong and for a private issue cryptocurrency to become the dominant monetary system, as many in the crypto community already believe is its destiny?

First and foremost—and again, we're discussing a private-issue currency here—this is more about socio-politics and government power monopolies than technology. The crypto developers are already the smartest kids in the class when it comes to digital currency technology. That's already clear. But the challenges won't be about the technology. Central bankers will realize the existential threat that crypto poses for them. To think "but there's nothing central banks can do because it's decentralized" is naïve. There's plenty they can do, starting with outlawing exchange of fiat currency for crypto tokens.

The only way for crypto to "win big" and for a cryptocurrency to become a dominant world currency is if the people of the world are so impressed that they refuse to allow governments to shut it down. The key would be for crypto to gain some political advocates—celebrities and public officials willing to take the crypto side of the argument on the public stage and openly advocate the replacement of government-issued money with something better. Such as the government of Malta already did while this book was being written.

The love affair the millennial generation has had with crypto was driven primarily by how much fun the speculative bubble was *on the way up*. As I've been writing this book, crypto has been crashing relative to fiat currency. And by the way, I'm not necessarily convinced that the crypto bubble is over. We could still have another speculative wave taking prices higher—maybe Bitcoin will reach $50k per coin. But it really doesn't matter. The phenomenon is not about crypto tokens gaining in *value* by any reasonable analysis. Just like late-'90s Internet stocks, they have seen a price bubble (perhaps not over yet) that has little to do with value.

Even if crypto could somehow overcome the regulatory challenges, there are still serious shortcomings. Crypto as we know it today should be thought of as an *alternative to M0 base currency*, not as a replacement for it. And to the credit of crypto's inventors, that's not a criticism. Today's cryptocurrencies were not designed to *replace* the global monetary system. They were designed to create a *viable alternative*. They've succeeded in that undertaking, at least while they're still allowed to exist.

The time to start designing a true *replacement* for the aging fractional reserve banking system, in which digital currency replaces all of M3, not just M0, is *right now*. So far the crypto community has been quick to denounce the shortcomings of FRB, but has yet to propose a viable replacement for the necessary credit functions FRB enables. What's needed is a total redesign of the entire monetary system, not just M0, but all of M3. That implies completely re-engineering fractional reserve banking to embrace digital technology. The real work has yet to begin.

But what *won't work* is to pretend that just because cryptocurrencies like Bitcoin have done a great job of providing an alternative to M0 so far, that they can somehow replace the entire fractional reserve system. We still need *lending* to make the global economy work. And we almost certainly need a variable money supply that contracts and expands in response to economic conditions. *There's still a whole lot of work left to be done before crypto or any other digital currency technology will be ready.*

My predictions for cryptocurrencies

Despite my opinion that governments will eventually seek to outlaw cryptocurrencies, I doubt it will happen anytime soon, and I won't be at all surprised if crypto continues to flourish for several more years.

China has been particularly proactive in restricting crypto exchanges, but that's driven by the fact that dirty Chinese politicians were using crypto to skirt capital controls and smuggle monetary value out of the country. The Chinese government understands that risk quite well and will continue to enforce strict controls on use of crypto within China. However, China's methods can rarely be used as a template for actions in Western countries.

Otherwise, crypto will continue to evolve as an *alternative to the mainstream global monetary system* and gain more followers and supporters, although mostly as an alternative to "regular money" that very few people (if anyone) will adopt as their primary system of payment for day-to-day expenses.

I doubt any major world government would adopt a cryptocurrency as its national currency, but it's quite possible that smaller countries might. Already Venezuela claims to have launched the first government-backed cryptocurrency, the *Petro*. All signs to date are that it's little more than a publicity stunt. While Nicolas Maduro claims to have raised hundreds of millions of dollars on the very first day the Petro was launched, the Petro's public blockchain tells a very different story—almost no transaction history, including no evidence of the supposed Day One fundraising that Maduro proudly announced as proof of the cryptocurrency's success.

But what if a more credible story unfolds elsewhere in the world and small countries whose money systems are in crisis start officially recognizing Bitcoin or another cryptocurrency as a national currency? That could do a lot to add credibility to the crypto movement, and might make it harder for other countries to outlaw crypto entirely.

Japan *has* officially recognized Bitcoin as a valid means of payment. Now to be clear, that's not the same as saying they have adopted it to replace the Yen. Rather, they have signaled that they don't see anything wrong with Bitcoin, and don't have any immediate intention to outlaw it.

So far, only law enforcement is taking exception to crypto—both in China and the U.S. That's because crypto facilitates doing illegal things. But that's a completely different issue from central bankers worrying over something replacing the global monetary system. Really, they show zero signs of even understanding that could happen.

Bottom line, to my thinking if there's a way for crypto to evolve to hold a meaningful role in the global financial system, it can only happen through government endorsement. If more countries follow Malta's example and start declaring their intention to use cryptocurrencies as their national currency, that would be a whole new ball game. I would interpret such an outcome as a form of government-backed digital currency. My point is not that government has to develop it's own digital currency. My argument is that government will decide what digital currency systems advance to become serious players in the global economy. If a cryptocurrency wants to achieve that title, I don't see how it's possible unless government endorsement plays a big role in the process.

Chapter 18:
Other Cryptocurrencies

I feel obliged to begin this chapter by emphasizing that my analysis of the various currently available cryptocurrencies is inspired by my desire to understand technology innovations that will help to build the digital currency systems of tomorrow. If your interest is in speculating on the price of crypto tokens (a foolish undertaking in my opinion—I've never owned a crypto token) or in mining cryptocurrency yourself, then you'll need a whole lot more information beyond the intent of this book.

I've limited explanations thus far to Bitcoin because it more than adequately satisfied our needs as an example to show what cryptocurrency is and how it works at a very high level—and for the purpose of illustrating how I think digital currency will eventually take over the global economy. There was no need to complicate that discussion by bringing up other cryptocurrencies.

Other cryptocurrencies *have* made some important advances beyond what Bitcoin first accomplished, and these technology innovations will definitely influence the design of the future digital currency-based global monetary system. This chapter explores some of them.

Ethereum and Smart Contracts

For IT-savvy readers, Ethereum offers a Turing-complete virtual machine architecture which allows the execution of "smart contract" financial scripts in a peer-to-peer distributed network, including provisions for payments of monetary value between independent actors in that network through a cryptocurrency system accessible to scripts executing within the Turing-complete virtual machine environment.

For those of you prefer plain English to geek-speak, here's the layman's version: If you think of the Bitcoin currency and payment network as a distant cousin to a sophisticated computer *program* such as Microsoft Excel, then think of Ethereum as a distant cousin to a computer *operating system*, such as Microsoft Windows. Yes, Ethereum includes a cryptocurrency system (the unit of currency is called an *ether*), but it's a lot more than just a cryptocurrency system like Bitcoin. It's an entire operating system designed to allow sophisticated financial application programs to be developed on top of it.

Smart contracts are the "programs" that run in the Ethereum system. I'll elaborate on their history and capabilities in Chapter Twenty-Three.

Ethereum has had a few false starts and mishaps. Notably, a scandal occurred in 2016 when an anonymous entity exploited an application system called DAO built on top of the Ethereum network. To make a long story short, someone basically stole US $50 million worth of ether. Oops!

But I don't think such things even matter to the longer-term picture. Sure, if you're a crypto speculator you care about security events like this—a lot. But will Ethereum take over and become *the* cryptocurrency or will it fade into crypto oblivion and be forgotten?

Really, I don't care.

However, the integration of smart contracts with digital currency was a really important technological milestone. Whether Ethereum leads the charge from here or gets upstaged by an even more impressive entrant to the crypto space doesn't much concern me. What I care about is the evolution of smart contract technology in concert with digital currency and, at the moment, such advances are occurring primarily under the guise of the Ethereum cryptocurrency—and that's why I pay attention to it.

Ripple (XRP Ledger): The crypto that's not really a crypto

As I've said many times now, the proof-of-work validated *blockchain* distributed ledger was an important breakthrough invention, but I don't think it's ready for prime time. It was a brilliant way to prove a concept possible, but the performance and scalability limitations caused by the inefficiency of proof-of-work make it impractical.

Similarly, the whole concept of "mining" in cryptocurrencies isn't suitable for a global digital currency system. More to the point, mining shouldn't be necessary once someone "breaks the proof-of-work barrier".

XRP Ledger, formerly known as *Ripple*, is a notable exception that doesn't rely on some interpretation of *blockchain*. Unlike the other cryptos, XRP doesn't use a proof-of-work validated blockchain and there are no "miners". For these reasons alone, XRP has a very shaky reputation in the crypto community. No mining? Meaning that there's no way for the guys with big gaming computers to print their own money? That's sacrilege!

Chapter 18:
Other Cryptocurrencies

How is it possible that XRP is working without proof-of-work or mining when nobody's figured out how to design a decentralized distributed ledger without proof-of-work? XRP *isn't* fully decentralized. It uses a *permissioned* ledger design to achieve much better performance than Bitcoin, but at the cost of partial centralization.

Promoting to the crypto community a currency system that uses a centralized ledger and doesn't have mining is like walking into an Irish sports bar next to Boston's Fenway Park wearing a New York Yankees sweatshirt and cap. Not a good idea.

XRP is completely unsuitable as a cryptocurrency if your definition of cryptocurrency is that it should be immune from government attempts to shut it down, and offer miners providing computing power an opportunity to make lots of money. No surprise, most cryptophiles hold XRP in low esteem.

But if your desire is to understand how government-sponsored digital currency systems of the future might work, XRP gives some interesting early insights into the challenges and benefits of a currency system that relies on a permissioned ledger system. That's the reason I'm keeping an eye on it.

Monero: A less transparent blockchain

Recall the scenario I described in Chapter Ten, where I suggested that a future digital currency system might require lenders to encode metadata about the loans they make such as loan-to-value metrics and creditworthiness of the borrowers onto the distributed ledger. The goal was to make possible instrumentation and incentive-based monetary policy tools allowing central bankers to know exactly what's really going on in the private credit system so that they can administer monetary policy more intelligently.

There's a big problem with that scenario. In the case of the *blockchain* distributed ledger as it was designed for Bitcoin, the ledger itself is completely public. Everyone can see all the data it contains for all time. Nothing is private. The identity of the transaction participants is *pseudonymous*, but the exact audit trail of payments is public knowledge. And forensic analysis firms like *Chainalysis* are already building detective tools to figure out the legal identity of pseudonymous participants in the Bitcoin network.

If we ever wanted to require lenders to provide metadata that regulators could use to administer better monetary policy, we'd have to address some privacy and disclosure objections first. For very good reason, commercial banks would strongly object to being required to make such disclosures on a public ledger that anyone anywhere could analyze to gain competitive advantage. *In other words, we need to figure out how to build some degree of privacy into the distributed ledger.* But the Bitcoin blockchain is designed to make everything transparent and publicly visible.

The reason I keep a watch on the *Monero* cryptocurrency is that its focus is on advancing the design of cryptocurrencies toward a *semi-public blockchain*, where much of the data on the blockchain is "obfuscated", meaning it's designed to make things at least difficult for anyone inspecting the blockchain after the fact to figure out who's who and what transactions they were party to.

To be clear, the primary motivation driving the design of *Monero* is to thwart the ability of firms like *Chainalysis* from figuring out the legal identities of the people transacting in Monero. This makes Monero cryptocurrency enemy #1 in the eyes of law enforcement, quite understandably. If you are a criminal selling black market services on the dark web, Monero is likely to be your payment method of choice, because it's much more difficult for law enforcement to discover the legal identity of a Monero transaction participant than a Bitcoin transaction participant.

My interest in Monero isn't about avoiding the law, and I have no intention of ever buying a single Monero token. But the techniques they're developing for *privatizing blockchain* may be relevant to the design of future global-scale digital currency systems which want to protect confidentiality of some of the information encoded in the distributed ledger.

A brief summary of the "me too" market

I'll close this chapter with a brief analysis of the many other cryptocurrencies that have come into existence in recent years and offer no apparent technological advance beyond what's been already accomplished. Something that's probably occurred to you already is that while Bitcoin seems like a really cool invention, the only reason there's any scarcity value to Bitcoins is because the Bitcoin software imposes a 21 million coin cap on the money supply. But it's open-source software. What's to stop someone with solid marketing skills from simply copying the Bitcoin software, calling it something else, making a few largely irrelevant

Chapter 18:
Other Cryptocurrencies

changes just to be able to say it's different, and then launching their own cryptocurrency?

Nothing is stopping them from doing this, and many of the countless cryptocurrencies amount to little more than that. Copy what someone else did, call it something different, and then launch a *marketing campaign* designed to exploit the greed of the masses who are obsessed with "getting in on the ground floor" of a new crypto early on before the "big move" up in price—like Bitcoin.

There might well be other advances out there rather than copycats, but from my vantage point most of them are just "me too" entrants. After all, the developers of a new cryptocurrency usually "pre-mine" and retain a sizable chunk of the money supply for themselves, so it's a very lucrative enterprise if you can sucker a bunch of speculators into buying tokens in your "me too" crypto.

So-called *Initial Coin Offerings*, or ICOs are an even less interesting sideshow than the "me too" cryptocurrencies. The essence of it is that every con man around the globe has figured out that crypto is hotter than hot, and many of them are creating their own digital "coins" because a whole bunch of people who have no idea what they're doing are buying any low-priced crypto token they can get their hands on, hoping it will make them rich. The vast majority of them will be sadly disappointed by the outcome.

Ethereum, Ripple, and Monero are each doing something *different*, and it's different in a way that I think could be relevant to the advancement of the field of digital currency technology more broadly. That's worth watching.

Beyond Blockchain: The Death of the Dollar and the Rise of Digital Currency

Chapter 19:
Global-Scale Digital Currency

Obviously, I have plenty of ideas to share with you regarding what a global-scale digital currency system might look like, and how it might ultimately evolve to dethrone King Dollar as global reserve currency. I'll leave plenty of questions unanswered as well; my primary goal is to *get everyone thinking about how a digital global reserve currency system should work*. It's going to take a lot more brainpower than just my own to figure out how to completely re-engineer the entire global monetary system. But one way or another, this business of central bankers running the global economy with monetary policy tools one step more advanced than a rain dance must come to an end!

Digital Currency doesn't by any means achieve that by itself. The fractional reserve banking system is long-overdue for overhaul. Monetary policy tools available to central bankers are primitive at best. There's a whole lot that technology can do to modernize the global monetary system well beyond switching to digital currency.

But digital currency will be the primary catalyst to bring about a much broader change. More precisely, the desire of other governments to dethrone King Dollar is likely to be the primary driver. The benefits of digital currency and the door that's been opened by the popularity of cryptocurrency will be a major impetus. Still, there's a whole lot of thinking left to be done about what else needs to be encoded on a distributed ledger and how better monetary policy tools could be engineered. This book is only going to scratch the surface, at least in this first edition.

To create a true global-scale digital currency system, we're talking about something on a completely different scale than a cryptocurrency. To put this in perspective, due to the inefficiencies of its proof-of-work validated blockchain distributed ledger, the Bitcoin network[34] can only process about seven transactions per second. Ethereum is much faster at fifteen transactions per second. By using a permissioned ledger XRP (formerly Ripple) is able to achieve 1,500 transactions per second.

---

[34] This figure is for the foundational Bitcoin architecture, and does not include the *Lightning* off-chain clearing network which is faster.

Consider that the Visa credit card network alone processes about 24,000 transactions per second. A global-scale digital currency system would need to process at least 250,000 transactions *per second* (and probably more) to function reliably and replace every payment that is now made by cash, check or credit card. That's not at all impossible, but we're talking about a completely different scale (by several orders of magnitude[35]) than today's cryptocurrencies.

Time Horizon and the De-Dollarization Catalyst

I've predicted that digital currency technology will be used to re-engineer (at minimum) a major global currency system, and lead to an effort to redesign the entire fractional reserve banking system upon which the global economy has operated for hundreds of years. Needless to say, that's a pretty big change. So *when,* exactly, will this happen? Is this something that will occur over the next few years, or will it need several decades?

The answer will depend entirely on whether I'm right about the *De-Dollarization Catalyst* leading to a new *Space Race.* If the nations around the world who would like to dethrone King Dollar recognize digital currency technology as their best chance of achieving that goal, we could see a global-scale digital currency begin to displace the dollar as global reserve currency by the mid- to late-2020s. The most likely sequence of events would be that Russia and/or China start the ball rolling, and then the U.S. recognizes that it *is* a race, and suddenly all major governments around the world are choosing sides and competing to see who can win.

But what if I'm wrong and the De-Dollarization crowd doesn't see the opportunity I see for them to advance their goals using digital currency? In that case I still predict that the global monetary system will eventually be re-engineered using digital currency technology. But now we're talking about a really, *really* big project that has to occur at the natural pace of government bureaucracy. It could easily take several decades, and would probably only come to fruition with the advent of some other major catalyst to bring it about.

The most important thing to watch will be China and Russia's actions. Maybe China hired all those blockchain engineers just so they could better

---

[35] The phrase *order of magnitude* is geek speak for the number of zeros after the 1 when talking about how much something needs to change. One order of magnitude means 10 times faster. Two orders of magnitude means 100 times faster. Three orders means 1000 times faster, etc.

Chapter 19:
Global-Scale Digital Currency

understand the risk Bitcoin poses for enabling capital flight from China. Maybe Sergei Glaziev is giving keynote speeches to blockchain conferences because he just happens to have a personal fascination with Bitcoin. Maybe the real reasons that both China and Russia have been accumulating physical gold bullion in massive size for the last several years[36] is just that those Mr. T.-style gold jewelry chains are about to come into vogue in Eastern fashion circles. And maybe I'm just a crazy conspiracy theorist to instead think these guys might have a carefully planned strategy that's all about attacking U.S. dollar hegemony using digital currency as their weapon of choice. *Only time will tell.*

One thing is certain: Either way, this won't happen overnight. Just look at how long it took to implement the Euro currency system. That was just a matter of designing a *conventional* currency system which basically worked like most of the other currencies around the world. All they had to do was coordinate how to switch a bunch of small countries' national currency systems over to something new, and sort out a few details like how to track imbalances created when different countries' central banks issued fungible units of the same currency. And just doing that took European bureaucrats *twenty years.* We're talking about something much bigger here.

Scope of the new system

The most obvious starting point is to simply replace the *monetary base* (MB) of conventional currency with a digital currency system, and leave the rest of the monetary and fractional reserve banking systems alone. The new digital currency system would be built using a *permissioned distributed ledger* and designed to scale to meet the needs of a global currency system several orders of magnitude bigger and faster than any current cryptocurrency.

The fractional reserve commercial banking system would work exactly the way it always has, except that it would be fractionalizing a digital currency rather than a paper one. *Bank money* would continue to be created and accounted for on the books of commercial banks, and there would be no change to the design of the fractional reserve system. Monetary policy would presumably work the same way it does today, except there might be better instrumentation to help central bankers better understand metrics like the *velocity of money*[37] within the monetary base.

---

[36] The relevance of this gold bullion accumulation to the digital currency story will be the subject of Chapter 21.
[37] https://en.wikipedia.org/wiki/Velocity_of_money

The above scenario represents only the first small step toward modernizing the global monetary system with digital currency. There's good reason to consider *starting there* because large, disruptive changes are always best implemented incrementally, in stages. But this is only scratching at the surface of what's possible.

Re-engineering fractional reserve banking

The really big "win" so far as I'm concerned would come from re-engineering the entire fractional reserve banking system to embrace and benefit from digital currency and other technologies. To be clear, I am *not* in agreement with my friends in the crypto community who think that FRB is the enemy and that it should be discarded. Rather, we need to preserve the *benefits that FRB presently delivers to society*, using technology to contain or eliminate the shortcomings of FRB and to enhance and improve upon the benefits it already delivers.

Any competent engineering effort begins with understanding *what needs to be accomplished*, and then works back from there to design the best system to achieve the desired goal. If we're talking about re-engineering FRB, we should start by understanding its benefits:

- FRB's fundamental purpose is that it enables *credit*. Society needs both consumer and business *lending services.* While it's tempting to criticize FRB because of the way it requires most people to keep most of their money in the banking system most of the time, we can't seriously entertain a change unless the replacement offers equal or better access to credit for both businesses and consumers.

- The re-engineering process should evaluate and consider how to best meet the needs of all forms of credit—not just conventional bank lending. This includes a close look at securitization of mortgages, credit card debt, auto loans, home equity credit lines, commercial lending, etc.

- FRB allows the free-market driven commercial banking system to expand and contract the overall money supply in reaction to economic conditions. We need to at minimum preserve the notion of a money supply whose size can change dynamically in response to changing economic conditions. Ideally, we should strive for a design that does a much better job than the current FRB system.

Chapter 19:
Global-Scale Digital Currency

- In addition to the "obvious suspects" of consumer and business lending, the current banking system includes some very important credit mechanisms which a redesign of FRB should consider. While these are not specifically functions of FRB itself, they are functions of today's complex FRB-based commercial banking system. The effort to re-architect the FRB system should include figuring out how to satisfy the needs currently serviced by these mechanisms and hopefully improve on them:
    - The *Tri-Party Repo System*[38] is a complex credit mechanism used extensively by financial institutions. The details of how it works are beyond the scope of this book, but the gist of it is that the world of high finance depends very heavily on a system of collateralized lending where the big banks' pledge investment assets to collateralize very large short-term loans. A redesign of FRB should include a thorough analysis of how "repo" works and should offer a replacement that delivers better instrumentation and controls.

        In particular, it has been alleged that banks have in some cases pledged the same collateral to secure multiple loans, in a practice known as *rehypothecation*. The extent to which this unethical practice has or has not occurred in the past is almost immaterial. The point is that distributed ledger technology enables a redesign of the system that would make *rehypothecation* categorically impossible, and that should be the goal.

    - The commercial *Eurodollar System* is another complex aspect of the current financial system. Once again, the full details are beyond the scope of this book.

        But in this case, I have a free resource for additional study to offer readers. I had the honor of producing a free 7-part podcast series titled *Eurodollar University*[39] featuring Alhambra Investments' Chief Investment Officer Jeffrey Snider, a recognized authority on the Eurodollar system. This free podcast series offers a thorough introduction to the history of the Eurodollar system and the role it plays in

---
[38] https://en.wikipedia.org/wiki/Repurchase_agreement
[39] http://www.macrovoices.com/EDU

the global financial system.

I consulted Mr. Snider in the course of writing this book, and he agreed that a redesign of the FRB system absolutely must include analyzing the role of the Eurodollar system and figuring out how to replace the useful benefits it delivers with a digital currency system.

- FRB is the mechanism through which central bank *monetary policy* operates. Therefore, a redesign of FRB should occur in concert with a redesign of monetary policy. The process should involve identifying a much better and more effective set of monetary policy tools. A further functional requirement of the FRB redesign then becomes enabling the desired monetary policy tools and also creating much more robust instrumentation over the entire banking system so that guesswork is eliminated from the central bank's oversight of the commercial banking system.

- There are several functional requirements that are specific to making a redesigned digital currency system an attractive long-term replacement for the conventional USD as global reserve currency. Those requirements would need to be identified and considered in the process of re-engineering FRB using digital currency technology.

That's a massive undertaking. As both a distributed systems technologist and a student of the global monetary system, I can't imagine anything more rewarding than working on the team that really takes this challenge on and has the influence to make a redesigned monetary system a reality. The opportunity to advance society is truly profound.

System should encompass all payment methods and credit instruments

Ultimately, all money in the system (meaning both base money and banking system money) should be digital money that can be tracked and managed through a distributed ledger system.

Furthermore, most financial transactions—mortgages, car loans, big bank repo transactions, consumer credit transactions, etc. should all be recorded and settled on a distributed ledger that encrypts proprietary information from public view, but allows central bankers robust instrumentation to see what's happening in the commercial credit system in real time. This means that through *permissioned analysis* of the distributed ledger, it should be possible to monitor the status of the overall monetary system—not just central bank money but the amount of loans outstanding and the rate of credit growth, the ability to accurately measure M0, M1, M2, M3 and MZM in real-time without need for estimation, the ability to accurately track statistics on debt service delinquency in real-time, and so forth.

Unlike cryptocurrencies which generally offer only a single method of payment that is cash-like, I envision a design that offers both cash-like and check-like payments. There are ample use cases for both, and a well-designed digital currency system should accommodate them. I also envision a *request for payment* transaction type—an *invoice* that can be sent requesting payment for a product or service.

Credit card purchases should be designed as part of the system as well. Credit card companies would still exist like today, but rather than offering merchants a parallel authorization and clearing network (today's credit card payment terminals), the same digital currency system that supports cash- and check-like payments should seamlessly support credit-based transactions. Just as you can make a payment *from* an address that contains money value (checking account), you could use the exact same system to transparently make a payment from an address that is a credit account. There's no good reason for the merchant receiving your payment to know or care whether it was made on a credit card or drawn from an account containing cash.

Zoned monetary architecture

I envision something I'm calling a *zoned architecture*, meaning that the global-scale system is intentionally segregated into distinct *monetary zones*. The most obvious zone boundaries would be international borders—the people of the United States and their money and credit accounts are in the *American Zone*, while the people of Europe and their accounts are in the *European Zone*. This would afford a number of benefits:

- International payments could be made subject to checks, balances, and limits. This is anathema to the values and philosophy of the crypto community, but my prediction is that governments will insist on having the ability to restrict or at least monitor international payments. From a distributed system design perspective, the most obvious way to achieve that is to segregate the global money system into national zones, and allow different rules to apply to inter-zone (i.e. international) payments than to intra-zone (domestic) transactions.

This zoned architecture could be hierarchical, so that the various nations of the European Union each have their own monetary zone within an over-arching Euro zone, and so forth.

- The zoned architecture could allow some aspects of *monetary policy* to be administered on a per-zone basis. This would mean that the Fed could continue to dictate U.S. monetary policy while the ECB retains authority over the Euro monetary zone, etc. The benefit would be to allow the existing balance of power between nations to remain status quo, eliminating what would otherwise be strong opposition to adoption of a system that disempowers the existing international central banking power structure.

- The zoned architecture would help address scalability challenges for the permissioned distributed ledger system.

Real-time Instrumentation and Monetary Policy

The redesigned system could offer central bankers new monetary policy tools far beyond their wildest dreams. This is a double-edged sword. Monetary policy tools that encourage immediate consumption for the sake of stimulating the economy (such as negative interest rates) serve to undermine more important priorities for society, such as encouraging prudent and responsible financial behavior by individuals and firms. Citizens demonstrating personal responsibility by saving for a rainy day should not be intentionally discouraged as a matter of government policy!

But once the risk of counter-productive monetary policy tools is addressed, the possibilities are endless. The system could be designed to give central bankers real-time instrumentation allowing them to monitor the banking system much more accurately than they can today. Similarly, much more precise and effective monetary policy tools could be designed to more directly influence the behavior of lenders and other actors in the private sector.

I alluded to one possible monetary policy innovation earlier—the idea of allowing quantitative easing to create a special restricted category of base money that can only be used for specified purposes initially, but which reverts after an expiration date to regular M0 money. The objective was to provide a way for the central bank to expand its balance sheet and the monetary base in a way that assures the new base money created by QE is used for the purpose the central bank intended.

Chapter 19:
Global-Scale Digital Currency

But I'm not even sure that's the best way to solve that problem. Another approach (assuming the goal was to incentivize lending within the private sector banking system) could involve more precise instrumentation that rewards commercial banks that lend in designated sectors of the economy by granting them access to a lower cost of borrowing through a special discount window only available after certain qualifying thresholds. And there are myriad other ways you could use digital currency technology (and particularly, the ability to record all lending transactions on the distributed ledger) to otherwise achieve the same goal.

I don't mind admitting not knowing the exact solutions that will prove to best solve these problems. It will take lots of people and lots of creative thinking to figure out how to best re-engineer the global monetary system. But I'm excited to be a part of that thinking, and you should be too.

Offline Digital Cash

I'd like to see a capability not possible with current cryptocurrencies, which I call *Offline Digital Cash*. It allows some payments to occur even when no connection to the Internet or the rest of the global digital currency network is available.

Consider the scenario where your home was flooded after a hurricane. The electrical power and Internet service is down throughout the city. You're able to get to a lumber yard which is running on emergency generator power, but has no Internet access. You urgently need to purchase supplies to make emergency repairs, but the lumber yard's cash registers are likewise unable to connect to the Internet or the global currency network.

We already have a solution to this today, but it's a very primitive one: The lumber yard has the option to allow you to pay using a credit card. They can't obtain the *authorization code* that guarantees them payment, but if they're willing to take your word that your credit card has available credit limit, they can process the transaction and it will be presented to the credit card merchant network when the network comes back online. They'll get paid as long as your credit card really did have available credit, and if not, they'll have an audit trail to use to take you to court.

A digital currency system can do a much better job. I'll spare you the technical details of how encryption technology makes this possible, but the upshot is the merchant will (without being connected to any network) have systems which can deduce through reliable cryptography the information that "This payment source had sufficient balance to pay the amount in question as of (date/time)". So in other words, their system tells them that as of the moment the network went down, you had sufficient credit on your credit card or other digital currency payment address to complete whatever transaction is under consideration.

Of course the risk is that once the network went down, you could drive around to every store in town and make purchases that exceed the total amount of credit that was available. But presumably if the people running the lumber yard think you're behaving like a responsible person, they'll probably believe you when you tell them whether or not you've already made other purchases against that credit limit.

This same system would allow vending machines not connected to any network to operate on a form of trust credit. Suppose you want to buy a soft drink for one dollar from a vending machine. The machine might be designed to allow *any identity-linked* payment address to be charged without validation. Sure, there will be people who try to cheat the system by using payment addresses with no value attached to them. But if those payment addresses are also linked to the identity of their owners, the vending machine operator has recourse—they can sell their bad credit transactions to a collection agency that tracks down and prosecutes the deadbeats. Since the deadbeats know how the recourse system works, they will seldom be tempted to cheat it.

The crypto community would hate that last part, because it presumes that payment addresses are linked to a legal identity. But that needn't be true for *all* payment addresses. It could be an option chosen by the creator of the address. The vending machine only accepts payments from sources that are linked to legal identities, but citizens could have the option to own both that kind of address and other addresses which are not identity-linked.

Network scalability, availability, and parallelism

We're talking about a global digital currency system capable of recording every payment transaction presently made by cash, check, credit card, or wire transfer on a distributed ledger. One hundred thousand transactions per second would be the bare minimum system throughput for a digital cash system intended to replace a major national currency, and a digital global reserve currency would require at least twice that, probably more. Translation: We're talking about the biggest and most sophisticated distributed computing system ever conceived, and it would need to offer availability, reliability and security features more robust than any computer network has ever achieved before.

Chapter 19:
Global-Scale Digital Currency

That's not to say it's impossible. We have the technology to build a massive parallel distributed system to meet this need. But it will be several orders of magnitude bigger and more sophisticated than any cryptocurrency, and it will require a different architecture.

This wouldn't be a project on the scale of merely modernizing the postal system to use barcodes. This is closer to landing a man on the moon. It's all about distributed systems technology—no rocket science is required. But this is so far beyond what Bitcoin's blockchain could ever deliver that it's hardly even worth thinking about blockchain. It's a completely different scale factor, and will require different technology. It's all possible and within reach, and my prediction is that progress will be rapid once the new *space race* begins.

Right now we're still at the *comic book phase*, where everyone knows about flying saucers and little green men from Mars, but nobody is taking space travel seriously. When Russia, China, or someone else introduces a global-scale digital currency system to replace SWIFT—that will be the *Sputnik* moment when the pace of change increases dramatically.

Who will design and build it?

It's conceivable that Russia and China aren't as far along as I've given them credit for, and that the U.S. is already secretly in the lead. If that's the case, they're really, *really good* at playing dumb. My strong impression is that the U.S. Government isn't taking digital currency seriously yet, save perhaps for the FBI's frustrations with Bitcoin and Monero. It's known fact that China and Russia's governments have taken an interest in the technology, but I'm speculating about the reasons behind that interest and their future intentions.

The Challengers

The clearest indication that someone is working on what I've described is the *Peoples Bank of China* (PBOC, the Chinese central bank) openly advertising that they are hiring blockchain engineers. In the beginning they said openly that the reason they needed these new hires was to "work on the digital RMB"[40]. But more recently they've been very quiet about what these people are actually doing. The PBOC also filed more digital currency related patents in 2017 than anyone else. They're obviously hard at work on *something*.

---

[40] The *Renminbi*, abbreviated RMB, is China's current conventional currency system, and is also known as the *Yuan*. Presumably the *digital RMB* refers to creating a digital version of China's current currency system. In other words, China's "Digital Dollar".

Meanwhile, Sergei Glaziev's activities show that Russia is at minimum interested and watching the space carefully. I find it particularly telling that Glaziev was the one to give the keynote address to the European blockchain conference. Russia has plenty of computer scientists with esteemed international reputations who would presumably be more credible in the blockchain crowd's eyes. So if Russia's intention was to impress them that Russia is onboard with the blockchain revolution from a technology perspective, they would have chosen a different spokesman.

But Sergei Glaziev? He's known primarily as the father of de-dollarization—the campaign to persuade other countries to ditch the dollar in international trade. I have to assume at the very least that Mr. Glaziev is interested in whether and how cryptocurrency can offer an alternative to SWIFT for international trade settlement. But this wasn't a cryptocurrency conference *per se*. It was a *blockchain* conference. That's the enabling distributed ledger technology that you need to learn about if you want to build *your own* digital currency system. The evidence is circumstantial and inconclusive by itself. *But something's going on here.*

I have little to offer about how the Challengers' side of the effort would occur. Would Chinese and Russian engineers work together on a secret team, or would they break the program up so that one country figures out the permissioned ledger issues while the other designs the currency system? Or might they agree to each take on the whole problem using their own personnel, and then collaborate to see which team comes up with a better solution, and then jointly promote whichever solution wins the bake-off, so to speak?

I don't know anything about Russian and Chinese government interaction with their private sectors. Russia and China *should be* commissioning something akin to America's *Manhattan Project* — a top-priority government program that taps the most talented engineers in each country to work on a focused project, whose goal is to secretly design and build a global-scale digital currency system, which will be rolled out publicly in a moment reminiscent of October 4th, 1957, when *Sputnik* first orbited the earth.

The U.S. Response

Several people I've spoken with in the course of writing this book think I'm crazy to assume the U.S. Government doesn't "get it" yet. They think the U.S. understands exactly what's at risk and already has a modern-day

Chapter 19:
Global-Scale Digital Currency

Manhattan Project of its own working on a central bank-sponsored Digital Dollar that will beat anything Russia and China might create.

If it's *not* already occurring, the U.S. Government will eventually figure out what's at stake here. My expectation would be that the banking industry would be the primary contractor hired to design the Digital Dollar. All the big banks are already working with distributed ledger. The distributed currency technology knowledge that's rapidly growing within the banking industry may not be *ahead* of the crypto designers, but it's catching up rapidly. And the bankers will be much more amenable to selling out Satoshi's view of the future to make a buck for themselves.

I'd be shocked if there's already a U.S. digital currency *Manhattan Project* underway. When the time comes for one, they're going to need expert banking knowledge every bit as much as digital currency knowledge. Whether it's part of a clandestine secret project or just for the purpose of advancing banking technology, the big banks are already learning the relevant technologies. When it comes time for the U.S. Government to launch its own digital currency *Manhattan Project*, the people they'll tap will be the big banks and the people in those banks who have the most knowledge of permissioned distributed ledger systems. Big IT players like IBM are already building permissioned ledger products. So when the U.S. Government is ready to get serious about a Digital Dollar, it's pretty clear who they'll call for tech support.

The coming Central Bank-Fintech complex?

Invoking the memory of President Eisenhower's infamous parting words to the American people warning us of the risks inherent to allowing the *Defense-Industrial Complex* to gain too much power, are we headed toward a moment in history when the *Central Bank-Fintech Complex* becomes the modern-day equivalent? I like to hope not, but the proverbial writing is on the wall.

Once governments figure out what's possible, they will realize that nobody benefits from digital currency technology more than those in government who would like to impose Orwellian control and surveillance over all of society. The opportunity to abuse digital currency technology toward that end is probably bigger than the opportunity to do positive things with it. And if what they need to pull it off is a private-sector partner who won't mind betraying the public trust if they can make a few bucks in the course of doing so, who better than Wall Street for that mission? *We the people* need to watch closely when the new space race gets going.

Beyond Blockchain: The Death of the Dollar and the Rise of Digital Currency

Chapter 20:
Digital Global Reserve Currency:
What would it take?

If you want to run a profitable nightclub, you design it to appeal to attractive young women. Catering to the musical taste of the middle-aged men who are actually your biggest source of revenue isn't important; they'll show up in droves regardless of the music's appeal so long as you figure out how to get plenty of young women into your club. Promoting a global reserve currency works the same way. The young women in the story are the central bankers. Make your currency system appeal to the central bankers' need for reserve assets, and the rest of the world will adopt your currency as their standard for everything else.

The part of the dollar hegemony story where the strength of the currency itself was the primary reason the dollar dominated the global monetary system ended with the Nixon Shock and the collapse of Bretton Woods gold convertibility in 1971. The Petrodollar system allowed King Dollar to retain its throne for several more decades, but now that, too, is rapidly losing relevance. The sole reason that King Dollar still holds the title is simply that *there is no viable alternative to the U.S. Treasury Bond market for central bank reserve assets.*

When someone comes up with a *superior alternative*, it will be like opening a new nightclub across the street that's full of Victoria's Secret lingerie models. The whole world will forget about the old club and flock to the new one. *The key to success lies in offering the central bankers something so far superior to U.S. Treasury bonds, they feel inclined to change a seventy-five-year-old standard.*

Russia and China's own sovereign bond markets will not suffice. They each have their own problems, and neither of them is ready to serve as the new standard for central bank reserves. The conclusion is inescapable: the best way to dethrone the Dollar as global reserve currency is to use technology to design and build a *digital sovereign bond market* which offers features and capabilities that go far beyond what was possible in a conventional bond market.

Thus one of my strongest contentions in this entire book: *the key to taking the title of reserve currency away from King Dollar lies in designing and building a digital sovereign bond market.* A market designed from the ground up for the express purpose of *exceeding* the depth and liquidity characteristics of the U.S. Treasury market is an essential component of a strategy to dethrone King Dollar.

The opportunity a digital sovereign bond market provides is not by any means limited to Russia and China's own sovereign debt. Redenominating that debt in a new digital currency would achieve very little. The reasons those nations' sovereign debt didn't appeal as central bank reserve assets wouldn't change much if they were digitized.

On the other hand, the rest of the world depends for the most part on dollar-denominated sovereign bonds. Smaller nations (known as *emerging markets* in finance parlance) are generally unable to borrow in their own currencies. As a matter of convention, their national debt is usually denominated in U.S. dollars, and the U.S. banking system is usually involved in underwriting their sovereign bonds. This gives the U.S. Government an additional lever of control over these nations' financial systems, and that's something many of them have come to resent. That resentment makes them far more likely to welcome a change to a new sovereign debt system.

Furthermore, there are serious risks for emerging market economies when the U.S. dollar begins to appreciate against their own currency. Imagine that you're the government of a small country, and all of your debt is owed in U.S. dollars. But now your own currency starts to lose value against the dollar in international foreign exchange markets. Before you know it, your debt has *increased* by as much as 50% or more in the sense that the amount of your own currency needed to repay the same principal balance of dollar-denominated debt has increased. What's more, this creates a self-reinforcing vicious cycle. That condition where your debt service obligations have increased puts serious pressure on your own economy. The result—your own currency depreciates even more on the international foreign exchange market, and the problem worsens.

You might be tempted to assume that the United States Government must understand this phenomenon and surely must take measures to help smaller nations struggling to repay dollar-denominated debt during periods of U.S. dollar strength relative to other currencies. But you'd be mistaken. U.S. Treasury Secretary John Connally famously made clear the American government's position on the issue when he responded to a group of

Chapter 20:
Digital Global Reserve Currency: What would it take?

European finance ministers expressing grave concern about exported U.S. dollar inflation. Connally responded to them by saying, "The dollar is *our* currency and *your* problem." At least he didn't mince words in letting them know the U.S. Government was unsympathetic to their concerns.

But what if someone were to use technology to design a *digital sovereign bond market* whose primary design *purpose* was to make it possible for all of that emerging market debt around the world to be refinanced with digital sovereign bonds denominated in a new global digital currency? That would result in the dollar-denominated debt being paid back, meaning the global U.S. dollar money supply would shrink, and the artificial international demand for dollars that has allowed U.S. trade deficits to continue for decades would start to dry up. Can you see why Russia and China might like to bring about that outcome?

Meanwhile, the European Union is struggling. It remains to be seen where the Euro currency is headed long-term. I've spoken with quite a few experts who are convinced that it's only a matter of time before both the Euro currency and the European Union fail. That's anything but a unanimous view—plenty of people disagree. But it's hard to dispute that the European Union faces its share of challenges right now.

What if European nations questioning their commitment to the Euro were presented with a new alternative? What if a new global-scale digital currency system could allow them to diversify away from the Euro and redenominate some (or all) of their sovereign debt in this new digital currency? The momentum would probably have to start in emerging markets. It's hard for me to envision Russia and China making a sales pitch and having European countries just up and walk away from the Euro and the ECB. But if a groundswell began first in emerging markets and then continued in Eastern Europe, I could easily see it gaining momentum. The key would be to offer both sovereign governments and investors new features that make the new system better than the old one.

Are you starting to see how a plan to dethrone King Dollar that *might actually work* is starting to take shape? Well, I don't think we're there quite yet. A new digital sovereign bond market integrated with the digital currency system *would* be extremely compelling. But we're still talking about the digital equivalent of fiat money. Yes, it might be a robust, global-scale digital currency and that's really cool from a technology perspective. But at the end of the day it's still just a digital form of fiat currency. And if that digital fiat money is issued by Russia and China jointly, it's questionable how much appeal it would really have beyond those nations' paper fiat currencies, which have both had a rough time in recent years. So I don't think a digital version of the RMB (Yuan) or the Ruble would cut it as global reserve currency.

But now suppose that Russia and China were to back this new digital currency system with gold. That's right—bring back good old-fashioned *representative money*. Both of them have been accumulating gold bullion in size for the last several years—a widely reported fact. What's all that gold for? One plausible answer is they're buying all that gold for their own reserves, so that they can divest their U.S. Treasury holdings. But I suspect there's much more to the picture.

Put yourself in global *investors'* shoes. Not the governments, but the investors who *buy* the sovereign debt. You have a choice to make. Do you want to own reserve assets denominated in a pure fiat currency like the dollar or the Euro in a day and age when sovereign debt markets have been propped up by central bank largesse, and many experts have expressed concern over a *global sovereign debt bubble*? Or would you rather invest in *digital sovereign bonds* which most people will see as the way of the future, and which are denominated in a digital currency *backed by and redeemable for gold bullion stored in a vault?* That's an easy decision.

So now we're talking about a new global digital currency system engineered from the ground up for the express purpose of dethroning King Dollar as global reserve currency. It starts with a robust global-scale digital currency system backed by and convertible into gold. An integral component of the overall system is a digital sovereign bond market designed to allow emerging market nations at first, then Eastern Europe, and ultimately any nation on earth, to dump the dollar and the Euro, and redenominate their sovereign debt in the new digital currency. What's more, since that new currency is backed by gold, investors will favor those bonds over conventional (fiat-backed) bonds, *and that investor preference will translate to a lower cost of borrowing for emerging market governments*. It's a win-win scenario. For everyone but the United States, that is.

There's one more carrot that China and Russia are probably already thinking about: If they can figure out how to use technology to engineer better *monetary policy* tools that allow nations moving to this new global currency to control their own destiny to some extent, it will be much easier to sell the central bankers on the change. This is the reason I've described a *zoned architecture* for the digital currency system. What matters at the end of the day is that the prettiest girls like your nightclub better than the competition. Appealing to all the central bankers around the globe is the name of the game.

Everything possible should be done to design both the digital currency system and the digital sovereign bond market to include features that give central bankers more control over their own economies and/or better instrumentation to understand what's going on in their economies. Those are the features that will sell the new nightclub to the people that matter. In other words, if you can deliver new monetary policy tools that far exceed the central bankers' wildest dreams, you can easily woo those same central bankers into your new nightclub (digital currency system).

In short, the whole world's monetary systems have been running on the equivalent of paper spreadsheets and an abacus for the last several hundred years. The technology now exists to give them Microsoft Excel and advanced computerized accounting systems. The question now is one of *time to market*. Can Russia and China really pull this off, or will the U.S. Government beat them to the punch by delivering a Digital Dollar with its own digital sovereign bond market?

Summarizing the strategy to dethrone King Dollar

This was just a high-level view. Here's a brief summary of what I believe it will take for one or more foreign governments to mount a viable plan to dethrone King Dollar:

1. **Introduce a global-scale digital currency system** which embraces the crypto community's invention of *double spend-proof digital cash*. But to make it global-scale, it will have to be built using a *permissioned distributed ledger* rather than *blockchain*.

2. **Back the new digital currency system with a gold-convertibility standard.**

3. **Create a *digital sovereign bond market*** which is integrated with the new digital currency system, and which is designed to offer both investors and central bankers a superior alternative to the U.S. Treasury Bond market.

4. **Offer *superior monetary policy tools*** that embrace technology to enable functionality well beyond central bankers' wildest dreams. The whole idea here is to offer central bankers something so appealing that they wouldn't hesitate to move away from the

seventy-five-year-old King Dollar standard when a superior alternative is offered to them.

My prediction is that something similar to this plan will be attempted by one or more foreign governments. A joint effort between China and Russia is the most likely scenario.

When does the new Space Race begin?

My suspicion is that Russia and China are already hard at work on this. All the signs are there. Some people think the space race has already begun and that the U.S. Government is developing a Digital Dollar. I don't buy that story. Unlike Russia and China, the U.S. would stand little to gain from the element of surprise. If the U.S. Government really understood what's at stake, it would make perfect sense for them to be very public about their commitment to designing a Digital Dollar. They already have the title of global reserve currency. Why would they risk letting Russia and China make a big splash with a *Sputnik Moment* where they announce their new digital currency with great fanfare? The U.S. could pre-empt that by announcing *right now* that it's committed to modernizing the dollar as a fully digital currency, thereby building further confidence in the U.S. as the anchor of the global financial system. But they're not doing any of these things.

Both the U.S. Banking industry and the FinTech companies already engaged in designing permissioned distributed ledger systems have probably figured most of this out already. Sure, it makes sense to explore how distributed ledger could advance the commercial banks' domestic affairs. But the utter obsession with "blockchain technology[41]" across the entire finance industry is taking on astronomic proportions. *As if the smartest guys at the bank already know what's coming, and understand that the bankers most talented in the use of permissioned distributed ledgers are the ones who will be first in line to bid on the design of the Digital Dollar.*

So to be clear, when I say the U.S. "doesn't get it yet", I mean that I don't believe the Federal Reserve or the U.S. Treasury have figured out how much opportunity digital currency technology offers. But the U.S. banking industry is another story. There's plenty of evidence that the bankers see

---

[41] People who say "blockchain technology" usually mean to say Distributed Ledger Technology. To call it *blockchain* technology would specifically imply a proof-of-work validated de-centralized ledger, but in my experience they usually don't mean that. They're talking about Distributed Ledger technology in general.

Chapter 20:
Digital Global Reserve Currency: What would it take?

what's coming and are preparing to be part of it. They may even be designing *digital dollar* systems on speculation, intending to sell them to the U.S. Government when the time is right. In any case, the things to watch for are:

- Signs of the *Challengers* showing their cards. If Russia and/or China start talking about rolling out a new "payment system" or "alternative to SWIFT" or "Digital RMB", it will be critical to closely analyze what they do. Please note that the *System for Transfer of Financial Messages* developed by Russia doesn't count. That is nothing more than a Russian-made alternative to SWIFT that uses the same technology and does exactly the same thing. What I'm referring to here is a technological *advancement* that obviates the need for SWIFT by offering something much better.

- Signs of the U.S. Government funding anything related to "blockchain technology" or any other "research" that the commercial banking sector receives federal funding for that might be in preparation for a digital dollar initiative.

- A trend of large U.S. banks acquiring FinTech companies involved in designing permissioned distributed ledgers, or other elements of technology used to design and build a global-scale digital currency system.

- Public announcements from the U.S. Government that appear to be setting the stage for an announcement of a government-sponsored initiative that amounts to hiring Wall Street bankers to design a Digital Dollar system.

I don't know exactly how this will play out—I don't think anyone does. But if central bankers like Klaas Knot and Mark Carney fully appreciate the importance of digital currency and are just playing dumb for the cameras, they should be nominated for an Oscar. Best acting *ever*.

Beyond Blockchain: The Death of the Dollar and the Rise of Digital Currency

Chapter 21:
Gold-backed Digital Currency

If you want to know what it would take to make a global-scale digital currency appeal to central bankers and investors alike, I can't think of a better answer than backing it with gold. The smartest people in finance already understand that the global economy is in a very precarious condition. Since the Great Financial Crisis, central bankers have been supporting the economy with quantitative easing and other monetary policy slight-of-hand that amounts to conjuring money out of thin air and using it to prop up the prices of financial assets, government bonds in particular.

We're in uncharted territory and nobody really knows the full extent of the systemic risks for certain, but everyone knows that at some point, *something's gotta give.* If there was ever a time when a safer alternative to pure fiat currency would be welcomed with open arms by investors, now is that time.

Suppose once again that China and Russia were to jointly engineer a new global-scale digital currency system. In its first version it replaces base money (MB) with digital currency. But suppose that they're working behind the scenes on a complete redesign of the entire fractional reserve system. Let's call this new digital currency the *Nuevo*.

The *Nuevo* is a government-issued digital currency built on a permissioned distributed ledger. It has a variable money supply regulated through digital monetary policy tools in a *zoned architecture* that allows some variance in monetary policy between national territorial zones. There is no concept of mining or miners. The system is secured through a permissioned distributed ledger so it doesn't need them. A newly formed *Banco Nuevo* central bank jointly chartered by China and Russia oversees the new currency.

The day it's introduced, a key feature is that *Nuevo* digital currency tokens are redeemable for gold at a guaranteed fixed exchange rate of 2,000 *Nuevo* per troy ounce of gold. Using a US $1,200 per ounce gold price as of this writing, this equates to each *Nuevo* having a gold redemption value (alone) of US $0.60.

The Governments of Russia and China sell the massive gold reserves they've accumulated in recent years to *Banco Nuevo* in exchange for *Nuevos*. This makes *Banco Nuevo* one of the largest holders of gold in the world (if not *the* largest), and supplies the governments of Russia and China with a large reserve of *Nuevos* to replace the gold they gave up to create *Banco Nuevo*.

Now *Banco Nuevo* (and/or Russia and China, for that matter) can begin selling the new gold-convertible *Nuevo* on the open market. There's no reason for them to even think about selling it for only US$0.60, its gold-redemption value. Just look at the mania that has erupted over cryptocurrency. It's *the way of the future* … It's the *new thing* … It offers so many advantages over conventional currency. So the digital currency token has to have some value unto itself, above and beyond its gold redemption value.

Consider that Bitcoin is a digital token convertible for precisely *nothing*, and isn't backed by any national government. But just the hype and excitement over digital currency being the way of the future led to Bitcoin tokens selling for as much as U.S. $19,666 each. So clearly, the world is ready to pay a big premium to get in on the ground floor of what they *perceive* to be the way of the future—and there was never even a *good reason* to think Bitcoin would be the way of the future. It was never suitable for anything beyond serving as an *alternative* to government-issued money.

Now we have a new International institution, *Banco Nuevo*, offering a gold-convertible currency designed to be the global digital currency system of the future and to eventually be recognized as the new global reserve currency. Demand would be off the charts. Investors wouldn't hesitate to pay a big premium above the gold value for *Nuevo* tokens.

Banco Nuevo could begin by selling *Nuevos* for US $1.00 just to get some traction in the market. That would be an easy sell, and would give them a *seigniorage*[42] profit of 66% on their gold. They could use the dollars and Euros they receive selling *Nuevos* to buy more gold bullion. But as demand grew, *Banco Nuevo* could easily slow the rate at which it is willing to issue and sell more *Nuevos* to allow the price to increase. They needn't be in a hurry. At this point, *Banco Nuevo's* digital sovereign bond market system wouldn't be ready for release yet, so they'd have plenty of time to get

---

[42] Seigniorage is the profit a government or central bank makes by issuing currency. It is defined as the price the currency is sold for minus the cost of producing that currency. In this case, it's the difference between what a *Nuevo* could sell for on the open market and the cost of the gold that backs it.

Chapter 21:
Gold-backed Digital Currency

Nuevos into circulation before they'll need an investor market flush with *Nuevos* to buy up new sovereign bond issues.

It would make no sense at all for *Banco Nuevo* to allow a dramatic appreciation of the *Nuevo* to occur on anything remotely close to the scale of what happened to Bitcoin. While the speculative mania in Bitcoin made millionaires out of a handful of young speculators who got lucky with the timing, it also set the market up for a subsequent crash. That kind of price volatility is exactly what central bankers would avoid like the plague. So the goal of *Banco Nuevo* would be to only allow their new digital currency to appreciate slowly and gradually, with minimum volatility.

And *Banco Nuevo* could achieve that goal easily through its own *open market operations*. By buying and selling its own *Nuevo* currency at whatever pace is necessary to maintain *stable pricing targeting approximately 175% of its gold-conversion value*, Banco Nuevo would be selling the hottest new thing the world has seen in a long time, and using the proceeds to buy even more gold bullion, making the gold-backing stronger than ever.

By maintaining a constant premium over the gold-conversion value of the *Nuevo*, the new *Banco Nuevo* would be running a profit-making digital money machine. They sell more *Nuevo* at whatever pace satisfies market demand while maintaining a *slow and gradual price appreciation*, and they use the fiat proceeds to keep increasing their own gold reserves. The appeal of digital currency generally has already been proven by the cryptocurrencies. The *Nuevo* could capitalize on this while growing *Banco Nuevo's* gold reserves and still deriving an enormous seigniorage profit along the way.

The *Nuevo* could very quickly grow to massive proportion. As it caught on with investors more and more, *Banco Nuevo* would be forced to respond by issuing and selling *lots and lots of Nuevo* to keep up with demand and avoid a price appreciation that could spook central bankers' confidence in the Nuevo's price stability. Furthermore, *Banco Nuevo* would be accumulating both gold and fiat cash so fast that it would have no trouble *defending the Nuevo* in the event of a market rout.

The key to success would be showing the rest of the world's central bankers that *Banco Nuevo* was committed to the *Nuevo*'s price stability— what they care more about than anything else. And that would mean that when the digital sovereign bond market is introduced, it would find plenty of investors welcoming the opportunity to invest in interest-bearing *Nuevo*-denominated bonds.

The risk of a 1971-style "run on the gold" attacking the Nuevo for the sake of its gold convertibility would be negligible. It would be easy for *Banco Nuevo* to manage the *Nuevo* to maintain market value well above the convertibility price. If the price started to decline, *Banco Nuevo* could easily intervene by spending their cash and/or gold reserves to defend the value of the *Nuevo* well above its conversion price. Unlike late 1960s America, *Banco Nuevo* wouldn't start any unfunded wars in Southeast Asia, and therefore would not be at risk of a "gold run" like the one the dollar suffered leading up to the Nixon Shock.

The next step: Government Independence

The scenario described thus far would involve the *Nuevo* being backed by and convertible for gold. That guarantee could be made by the governments of Russia and China. But already, this starts to feel like an old story. You can trust the government because the government is more trustworthy than anybody. Right up until the moment that they default on the deal, as happened with the Nixon shock. I doubt that the governments of Russia and China would be perceived as *more* reliable than the American government. It's easy to see how geopolitical situations involving Russia and China could bring rise to pressures on the *Nuevo* currency system.

Now suppose that *Banco Nuevo* was formed as an independent global central bank, whose sole charter is to govern and administer the *Nuevo* gold-backed global digital currency system. It might be headquartered in Switzerland to take advantage of that country's neutrality and legal system. The charter might allow other countries that adopt the *Nuevo* as their national currency to obtain seats on *Banco Nuevo*'s Board of Governors so that Russia and China would be on even footing with other nations participating in the currency bloc.

Russia and China would still need to seed *Banco Nuevo* with thousands of tons of gold to make it viable. At first glance it would seem that handing over all of their gold is the last thing they'd ever consider. But I don't think it out of the question. Suppose that Russia and China got a one-time bargain deal for supplying the *seed* bullion needed to launch *Banco Nuevo*: They exchange their gold bullion for *Nuevos* at a 1:1 ratio to the gold redemption price.

Chapter 21:
Gold-backed Digital Currency

In other words, they would retain the right to take their gold back (in the same amount) if they ever changed their mind. But far more likely, they would take some profits by selling *Nuevos* on the open market. If their cost to acquire billions of *Nuevos* was U.S. $0.60 but the *Nuevo* was introduced at par to the dollar (meaning a price of $1.00 at time of introduction), Russia and China would show an instantaneous 66% profit on the value of their gold. They would need to show restraint and not sell too many *Nuevos* too quickly to avoid upsetting the price objectives of *Banco Nuevo*, but their vested stake in the project would assure their prudence.

For the sake of giving the appearance of impartiality, the same 1:1 deal could be offered to anyone else who wanted to participate, but Russia and China would know it was coming and would wind up with lion's share of the discounted charter issue of *Nuevos*.

The end result would be a new supranational central bank, headquartered in Europe, offering a gold-convertible ultra-modern high-tech digital currency. This would come at a time when the European Central Bank is struggling and many people in finance are already beginning to question the long-term viability of the Euro currency. Russia and China could first introduce a superior alternative to the Euro, then step back and allow the countries joining the bloc to also participate on equal footing in the long-term governance of the system.

Russia and China would have already made a 66% seigniorage profit, and they would have had control over writing the initial charter and organizing rules of *Banco Nuevo* so as to assure their long-term objectives were met. They would also retain controlling interest in the voting structure of *Banco Nuevo* until such time as enough outside capital joined the system that Russia and China's "founder's share" of the currency issuance they obtained for their gold became a minority share of the total outstanding issue of *Nuevos*. And if things didn't work out, they'd still have the option to take their gold back.

This scenario of a completely independent *Banco Nuevo* represents Russia and China's best strategy by far to upstage the dollar as global reserve currency. As much as the world is hungry for a global reserve currency over which the United States exerts less domination and control, the world would be very skeptical of taking the keys to the kingdom away from the USA and handing them to China and Russia. But handing them to an independent global central bank headquartered in Europe, answering directly to no government, but *supported* by several governments, would play very well.

China and Russia really don't have that much to lose by giving up control. The seigniorage profit they would derive from selling all their gold at the initial offering 1:1 exchange for *Nuevos* would be reason enough to do the deal, and they'd get the independence from American hegemony they've always wanted as a fringe benefit, effectively for free.

Gold Standard or Gold Convertibility Standard?

If *Banco Nuevo* offered gold *convertibility* but not a true gold standard, the system probably would work fine. Initially, there would be 100% gold backing for every *Nuevo* in circulation, because Russia and China exchanged gold for their initial 1:1 issue of *Nuevos*. But as soon as *Banco Nuevo* started to issue and sell more *Nuevos*, the money supply would increase, and by definition, the gold backing would drop below 100%. So it seems that *Banco Nuevo* can only offer gold *convertibility*, not a true *gold standard*.

Consider that *Banco Nuevo*'s operating expenses would be minimal once the digital currency system had been built, and they would be selling freshly minted *Nuevos* at a considerable *premium* to their gold-convertibility price. This means that *Banco Nuevo* could easily use the proceeds to maintain their gold reserves at 100% backing. In theory, they could even increase the gold reserves to *more than 100% backing*, by reinvesting some of their *seigniorage premium* toward increasing gold backing.

Imagine a situation where *Banco Nuevo* is an independent global digital currency-issuing central bank, headquartered in Switzerland, and that by charter mandate, it always maintains a *minimum gold backing of 90%* of the *Nuevos* in circulation backed by gold bullion vaulted in Switzerland. That means that anyone investing in *Nuevos* at par to the U.S. dollar has an absolute worst-case 40% loss risk if the currency collapses and has to be redeemed for gold. Compare that to a 100% loss risk for the pure fiat Euro, a currency plenty of people are concerned has a very real and growing risk of failure. Can you hear the salesman in your head saying, "*Now how much would you pay for a Nuevo?*" I sure can.

What if the charter mandate said that *Banco Nuevo* must maintain a 90% minimum gold backing, but after the first year of operations, audited financial statements showed that *Banco Nuevo* had actually amassed a 105% gold backing for all of the *Nuevos* in circulation, by reinvesting part of their *seigniorage premium* in more gold bullion? *Now how much would you pay?*

Chapter 21:
Gold-backed Digital Currency

There's one big risk in this strategy—it could be the catalyst to cause a massive speculative rally in the price of gold. That would (for good reason) cause a big rally in the value of *Nuevos* relative to other currencies. This would be great news for holders of the *Nuevo* currency, but still be a caution flag for central bankers who know that a new digital currency would not be viable as a global reserve currency if it was prone to uncontrollable price appreciation versus *pure fiat* currencies. But this could be managed by *Banco Nuevo* having the latitude to allow its gold backing to drop to 90% of *Nuevos* in circulation. By taking a break from buying gold, the self-reinforcing vicious cycle driving a speculative gold bullion mania could be broken.

It's an interesting debate whether *Banco Nuevo* would be best off with or without a *charter mandate* to maintain a high percentage backing of gold. But I'm convinced it would benefit from transparent reporting of its holdings, and a managerial bias toward accumulating excess gold reserves to whatever extent it was possible to do so without igniting a speculative mania in gold. If Banco Nuevo could show the world that it intended (regardless of mandate) to maintain the highest possible gold backing for the new digital currency, I just don't see how any fiat currency could compete.

Conclusions

The hypothetical *Banco Nuevo* could rapidly advance a viable supranational digital currency that BRICS countries and others could use immediately as an alternative to the dollar for trade settlement. It wouldn't take long to entice Eastern European nations at first and eventually, the major Eurozone nations such as France and Germany to join the *Nuevo* bloc. But I don't think it would be enough to remove the dollar as the reserve currency. That wouldn't occur until *Banco Nuevo* introduced its *digital sovereign bond market* a couple of years later. We'll explore how that could occur, but first we need to spend a couple of chapters on some more enabling technology you need to understand first.

Beyond Blockchain: The Death of the Dollar and the Rise of Digital Currency

Chapter 22:
Permissioned Distributed Ledger

Let's quickly review some concepts introduced much earlier in this book. A *distributed ledger* is a computer database that has no single owner and no master copy. The database is replicated across a network, and many different participants in the distributed network validate transactions being added to the ledger to make sure they are legitimate. In the case of a digital currency, this pertains in particular to making sure that no digital coin ever gets double-spent.

The *distributed ledger* Satoshi perfected for the Bitcoin cryptocurrency is known as *blockchain*. On one hand it represents a breakthrough in computer science—prior to blockchain, nobody had ever figured out a way to make a secure ownerless database work in a peer-to-peer network that has no central authority figure or point of control. This was the key innovation needed to perfect the invention of *double spend-proof digital cash*, which the cypherpunks had been struggling with for well over a decade before *blockchain*.

But *blockchain* has a really serious problem: The only way Satoshi could figure out to make it work in a truly decentralized network was to use a system called *proof-of-work* that's slow as molasses. This is precisely the reason that you've probably heard statistics that the Bitcoin network consumes more electricity than entire nations, yet it is only able to process about seven transactions per second of network-wide throughput.

Ok, so what does all of this really mean when we net it down to the current state of the art? It means that decentralized cryptocurrencies are nowhere close to "ready for prime time" in the sense of scaling up to meet the demands of the global economy. To build a national or supranational digital currency system that could process all the payment transactions expected, we'd need to support *hundreds of thousands* of transactions per second. Today's state of the art fully decentralized cryptocurrencies can't even support *hundreds* of transactions per second.

The reason for this inefficiency and poor performance is all that busy work—the cryptographic math problems—intended to prevent the bad guys from outnumbering the good guys.

The unpalatable alternative (to the cypherpunks) is a permissioned distributed ledger. That means giving up true *decentralization* in its purest sense, but the benefits can be enormous. Simply put, a *permissioned distributed ledger* is a distributed ledger that works similar to *blockchain*, but without the *proof-of-work* (the busywork math problem) requirement to validate transactions on the network.

The performance benefits are enormous. XRP (formerly, Ripple) is the one cryptocurrency that uses a *permissioned ledger* rather than a decentralized ledger. The result is that it's more than two hundred times faster than Bitcoin and one hundred times faster than Ethereum. Other distributed ledgers now being developed have the promise of delivering performance thousands of times faster than Bitcoin. The downside is that they're not fully decentralized, and therefore cannot satisfy the cypherpunks desire to evade government authority. Some critics have suggested that XRP is not a *true* cryptocurrency for precisely this reason.

So if your goal is to build a cryptocurrency system the government can't shut down, a permissioned ledger just doesn't work. But if you *are* the government and you're designing a government-issued digital currency system, you're not concerned about making your system resistant to your own oversight and control. It's a pretty clear choice that a *permissioned distributed ledger* is the right place to start if you're designing a global-scale digital currency system with state sponsorship.

Permissioned Distributed Ledger still has no central "owner"

The breakthrough invention of distributed ledger is to enable a computer database that has no single owner or "master copy". The data is distributed across a network and many different network participants who all have a vested interest in keeping the system "honest" share in the process of keeping everyone else accountable and making sure nobody gets away with any monkey business.

A *permissioned* distributed ledger still has all these features. There is no owner or master copy for the data. Everyone with a vested interest still gets to monitor the integrity of the ledger, and make sure nobody is double-spending coins or otherwise cheating. So just like a fully de-centralized ledger such as *blockchain*, a permissioned ledger offers a whole new degree of independence and security that was never possible in the centralized database architectures that were the only known way of doing things before blockchain was invented.

Chapter 22:
Permissioned Distributed Ledger

So to be clear, in both permissioned and de-centralized distributed ledgers, the data itself is completely de-centralized in both cases. Only the *permissioning* function—deciding who's allowed to be a miner in Bitcoin parlance—is centralized in a *permissioned* distributed ledger system.

Hijacking Risk in Permissioned Ledgers

Permissioned distributed ledgers are not necessarily a panacea. They offer the opportunity to process transactions several orders of magnitude faster than a proof-of-work validated blockchain. That's the big plus, but the risks are significant.

The whole concept of a *permissioned* ledger is that there is a central authority who specifies which other computers in the network may participate in the critical task of validating transactions and adding them to the permanent ledger. If hackers could ever figure out a way to take over that central authority itself, they could completely hijack the entire currency system. So security of the *permission function* is absolutely critical. So critical, in fact, that some critics would say it's crazy to even consider using a *permissioned* distributed ledger to build a digital currency system.

We're not talking about the need for the kind of "strong security" required in something like an airline reservation system, or even the "super strong security" needed for a major bank's systems of record. We're talking about the security of the entire global economy. The security has to be absolutely *bulletproof*. There are a lot of companies working on advancing permissioned ledger technology using very sophisticated security models to protect against this risk. I'm confident that someone can come up with adequate security—conceptually it's definitely possible. But until then, it can't be taken for granted.

Breaking the Proof-of-Work Barrier

If the last couple of paragraphs shook your confidence in *permissioned distributed ledger* being the answer to everything, I'm glad—that was point. We need to be cognizant of the fact that a *permissioned* ledger is only as good as the security of its *permissioning system*. If a global digital currency system the size of the dollar or the Euro relies entirely on the security of its distributed ledger, that ledger has to be absolutely safeguarded. *Almost* isn't anywhere close to good enough.

Keep in mind that the only thing *wrong* with a *permissionless decentralized* distributed ledger such as blockchain is that so far, nobody has figured out how to design one that doesn't rely on the incredibly inefficient, resource-wasting *proof-of-work* architecture for its *security*.

So the fully decentralized *permissionless* distributed ledger that doesn't depend on proof-of-work and which could realistically scale up to support a global-scale digital currency system *has yet to be invented*. That doesn't mean it won't be; it just hasn't happened *yet*. But plenty of very smart people are working hard on inventing it. *Very hard.*

The jury is still out on how the distributed ledger system to support a global-scale digital currency system will work. For the moment, *permissioned* ledger is clearly in the lead when we evaluate performance. The *proof-of-work* validated de-centralized ledgers are literally thousands of times slower, and therefore nowhere close to "ready for prime time" when it comes to supporting a global-scale digital currency system.

We need *either one* of two potential scenarios. One possibility is a *permissioned* distributed ledger whose permissioning mechanism is so secure that we can entrust the integrity of a major global currency system to it. The other possibility is that someone "breaks the proof-of-work barrier" and figures out how to make decentralized ledgers operate several orders of magnitude faster and more efficiently than they do today. Either one would suffice.

Distributed Ledger State-of-the-Art: Not quite there yet

Today's *permissioned* distributed ledgers can operate one thousand times faster than Bitcoin's blockchain. Wow—that sounds impressive, but hold on … a thousand times faster than Bitcoin is still only 7,000 transactions per second. That's still not enough if we're talking about a major national or supranational currency system. We still need more than *another full order of magnitude* performance improvement to support a major national currency system, and we also need to achieve near 100% reliability and availability characteristics. A global-scale digital currency, when it is developed, will almost certainly represent the most sophisticated and advanced distributed computing system in existence.

The design of blockchain involves all of the computers in the network maintaining a copy of the cumulative transaction history of the entire currency system since Satoshi mined the first block in 2009. Every time somebody buys a pizza and pays with Bitcoin, that transaction gets added to the blockchain and every miner and full node in the network is updated to reflect the addition of that transaction.

Chapter 22:
Permissioned Distributed Ledger

That's fine for a cryptocurrency, but if we're talking about the entire global economy, the transaction volume and size of the ledger itself would quickly become overwhelming. A different architecture is needed which doesn't require every single transaction to be stored on every single computer in the network. It just wouldn't be realistic to run an entire national economy on the *single-channel ledger architecture* that has been used by the cryptocurrencies thus far.

I'm not too worried about this, however. I can easily envision a *segregated* architecture where the overall money supply is segregated into zones. Within a single zone, the design would be similar to the way cryptocurrencies work, with all the network participants tracking all the transactions. But the transactions would only be kept and tracked by the computers within that zone. Intrazone payments would work similar to how cryptocurrency transactions work, but inter-zone payments would be more complicated. Any time a coin is spent across zones, it would be necessary for that coin to be re-registered as resident in a different zone, and therefore stored in a different segment of the distributed ledger.

This is convenient in the sense that governments would probably insist on special rules applying to international payment transactions anyway. If each national economy were a separate zone (and perhaps contained several sub-zones within that national zone), it would naturally lend to a design in which special reporting or accounting rules apply to international transactions, which are also inter-zone transactions. Intra-zone transactions would operate with a higher performance, lower overhead set of transaction settlement rules.

The cypherpunks would hate some of these ideas. Their philosophy is that international payments should work exactly like any other payment, and that governments should not have the authority or power to regulate or control international movement of money. But as much as these ideas appeal on some level to my libertarian instincts, I just don't think they're realistic in this day and age. Whether we like it or not, governments want to regulate and control international money flows, and most people support giving government the authority to do so.

Bitcoin and other cryptocurrencies will continue to be popular long after the advent of global-scale government-sponsored digital currency, because there will always be a niche market (and probably an illegal one) for people who insist that government should have no authority to regulate or oversee international capital flows. But the vast majority of society will accept government's desire to regulate such matters, and that global-scale state-sponsored digital currency systems will be designed to provide such controls.

Conclusions

Building a truly global-scale digital currency system capable of processing 100,000+ transactions per second would require distributed ledger technology which doesn't exist yet. But I'm not at all concerned by this. The first versions of any new technology almost always suffer performance and scalability shortcomings, and these problems have always been overcome with a little time and ingenuity.

The really hard engineering problems have already been solved. The key breakthrough was the invention of *Distributed Ledger* itself—the notion of a computer database that has no owner and which allows everyone with a vested interest to help keep it secure. The remaining technology challenges will solve themselves faster than the social and regulatory challenges will be overcome.

In short, the biggest and hardest problems have already been solved. Now we need to make existing inventions go faster and work even more securely. I have far more faith in the ability of technology innovators to step up to that challenge than I have in the central banking establishment to get their heads around even the most basic concepts that should have been obvious to them years ago.

Chapter 23:
Smart Contracts

The phrase *smart contract* was coined in 1994 by Nick Szabo, a computer scientist who is so accomplished and well respected in the field of digital currencies that quite a few experts have speculated that he may actually be Satoshi Nakamoto—something Szabo has denied. But regardless of whether or not he might be Satoshi, one thing that's not in dispute is that Szabo has been a thought leader in the digital currency space for a long time. In 1998, he proposed a hypothetical digital currency he named *BitGold*. The rationale for the name was that Szabo's goal was to create a digital currency system that mimicked the characteristics of gold bullion as closely as possible. Most of the key features of Bitcoin were originally proposed by Szabo in his *BitGold* design, fueling the speculation that he might be Satoshi.

The meaning of the phrase *smart contract* has evolved considerably since Szabo first proposed the concept in 1994. At that time, the idea was very specific. Legal contracts[43] are normally written on paper according to a set of rules and accepted procedures known collectively as *contract law*. The purpose of a contract is to document in writing an agreement between two or more parties, and in most cases one or more required payments of money to be paid by one party to another are specified within the *terms* of the contract. In conventional (paper) contracts, if there is a disagreement between the parties with respect to each fulfilling its obligations as set forth under the contract's *terms and conditions*, the court system *enforces* the contract by hearing arguments from the parties to the contract and then passing judgment on what the parties are actually required to do in order to satisfy their obligations under *contract law*.

Szabo's original proposal in 1994 was to replace or supplement the function of the court by codifying the contract as a special type of computer program, rather than just a document written on paper. The idea was that if the contract says that Party A must pay $100 to Party B when some condition is met, then the computer program could detect when the condition had been met and automatically effect the payment without Party A having to take any action to send it. Put another way, the concept of a

---

[43] https://en.wikipedia.org/wiki/Contract

legal contract that is interpreted and enforced by a court of law could be replaced or extended by the concept of a contract *program* enforced by running it in a special computer programming environment that allows the *smart contract* program to cause payments to occur between accounts owned by the parties involved in the contract.

Szabo's original concept was that contracts would be *programmed* by programmers rather than being written by lawyers, and the computer system would automatically enforce the terms and conditions of the contract. A principal advantage of these *smart contracts* over conventional contracts is that many routine enforcement needs could be met through automation without the need to involve the court system. For example, if a contract sets forth a cancellation policy that requires notification by midnight Eastern time on January 1st, but a party who waited until 1:00 a.m. is trying to weasel out of paying, the computer program can detect the timestamp of the cancellation message and enforce the terms and conditions as codified into the *smart contract* without the need for a court hearing or judgment.

This concept has evolved considerably since it was first proposed by Szabo nearly twenty-five years ago. As used today, the phrase *smart contract* refers to any program that runs within a digital currency *scripting environment*, which is a special type of computer programming language. Among today's cryptocurrencies, Ethereum has done the most to embrace and advance the notion of *smart contracts*. Several other cryptocurrencies offer smart contract support as well, including an extension to Bitcoin which allows a type of smart contract script to run as an extension built on top of the Bitcoin payment network.

Visualizing smart contracts

To illustrate how smart contracts work, let's start with the simple function of a system that does *not* support them. For example, in the Bitcoin system, when you send a payment to address A1[44], the Bitcoins you send go straight into address A1 and nothing else happens. There is no way for the owner of address A1 to ask to have something different happen.

---

[44] Real Bitcoin addresses are long hexadecimal numbers. I'm using the shorthand "A1" to mean some arbitrary Bitcoin address. To make an actual Bitcoin payment, a full-length address would of course be required.

Chapter 23: Smart Contracts

Now suppose we're talking about a cryptocurrency which supports smart contracts. The function of receiving that payment and depositing it entirely into address A1 is represented by the following pseudo-code[45]:

```
function ReceiveDeposit(IN AmountReceived, IN
ReceivedToAddress)
        ; This function receives two inputs, the amount
received
        ; and the address specified to deposit that amount
into.
DepositToAddress( AmountReceived, ReceivedToAddress )
        ; Deposit all of the funds received into the target
address
        ; without taking any further action.
end function
```

In this first form the *smart contract* simply deposits all the money received into the account it was sent to—the same action that would be expected if there was no smart contract. But now suppose that a tax authority imposes a 10% sales tax on whatever is being sold through this address. Furthermore, they specify that as soon as the accumulated tax that any merchant has collected exceeds 1,000 units of currency, the merchant is required to deposit the full amount of taxes in escrow to the taxing authority promptly. What's worse, there's a twenty-four hour deadline and stiff penalties for late compliance.

In a normal system it would be necessary to develop a business process for keeping track of revenues, calculating taxes and putting them in escrow, then ultimately sending them to the taxing authority. But using *smart contracts*, the whole thing could be codified into a new version of the same function that receives a payment:

```
function ReceivePayment( IN AmountReceived, IN
ReceivedToAddress )

myTaxEscrowAccount = Lookup( "TAX_ESCROW_ACCOUNT")
TaxAuthorityPmtAddr = Lookup(
"TAX_AUTHORITY_PAYMENT_ADDRESS")

DepositToAddress( (AmountReceived * 0.1), myTaxEscrowAccount
        ; Put the first 10% in escrow for the tax man
DepositToAddress( (AmountReceived * 0.9), ReceivedToAddress )
        ; Deposit the rest to my regular revenue account
```

---

[45] The phrase *pseudo-code* means a shorthand written to follow the usual form of a computer program, but using self-explanatory English statements that show the logic of the program without all the special syntax and keywords of an actual computer program. Pseudo-code would have to be translated into an actual programming language to actually make this work, but I'm sticking with plain English for the benefit of readers who are not experienced in computer programming.

```
        If GetBalance( myTaxEscrowAccount ) > 1000 THEN:
            DepositToAddress( GetBalance( myTaxEscrowAccount ),
   TaxAuthorityPmtAddr )
            ; As soon as the escrowed tax balance exceeds
            ; 1,000 deposit it to the tax authority automatically.
    end function
```

This version deposits only 90% of the revenue received into the target address, after deducting 10% tax and placing it in escrow. The instant that a new payment causes the tax escrow account to exceed 1,000 units of currency, it is automatically sent to the government tax authority's payment address, satisfying the regulatory requirement automatically.

I've intentionally avoided showing you the actual programming syntax used in Ethereum smart contracts or describing the capabilities and limitations of Ethereum smart contracts, because I don't want your imagination to be *limited* by such details. Obviously, if your goal is to start developing *smart contract* financial applications on the Ethereum platform you need to know such things, but this is not the book for that.

You're probably wondering, *what are the capabilities and limitations of these "smart contracts" in a digital currency system?* For the purposes of this book, I want you to imagine that the possibilities are limitless. Yes, of course there are limitations to what is possible *today*. But this is a field that is advancing rapidly and the capabilities currently in existence are already quite impressive[46].

By the time we get past all of the regulatory, social, and bureaucratic hurdles necessary to introduce a global-scale digital currency, *smart contract* technology will have evolved considerably too. So indulge your imagination and assume that these financial application programs will be able do absolutely anything.

Relevance of smart contracts to global-scale digital currency

Think about the difference between a *computer program* such as *Microsoft Excel* and a *computer operating system* such as *Microsoft Windows*. A computer program performs some useful function for the user, whereas a computer operating system provides the environment in which computer

---

[46] For readers with a software background, Ethereum runs its smart contracts in a Turing-complete, fully sandboxed virtual machine architecture. The virtualization engine is distributed across the Ethereum network so the exact location of the node(s) running the VM is transparent to the smart contract developer. It's a very impressive architecture and it's clear that the Ethereum developers have a vision that involves smart contracts growing in capability to eventually support very sophisticated distributed financial application systems in their own right.

Chapter 23: Smart Contracts

programs can be created. The job of the operating system is to organize the computer's disk drives into *files* and *folders*, and to provide services that make it easy for application programmers to create files, read and write data to and from files, and so forth.

Start thinking about the future global digital currency system more like a computer *operating system*, not just a computer *program*. In other words, just as the Windows operating system offers application programmers a bunch of technical services such as creating files, deleting files, and reading and writing data to and from files, imagine the future digital currency system as offering *services* such as sending payments, receiving payments, creating new payment addresses, and so forth. The currency system provides the basic functions of money (tripartite definition), and it provides *services* which allow financial application software developed on top of the currency system to send and receive payments within that system. Examples of such applications might include things like *Accounts Payable* or *Accounts Receivable* programs for businesses.

But unlike the conventional versions of these programs which just print reports on paper, the future digital currency system will allow these application software systems to send payments, receive payments, send invoices and dunning notices to customers, and so on. The digital currency system upon which they are built will provide all these general-purpose services for use by custom application software.

These capabilities already exist today in the Ethereum cryptocurrency. These days, when people talk about *smart contracts,* they're usually referring to this general architecture of the currency system acting like an operating system upon which financial applications can be developed. Among the existing cryptocurrencies, Ethereum is currently in the lead (in my opinion) with respect to designing the currency system as a platform upon which application programs can be developed. But Ethereum is still a *cryptocurrency*—an *alternative* to mainstream government-issued money. In its current implementation, it cannot scale to support the needs of a global digital currency system.

So where exactly does this fit into our story about the quest for the *Challengers* to try to displace the dollar as global reserve currency? The answer is that if ever there was a *perfect* example of how to really advance the condition of the global monetary system using an *application system* developed *on top of the digital currency platform*, that example is the *digital sovereign bond market.* Recall that the whole name of the game is to offer central bankers a superior alternative to the U.S. Treasury bond market for reserve assets. A *digital sovereign bond market* could achieve that, and the perfect way to design and build one is to create a *layer* of additional functionality.

If Sergei Glaziev is as smart as I think he is, Russia figured this out a long time ago, and knows that they need to create a new sovereign bond market capable of giving the U.S. Treasury market a run for its money. If they wanted to leverage technology to achieve that goal, the ideal way to do it would be to design a *digital sovereign bond market* that uses technology to deliver functionality and liquidity characteristics superior to the existing conventional U.S. Treasury bond market.

If Russia were inclined to start with an existing cryptocurrency system as the basis for building their dollar-challenging digital currency system, and saw the need to create a digital sovereign bond market, the logical choice would be the cryptocurrency with the best support for *smart contracts*, since that's the feature most needed to create the critically important digital sovereign bond market that plays a critical role in ending dollar hegemony. Ethereum is the leader in this regard at the moment among the cryptocurrencies.

Say, who was that kid I mentioned earlier in this book who managed to get a personal meeting with Russian President Vladimir Putin? *Vitalik Buterin, the Russian-Canadian inventor of Ethereum.* Small world, eh?

Chapter 24:
Digital Sovereign Bond Market

If your goal is to replace the U.S. dollar as global reserve currency, the way to achieve that is to offer central bankers a superior alternative to U.S. Treasury bonds. Until now, everyone has assumed that meant that a viable alternative *bond* was needed. The notion of offering a superior bond *market* has never been perceived as a significant differentiator. Technology could change that. I see three distinct categories of opportunity for a *Challenger* to use technology to change the balance of power away from continued dollar hegemony:

1. **Use technology to create a better sovereign *bond*,** meaning that a digital sovereign bond could offer features that make it more desirable as a central bank reserve asset than a conventional bond, with other factors such as credit strength and market capitalization being equal.

2. **Use technology to create a better sovereign bond *market*.** Most people have always assumed that the primarily determinant of any bond market's *depth* and *liquidity* characteristics is the market capitalization and market demand for the bonds. I'll propose other ways to achieve these goals.

3. **Offer emerging market governments an alternative to Dollar financing for the purpose of reducing the Dollar's dominance in the global financial system.** Although emerging market sovereign issues are unlikely to be central bankers' first choice for reserve assets, introducing a digital sovereign bond market which leads to widespread redenomination of EM debt in a non-dollar currency will have systemic effects that should accelerate the process of the dollar losing favor as global reserve currency. This is the Challengers' main goal.

I'll elaborate in detail on these three points later.

What's so great about U.S. Treasury Bonds?

First, it's essential to understand the appeal of U.S. Treasury Bonds as reserve assets. After all, we can't have a coherent discussion of what it would take to replace them until we first understand why central bankers prefer them to start with.

Size Matters!

The U.S. Treasury market is the biggest sovereign debt market on earth. It's also the most actively traded sovereign bond market in the world. The words *deep* and *liquid* are often used to describe the market characteristics desired by large traders such as central banks who need to trade *in size* when the time comes. *Liquidity* refers to how much of something can be sold at the currently quoted price, without the sale transaction exhausting all the demand that exists at that price. *Depth* refers to how much *more* liquidity exists at slightly lower prices. In other words, if the market will absorb $10 million at the quoted price, how much will it absorb one tick below the quoted price? What about two ticks below, or three? Central bankers are looking for an asset that can be sold in very large size, on a day when a crisis is developing, without their own selling activity forcing the price markedly lower.

This is all a complex way of saying the reserve asset has to be something for which constant demand exists, and where a motivated seller can quickly sell a *very large* amount of that asset simply by offering a *very small* discount to the actively quoted market price. The size of the U.S. Treasury Market and the widespread demand for U.S. Treasury paper makes it the best choice by far to satisfy these criteria.

Credit Matters Even More

While *depth* and *liquidity* are very important when it comes time to conduct a sale transaction at the price the bonds are valued at, nothing is more important than the question of whether the bonds will hold their value and still be worth what the central bank originally paid for them. Keep in mind that during "normal times", the central bankers aren't concerned with the need to sell their reserve assets. What they care about is their ability to sell those assets *during crisis conditions*. This means favoring bonds issued by countries least likely to suffer dire economic consequences from whatever sort of crisis might develop.

Historically, the title of global reserve currency has usually been held by the country with the *strongest navy*—an indicator of military might before the advent of air power. So while some smaller emerging market countries have fantastic economic outlooks, and the value of their sovereign bonds should appreciate greatly in coming years, *and* a profit-motivated speculative investor would favor them—countries without a powerful

Chapter 24:
Digital Sovereign Bond Market

military could easily be obliterated in a war. The United States' fiscal condition is less than ideal to say the very least, but the odds of the United States being defeated in a war to the point that its sovereign debt becomes worthless are extremely low.

At some point the merits of *size* and *credit* conflict with one another. What if the U.S. Treasury market was twice as big as it already is? Would that be even better? What about three times? For the U.S. Treasury market to be markedly bigger than it already is would imply that the U.S. national debt was also much bigger than it is. But many economists are already concerned that the U.S. national debt has reached a level where it *cannot be repaid in real terms*. The only way to repay the debt would be to encourage enough *inflation* that the real purchasing power repaid would be less than the amount borrowed. A rapidly inflating currency loses value relative to other currencies around the world, so this condition would be highly undesirable to central bankers shopping for reserve assets.

For the moment, runaway inflation risk in the U.S. dollar is not of much concern to most investors and economists, but this bears watching. Many macroeconomic analysts have become convinced that the thirty-six year bull market in bonds (meaning gradually *declining interest rates* over a long time period) has ended and a new secular bond bear market (meaning gradually *increasing interest rates*) has begun. If that's true, governments around the world including the U.S. will struggle with rapidly increasing cost of debt service, and this may cause central banks to change their reserve asset preferences.

Evaluating Alternatives to U.S. Treasury Bonds

Suppose that frustrations with U.S. foreign policy lead other nations to favor non-U.S. assets as central bank reserves for political (as opposed to economic) reasons. There aren't many appealing alternatives to choose from.

German Bunds

The German sovereign bond is known as the *bund*, and many investors and economists consider it to be second only to the U.S. Treasury bond in terms of safety and creditworthiness. Germany is widely regarded as one of the most fiscally responsible nations on earth, and its *bunds* are so highly regarded that even at the ten-year maturity, yields were pushed into negative territory. This means that investors valued the *safety* of the ten-year bund so highly that they were willing to keep bidding the price higher even after it reached the point where the bond would offer no investment return whatsoever.

Considering the fact that the primary reason for favoring sovereign bonds over gold bullion for reserve assets is that they produce income, it hardly makes sense to favor negative-yielding German bunds. And aside from the negative yield, bunds are denominated in Euros, a currency which some economists fear may be doomed as a result of other countries in the Eurozone having been far less fiscally responsible than Germany. The money you get paid back from an investment in bunds gets paid back in Euros, so unless you're unconditionally confident that the currency will hold its value, you cannot have complete faith in the bund as a reserve asset.

U.S. Treasuries offer a much higher yield than bunds and are denominated in dollars. Despite the rapidly growing frustrations with U.S. foreign policy, few people question the stability or longevity of the dollar. It's easy to see why central bankers have set aside their political frustrations with U.S. policy and have continued to favor U.S. Treasury paper for reserve assets due to its safety and stability.

But perhaps the biggest downside to bunds (when evaluated in comparison to U.S. Treasury Bonds) is the size of the market. Germany is a much smaller economy than the U.S., so both the market capitalization and the daily trading volume of bunds pales in contrast to U.S. Treasuries.

Other Eurozone Sovereign Bonds

Moving beyond Germany to the rest of the Eurozone[47], it's the same overall story, except the other countries are all regarded as less creditworthy than Germany. The peripheral countries Portugal, Italy, Greece and Spain are known in finance circles as the PIGS, an acronym derived from the names of those countries but intentionally carrying the connotation of poor creditworthiness. France and other core countries are stronger credits, but all the other criticisms described for the German Bund apply to them.

Japanese Government Bonds (JGBs)

The Japanese Government has been engaged in monetary policy designed to produce extremely low (or even negative) sovereign bond yields for several decades. Meanwhile, the amount of outstanding debt (as

---

[47] In finance parlance, *Eurozone* refers to the group of countries which use the Euro currency. This is not quite the same as the *European Union*, since some countries like Switzerland are E.U. members but do not use the Euro currency.

measured as a percentage of Gross Domestic Product) is astronomical—much higher than any other major sovereign bond issue. The result is that JGBs offer almost no income (so why favor them over gold?), and are less creditworthy than U.S. Treasuries or other alternatives.

British Gilts

The United Kingdom's sovereign bonds are known as *Gilt-edged securities*, or just "Gilts" for short. The Gilt market is relatively creditworthy in many regards, but the Brexit Referendum which obligates the U.K. government to leave the European Union casts a cloud of doubt and uncertainty over the Gilt. Some economists believe that Brexit will be the best thing that ever happened to the U.K., while others are convinced it will bring economic ruin. Obviously these are subjective matters of opinion, but central bankers shopping for reserve assets don't like uncertainty. Just the *question* of what unforeseen consequences Brexit may bring is reason enough to take pause.

Gilts are certainly used as central bank reserve assets to a certain degree, and are regarded as a high quality debt instrument in financial circles. But between the size of the market and these factors of uncertainty, most central bankers continue to prefer U.S. Treasury Bonds.

Everything Else

The aforementioned sovereign bond issues are the major ones in the global economy. Of course, there are dozens of other countries issuing sovereign debt, but none of them are big enough to appeal as preferable to U.S. Treasuries for use as central bank reserve assets. China and Russia's own sovereign debt is large in size, but Russia in particular has been forced to default on sovereign bonds in recent years and China is still a closed currency system. For these reasons the debt of these nations is unlikely to be favored *in its current form* as a central bank reserve asset.

I do believe that emerging market sovereign debt will play an important role in this story, but it won't be as a viable alternative to U.S. Treasuries for central bank reserves.

The inescapable conclusion—there really is no viable alternative to U.S. Treasury Bonds when it comes to choosing central bank reserve assets *based on the choices available today*. To change the game, someone will need to figure out a way to offer something *different* that will appeal as a central bank reserve asset even if the credit of the issuing government is not demonstrably superior to the United States.

Use Technology to Create a Better Sovereign *Bond*

Digital currency represents a significant advance beyond what was possible with conventional currency. My belief is that technology can be used to engineer a new kind of digital sovereign bond that is superior to the conventional variety. Specifically, I believe it is possible to start with the objective of *designing* a sovereign bond with the express goal of making it appeal to central bankers as a reserve asset. There are many ways digital technology can help achieve that goal.

Before going on, I want to return to my 1977 computer salesman analogy. The invention of digital currency systems upon which more complex financial software systems can be built using *smart contracts* is analogous to the invention of the PC. It will take the imagination and creativity of a lot of different people to figure out how to best leverage the opportunity this creates. I have some specific ideas of my own to share with you, but I want to emphasize that they will be the equivalent of that 1977 TRS-80 salesman saying you could balance your checkbook with a computer. You'll be able to do a whole lot more with digital currency technology than I'm able to predict in detail at this stage of the game. We're still very early in the story, and a lot of innovation lies ahead.

The Smart Contract Revenue Bond

Consider the current circumstances of a country like Venezuela. The good people of that nation are suffering through an economic nightmare at the hands of socialist 'leader' Nicolas Maduro. Eventually there will be regime change, and a new government's highest priority will be to rebuild Venezuela's oil production infrastructure, the primary source of that nation's wealth. This will require considerable foreign investment to finance the capital expenditure required to rebuild the oil production facilities.

Put yourself in the shoes of an international investor contemplating the purchase of a bond issue offered by the new government of Venezuela for the purpose of rebuilding. On one hand, it seems a sound investment—we're talking about the richest oil reserves on planet Earth, and there's sure to be global demand for oil. But what if this new government fails or is overthrown in a coup? Such things are common when a new government takes office in an emerging economy nation, so the foreign investor has no choice but to demand a very high *risk premium* in the form of a much higher interest rate than might otherwise be required for this financing. That's perfectly understandable on the part of the investor, but it leaves the new government with very expensive debt service—something that will cause them to take longer to recover from the mess left behind by the previous administration. The direct result is years of additional human suffering.

Suppose that we had a global-scale digital currency system with an integrated digital sovereign bond market. A form of *revenue bond* could be created using smart contracts to guarantee the servicing of the debt. The revenue bond smart contract would secure a claim on the payment address through which Venezuela receives payment for crude oil exports. Upon receipt of an oil revenue payment, the smart contract would first check to make sure that all required coupon payments had been made on the revenue bond before allowing the payment to flow through to Venezuela's national oil company. If there was a delinquency, the smart contract would automatically divert a portion of the oil revenue to the bondholder, making sure that the creditors' interests are always satisfied first. Once the debt service was made current, the remainder of the revenue would pass through to the national oil company.

The result would be a better deal for all parties involved. The creditor would have confidence that the smart contract would enforce their claim on oil revenue *even if the government failed and was replaced by a new one*. With this assurance in place, the investor can justify a much lower risk premium, thereby offering a much lower cost of borrowing. *And for a country like Venezuela, that could translate directly to a whole lot less human suffering as the country struggles to recover.*

This begs a few questions ... what if the national oil company just created a different payment address to bypass the smart contract claim? What if a new government abandoned the digital currency system entirely to avoid liability, and went back to selling oil in U.S. dollars to bypass the revenue bond? Obviously, there is no magic wand here and these issues would have to be addressed. But these are all surmountable problems, and while the safeguards such a system could provide might not be completely effective in every imaginable circumstance, they would be a lot better than no protections at all, as afforded by the conventional system.

I began with this example of a *smart contract revenue bond* because I'm fond of thinking about how to use technology to help disadvantaged people. The scenario could help an impoverished country like Venezuela to rebuild its oil infrastructure at a lower cost of borrowing, leaving more government resources available for humanitarian aid.

But that said, I'll be the first to admit that emerging market sovereign debt issued by countries like Venezuela will never be central bankers' first choice for reserve assets. This might make their bonds a little more attractive for a small position in a central bank's portfolio, but not as a primary reserve asset. So I'll move on to another scenario that could create a better bond that might actually be *preferred over U.S. Treasuries* by central banks selecting reserve assets.

Instantaneously reverse-callable digital sovereign bonds

Recall we're exploring ways that technology might be used to create a *better bond*. Let's now consider a new kind of sovereign bond with features making it more desirable than conventional bonds for use as a central bank reserve asset. I'll now propose a possibility that might make even a small nation's sovereign bonds not just a *viable alternative,* but a *superior alternative* to U.S. Treasury Bonds.

A *callable bond*[48] is a bond that the *issuer* has the option to redeem before it reaches maturity. The idea is that if the issuer has plenty of cash on hand and wants to avoid interest expense, they have the option to send the bondholder a check for the principal amount and effectively pay the loan off early. Now imagine a variation of that concept that was never possible before digital technology. I'll call it a *reverse-callable bond*, meaning that the *holder* rather than the issuer has the right to exercise an emergency early repayment option. The bond would be issued with the agreement that the holder of the bond has the right to press an electronic "panic button" at any time, forcing the issuer to pay back 95% of the principal amount owed. The 5% *haircut* is a nuisance fee that the issuer keeps as penalty compensation for having their financing cut off early.

What's more, the digital currency system automates the entire transaction, so it occurs *instantaneously.* In order to issue this type of bond, the issuer agrees to hold a certain amount of cash in reserve at all times to service emergency redemptions. Of course they won't always have enough cash to allow *all* the bondholders to redeem simultaneously, but they don't need to. They only need to keep a sufficient amount of reserve cash to satisfy the size of emergency redemption that a small nation's central bank might realistically require.

The deal is that the issuer gets a 5% discount on repaying money they would have eventually had to repay in full. So they should be delighted to have the bond extinguished this way. The central bank that owns the bond

---

[48] https://en.wikipedia.org/wiki/Callable_bond

Chapter 24:
Digital Sovereign Bond Market

gets the assurance that *no matter what*, even if there is a "no bid" market where it's impossible to sell *anything*, they will have a special recourse option. It's an expensive option—it costs them 5% of principal to push the panic button. *But unlike a conventional U.S. Treasury Bond,* they literally don't even need a willing buyer. They can liquidate this special *reverse-callable* category of bond at any time, raising cash instantly to defend their own currency. They don't have to wait for the market to open, and they don't have to care how wide the bid-ask spread is. They know that no matter what, if they accept the 5% haircut, they'll be able to liquidate that position and raise cash.

I simplified this example to make the concept clear. In reality, this wouldn't work quite as described because sovereign bonds routinely fall to less than 95% of their par value when default risk rises. If that were to occur, this option might be exercised (and the cash reserves of the bond issuer depleted) under conditions other than those the mechanism was intended to address. To solve this, the liquidation price would have to be 95% of the last price the bond *traded at* rather than its par value, and there might need to be additional provisions to increase the discount in fast-moving markets to avoid having the emergency mechanism used for purposes other than it was intended. But these are all solvable problems. The final solution would probably be complex and intricate, and that's why I simplified the example.

Assume we overcame those hurdles. Now we have a new kind of sovereign bond that offers central bankers a feature they *never had access to before*—a guaranteed way to liquidate a reserve asset even if there's no ready buyer in the market. And the power of smart contracts layered on top of a global digital currency system allows it to work *instantaneously*. The issuer might be satisfied with the discount below market as compensation for liquidating under these circumstances. If not, they could simply demand a lower coupon (interest) rate when issuing the bond. This way their cost of borrowing is reduced in consideration for offering this feature. The 5% haircut could be a feature of the bond itself, and other issuers could issue reverse-callable bonds with higher or lower haircuts in reaction to supply and demand.

Smaller central banks around the world would love this. *And more importantly, it could allow smaller countries that are able to maintain cash reserves adequate to meet the redemption risk to issue sovereign bonds that would be suitable as central bank reserve assets.* Take a moment to contemplate the significance of that. It would balance the playing field so that a much larger number of nations' sovereign debt could compete on much more even footing with U.S. Treasuries. And it would mean smaller nations with impoverished societies would gain access to funding sources never before available to them.

Yes, the market for U.S. treasuries might still be the deepest, most liquid market on earth. But if a new kind of bond allows the market to be bypassed entirely in a special emergency liquidation mechanism, who cares? Smaller nations could offer a better coupon (interest rate paid to the lender) and also offer this instantaneous redemption option, *making their bonds preferable to USTs.* Smaller central banks would start to scoop up these bonds in lieu of U.S. Treasuries for the sake of getting a better return on their investment, and they'd take the 5% haircut risk knowing that the likelihood of a crisis requiring them to exercise that option is low.

This is just one example of using technology to create a genuinely superior alternative to conventional debt instruments. I can't possibly be too emphatic in making this point: *we're still at the balance-your-checkbook stage in the very first chapters of the evolutionary digital technology story.* You might think of other ways that smart contracts could create new financial innovations superior to what was possible in conventional instruments. We're just scratching the surface here.

Already this one example illustrates how the global balance of power could be altered by using technology to create a superior kind of sovereign bond that is *intentionally designed to appeal to central bankers shopping for reserve assets more than conventional U.S. Treasuries.* Just imagine what would be possible if we had teams of talented engineers working on thinking up even better ways to improve the reserve asset system beyond what was possible before digital technology.

Use Technology to Create a Better Sovereign Bond *Market*

U.S. Treasury Bonds trade on electronic markets considered modern and sophisticated by today's standards. While the markets are highly available and highly reliable, the *function* they offer is very basic: a bid-offer system that 'discovers' market price by matching supply and demand. This is fine for routine transactions between casual buyers and sellers trading relatively small order sizes.

But nothing about this market is designed to meet the needs of central bankers who sometimes need to liquidate large holdings quickly. Is it possible to redesign these markets to better suit these needs?

Use commission rebates to incentivize liquidity providers

In contrast to bond markets, stock markets have become more sophisticated in recent years. One innovation has been to offer *commission rebates* to liquidity providers (the people who make offers to buy or sell stocks available to other traders) as an incentive to supply more liquidity. A simplified explanation is that the trader who first *makes* an offer to buy a stock will pay a lower commission than the trader who *takes* that offer. The idea is to incentivize the guys who are making the offers to be more forthcoming in doing so, thereby increasing the overall market's depth and liquidity characteristics.

A first step we could take in designing a digital sovereign bond market is to borrow and improve on this concept to design the entire system to incentivize traders to supply the depth and liquidity that central bankers value most. Put another way, in the current system, *depth* and *liquidity* are characteristics determined primarily by the market capitalization of the bond market. But by borrowing a few tricks from designers of stock markets, we can improve the depth and liquidity characteristics of our newly designed digital sovereign bond market so that even a bond issue with much smaller market capitalization than a U.S. Treasury bond might still offer superior depth and liquidity characteristics, due to improvements in the *market* as opposed to the bond itself.

Design the market to support central banks' priority use cases

To design a digital sovereign bond market, we should focus the design not on how bid-ask financial markets have worked in the past, but instead on the *use cases* most important to the system's most valued customers—the central bankers. Today's central bankers are forced to figure out how to design their *open market operations* to utilize the simple bid-ask market systems designed to support transactions between traders with completely different needs. We should instead design the market system around the *use cases* the central bankers care most about.

For the purpose of this discussion, we'll focus on the *use case* of a central bank needing to liquidate reserve assets in a hurry, potentially in difficult market conditions, to defend its own currency. In an actual design effort to build a digital sovereign bond market, we wouldn't even consider stopping there. We'd assemble a team of experts and do detailed analysis on *all the different use cases that both central bankers and their trading counterparties care about*. Then we'd design a system to optimally meet all of those use cases. But to keep this discussion simple, assume we're only concerned with the *use case* where a central bank needs to unload reserve assets in a hurry to raise cash.

The status quo involves central banks' open market desks trying to figure out how to liquidate large positions on markets designed to handle a constant flow of much smaller transactions. When the central bank starts selling, their large position size creates initiative selling volume the market isn't used to. This can have the effect of 'spooking the market', meaning that some traders begin to wonder if some breaking, newsworthy event somewhere has changed the fundamental value of the bonds in question. In reality, it's just a matter of a very large holder in sudden need of cash, but they don't know that.

Now consider a system *designed around the target use case*. Suppose that institutional traders were incentivized to place large "block order" bids below the current market price—to provide the *depth* central bankers care so much about. The system could be designed so that buyers are incented to make their best offers to buy *in size* up front, rather than in reaction to market 'tape action'. This would provide central bankers with instrumentation showing them exactly how large a position they could liquidate at a given price. By offering the bidders incentives to place these bids in advance, they could have a chance at buying large positions at a discount to market value. When the central bank needs to liquidate billions of dollars of bonds, they could do it at a push of a button, at a pre-negotiated price they know in advance, eliminating guesswork and uncertainty.

These large 'block trades' could bypass the small bids in the market—comparatively normal transactions. Large block order transactions to satisfy central bank needs could execute independent of the "order book" that governs day-to-day trading in the same bonds. The buyers get a slight discount below market price, and the sellers (central bankers) get the opportunity to move a very large position quickly at a price known in advance, something that's not possible with the design of current market systems. What's more, price spikes caused by open market operations could be eliminated as well.

I've cited just a couple of simple examples showing how a digital sovereign bond market could offer a better deal to all parties involved by being designed to meet the needs of its most important customers, rather than following the simplistic bid-ask market system developed on chalkboards and index cards over a hundred years ago, and subsequently computerized without much thought given to modernizing the process. Just

Chapter 24: Digital Sovereign Bond Market

imagine how impressive the design would be if we put a team of both distributed systems technologists and subject matter experts with central bank open market operations experience together to do a *real* use case analysis and figure out how to best design a digital sovereign bond market system.

Re-denominate Emerging Market debt in Digital Currency

If the goal is to design a market which can compete with U.S. Treasuries for central bank reserve assets, the apparent goal should be to use technology to improve the sovereign bonds which were already in 2nd or 3rd place behind U.S. Treasuries, on the logic that just a little improvement should make them competitive. So, it would seem at first that the goal should be to figure out how to create a digital German bund or British Gilt, these being the securities closest to competing with USTs now. A little help from technology should make them competitive.

But I don't think that's the best way for the *Challengers* to approach this problem. The European Union is such a bureaucratic mess it would take forever to bring about that sort of change. Meanwhile, emerging market nations around the world are much more ready to consider a new approach, and many are willing for political reasons to break ties to the U.S. and look for new ways to finance their external debt.

But wait, you say ... if we're talking about small emerging market nations, how can those *small* sovereign bond issues ever compete with U.S. Treasuries? *I don't think they need to*. The emerging market segment of the global economy is hungry for a solution to the problems posed by dollar-denominated external debt. There are plenty of good reasons to fear a considerable U.S. dollar appreciation versus other currencies. That would be crippling to emerging market economies. They're very ready to move to a new system, so if the *Challengers* we're talking about are Russia and China, it's entirely plausible for them to persuade the Philippines or Vietnam to redenominate their external debt in a new digital currency and digital sovereign bond market. This strategy is all about securing market share *where you can secure it*, not where you most want it.

No, I don't think that Vietnamese or Philippine sovereign bonds are going to become the favorite reserve asset choice of central bankers any time soon. But that's not the point. If a trend can be established to move small nations off the dollar standard for external debt, it could collectively result in a dramatic repatriation of U.S. dollars and a reduction of the effects of *exorbitant privilege*. There would be less reliance on the dollar around the world, and that's exactly what Sergei Glaziev has been focused on achieving for years.

And don't forget that even those Vietnamese sovereign bonds could have very real value to central bankers if the *reverse-callable* feature were used. In that case even those small-country issues would offer central bankers instantaneous liquidity, at least for relatively small position sizes.

Think about how Japanese automobiles broke into the U.S. market. In the 1970s the Honda Civic and Toyota Corolla were sold entirely on the selling point of economy—it was cheaper than an American car. Then over many years the Japanese manufacturers demonstrated high reliability and won more consumer trust. Today's Acura and Lexus automobiles (made by Honda and Toyota) are considered by many people to be superior in quality to any American-made car.

The analogy here is I think the *Challengers* will start with the emerging markets where they can gain market share. That will allow them to show off the benefits of their digital sovereign bond market just as Honda and Toyota demonstrated their superior reliability with the low-end economy car market. Eventually, it won't just be Vietnam and the Philippines. Eastern Europe will start to look seriously at the new digital currency and its digital sovereign bonds as the way of the future. Ultimately, the trend could spread to Western Europe, Australia, New Zealand, and the other major economies of the world. Of course, by then the U.S. Government will have recognized the need to design their own digital sovereign bond market. The new space race will be on.

Network Effect Revisited

Recall from earlier that *Network Effect*[49] refers to the self-reinforcing phenomenon where more people using the same thing makes that thing more useful. There's little reason to want to own a telephone if nobody else has one. But if everyone in society has one, it's impractical to survive without one.

In the case of central bank reserve assets, we're talking about the way that central banks prefer to own the same reserve asset that other central banks favor. If everyone else is using U.S. Treasuries, it means the other central bankers are likely to be ready buyers if you need to sell yours in a hurry. Central bankers tend to all favor the same reserve asset, and this

---

[49] https://en.wikipedia.org/wiki/Network_effect

has made the U.S. Treasury bond the most widely held and liquid sovereign bond.

A digital sovereign bond market could be designed so that *network effect* operates more on the *market* than on the individual sovereign bonds *in* that market. Once central bankers discover the benefits that a digital sovereign bond market offers above and beyond what's possible with conventional markets, they'll become addicted to the *market mechanisms* rather than just specific bond issues.

Consider for example the scenario where the *Challengers* have introduced a gold-backed digital currency with an integral digital sovereign bond market. None of the bond issues from small countries who are early participants in the system would be big enough in terms of market capitalization to compete with the U.S. dollar as a reserve asset. But now, for the first time, central bankers are presented with the choice of sticking with USTs vs. *diversifying* their holdings across many different issues that all offer features not offered by USTs. Ok, sure, Vietnam and Philippines bonds aren't exactly top-shelf. But what if they can both be liquidated instantaneously through a reverse-callable mechanism and turned into digital currency backed by and convertible for gold bullion? Whoa, that's a whole different story. Add a robust digital foreign exchange market to make it easier for central bankers to defend their own currency without needing dollars to do so, and you really have a winner.

My point is that it would be a very long time before any other nation's sovereign bonds could ever compete favorably with USTs as central bank reserve assets *on their own merits*. But a new *class* of sovereign bonds denominated in a global digital currency and traded on a digital sovereign bond market could very easily grow in popularity to the point where the *class* overall could in fact compare favorably to USTs as central bank reserve assets.

What does all of this have to do with *network effect?* Today we think of network effect as meaning "everybody wants to have USTs because everybody else is using them." Long before any one smaller bond issue could ever begin to compete, it's plausible to move to an environment where the thinking shifts to "Everyone wants to hold reserve assets that trade on the new digital sovereign bond market and are denominated in digital currency, because it's the direction everyone else is moving to". It's no longer about a specific *bond issue*. Rather, it's about the market system that bond trades in being perceived as the way of the future.

The Digital Sovereign Bond Market is a Major Undertaking

Before closing this chapter, I want to be clear that what I'm describing here is a big deal. A really big deal, in fact. On one hand, it could materially change the entire global financial system and the nature of how central banks choose reserve assets. And that, in turn, would play a major role in accelerating the demise of the dollar's hegemony over the global economy. It could also advance the way international finance works in ways that directly benefit humanity, such as the Venezuelan smart contract revenue bond example.

This is not something a few smart computer programmers could just put together in their spare time. Not even super-smart programmers like Satoshi and his cohorts. I'm talking about re-engineering how the world's sovereign debt is both issued and traded, and moving the entire market for sovereign debt off decades-old antiquated computer systems and onto a distributed ledger-based state-of-the-art system. This is a major undertaking that would change the way entire nations finance themselves. *It's a whole lot bigger in scope than inventing something like Bitcoin.*

What we need most to really do a good job of such an ambitious undertaking is a team with the same caliber of software engineering talent and the ability to see how to best apply technology to finance that went into designing Bitcoin. Klaas Knot and Mark Carney need not apply.

Chapter 25:
Satoshi vs. Orwell

Digital currency technology offers society the potential for profound rewards. We could modernize the global monetary system. We could improve protections against fraud and other crimes. We could create new financing options for emerging market nations where reducing cost-of-borrowing often translates directly to reducing human suffering.

We have the opportunity to take a fresh look at the antiquated fractional reserve banking system and *re-engineer* it to create a much better system that offers society all of FRB's benefits while eliminating its shortcomings. We have the opportunity to completely redesign and materially improve the sovereign bond system which finances all of the nations of the world. We have the opportunity to architect a sophisticated digital monetary system that will advance society in ways as significant as the personal computer or the Internet.

And we have the opportunity to design a foundational monetary system upon which the digital sovereign bond market is but the first of many complex financial application systems to be built on top of it. Within twenty years time we could completely re-engineer not only the currency system, but the entire commercial banking and financial system. We could democratize and improve credit systems to be fairer and create more opportunity for society to advance in ways beyond our imagination. It's tempting to say that the opportunities for digital currency technology to materially improve humanity are so profound that nothing could possibly go wrong.

But unfortunately, plenty can go wrong, and I fear that it will. I'll even go so far as to say that the risk may actually be greater than the potential benefit. Digital currency technology offers the *power* to change the monetary system. But technology is a double-edged sword. My greatest fear is that power-hungry governments will use that power to create a new monetary architecture which does far more damage to society than any potential benefits.

Just look at the United States' foreign policy. On the very day that I began writing this chapter, European Union foreign policy chief Federica

Mogherini stood shoulder to shoulder with Iranian foreign minister Mohammad Javad Zarif at the United Nations and announced their intentions to create a new payment system for the express purpose of defending the rights of European companies to conduct lawful business with Iran, a nation which has not been sanctioned by the U.N.

The whole point was to defend against America's *weaponization* of the U.S. dollar-centric global monetary system as a tool of coercion to unilaterally impose sanctions on nations it doesn't like. Consider the significance of this. Europe, perhaps America's longest-standing and strongest ally, is publicly *siding with Iran* and fighting back against what they see as American abuse of dollar hegemony. This is a really big deal, but few Americans seem to have taken notice.

The United States has the wherewithal to engage in *and win* the digital reserve currency *space race* I've predicted. But my desire to see America come riding to the rescue is based on my absolute and unyielding personal commitment to the *American values* I was taught in grade school in Concord, Massachusetts, the birthplace of the American Revolution. *What I see the U.S. Government doing today is a far cry from what I was taught America stood for when I was a kid.*

I really hope we get our act together and return to the principles and values the great United States was founded upon. If things went the other direction, it could get really ugly, really fast. It would be very easy to design a new digital currency system to include all sorts of "features" to advance an Orwellian socialist police state control structure. It would be quite straightforward, for example, to include the following:

- Central bankers could be given far more powerful monetary policy tools that operate by imposing unreasonably strong incentives on citizens to "start spending to stimulate the economy". It would be easy to design the currency system so that your savings work like frequent flyer points. They have an expiration date (set by central bankers), and become worthless if not spent by a certain date. Central bankers might decree that citizens have six months to spend 20% of the value of their savings accounts, or else the unspent remainder vanishes. *And there really are people in government today who think this sort of thing is exactly what we need.*

- Law enforcement could be given the authority to literally extinguish the value of money they believe to be held by criminals. By

Chapter 25: Satoshi vs. Orwell

knowing the payment addresses used by the criminals, special features could allow law enforcement to literally make the suspected bad guys' money disappear at the click of a mouse, perhaps without so much as a court order or warrant.

The first draft of this chapter listed twenty-seven examples of potential "features" that I think have no place in a digital currency system, because they threaten the rights of the people. Most of them were far more clever and less obvious than the very simple examples cited above. We could easily end up with a monetary system that would make George Orwell's *1984* look mild by comparison.

I literally did not dare to publish the original list for fear of giving the wrong people too many ideas. I left just these two examples in, because they're so obvious that even Klaas Knot and Mark Carney could have thought of them. I'll keep the less obvious ones to myself. *That's how concerned I am about this risk.*

We live in a day and age where people in government who are entirely well-meaning have become so obsessed with the "fight against terrorism" that they are discarding the very values of liberty and individual freedom the United States was founded upon.

Satoshi had exactly the right idea, but it was taken a little too far. I'm reminded again of the anti-war activists of the late 1960s. They had exactly the right idea—that the country needed to stop, take a step back, and re-evaluate some of its foreign policy decisions. But they became so obsessed that many of them advocated overthrowing the U.S. Government in a revolution. That clearly wasn't going to help the situation.

The cypherpunks have gone too far too. Designing cryptocurrencies for the express purpose of subverting government's oversight is just asking for trouble. Bitcoin and the other cryptocurrencies haven't been outlawed—not yet. But the approach the cypherpunks have taken is *asking for trouble* from government regulators.

We the people need to come together and call on the U.S. Government to return to the nation's founding principles. Not by designing cryptocurrencies to make it easy to break the law, but by demanding that the government serve the people; *not the other way around.*

We have the opportunity to *lead the world to a whole new monetary order based on a global digital reserve currency designed and built with good old American ingenuity.* And that should be our highest priority—creating a fair and equitable digital currency system in which no nation has undue power or authority over others, and which offers all of the people of the world the same standards of security and financial sophistication. The rights and needs of the people should always be first and foremost, and government oversight authority over the system should be limited and subject to public debate before any such powers are implemented.

Instead we're alienating the entire world by weaponizing the U.S. dollar as a tool of coercive influence.

We've gone astray before. Through McCarthyism, the Civil War, and many other times in American history, we've managed to recognize we were headed in the wrong direction and corrected our course. I hope that happens again soon, and that we return to our values and go back to *leading the world* by offering technology superiority in a constructive, positive way. Digital currency technology offers us that opportunity, or it could be used to pursue an Orwellian outcome. The American People need to involve themselves in holding their government accountable to doing the right thing.

Conclusions

I decided to throw out half this chapter *because I do not want to be responsible for giving the United States Government—the very same government I grew up respecting unconditionally—information that it might use against its own people.* If they decide to do the *right* thing, I'm available to help. If they go full Orwell on us, I'll be first to join the resistance.

Chapter 26:
If I were in charge

I have no delusions about ever having the opportunity to lead a team to design the digital monetary system of the future I envision. But in this final chapter I'll indulge that fantasy and share with you what I'd do, if I were in charge of the world.

The world needs an *Independent* Banco Nuevo

The world really needs the hypothetical *Banco Nuevo*, except that I'd prefer that Russia and China not be in the driver's seat. Ideally, the United States would return to its founding principles and return to its heritage as a world *leader*. American technical ingenuity is exactly what's needed to build a new digital monetary system.

The ideal solution would be to create an *independent* central bank that doesn't answer directly to any government. Similar to the United Nations, it should exist to advance the needs of humanity, and should be governed by an international community of leaders in which no country has absolute authority over any other. This independent *Banco Nuevo* should be chartered to design and develop a new world monetary system incrementally. The rough chronology should go something like this:

1. Design and develop a global-scale digital currency system using double spend-proof digital cash and a permissioned distributed ledger. Design the system to be gold-backed. In its first version the system replaces M0 base money, but doesn't attempt to change the fractional reserve banking system.

2. Offer any country that wants to participate a one-time opportunity to seed the system with gold bullion exchanged at a 1:1 ratio to the new currency's gold redemption value, meaning that they can redeem their *Nuevos* and take back their gold at any time. Agree to restrict the resale of *Nuevos* sourced from this initial transaction for the first three years to a pace determined by *Banco Nuevo's* board of Governors not to flood the market. No restrictions after the three-year incubation period.

3. After the initial funding transaction, *Banco Nuevo* begins open market operations, selling *Nuevos* on the open market for fiat currency, at an initial price of 166% of the gold redemption value. If the market price falls to 150% of gold redemption value, *Banco Nuevo* should buy *Nuevos* back to defend a minimum price at 150% of gold redemption value.

4. As fiat currency accumulates from open market operations, *Banco Nuevo* should buy more gold bullion on the open market to increase its reserves proportionate to money supply growth.

5. Member nations are encouraged to officially adopt the digital *Nuevo* as a second official currency, and encourage their citizens and businesses to begin adapting to the use of digital currency rather than conventional currency for most commerce.

6. Banco Nuevo charters parallel efforts to both design and build a *digital sovereign bond market*, and to re-engineer fractional reserve banking such that all money (M3) becomes digital currency, and is accounted and tracked on a global-scale segregated permissioned ledger.

7. Long-term, *Banco Nuevo* is governed by two principal committees. The *Banking Committee* is the central bankers whose knowledge focuses on monetary policy and financial affairs, and the *Technology Committee* includes the thought leaders of digital currency technology. The two teams work in partnership to advance the state of the art global monetary system without undue influence or control falling into the hands of any one government.

8. National currencies can eventually be phased out as the *Nuevo* offers the world a much improved monetary system, built on a *zoned monetary policy architecture* allowing economic priorities of each national region to be met with appropriate monetary policy measures.

Assembling the Team

My first step would be to reach out to all the brightest minds in the crypto community. I'd want Nick Szabo, the father of smart contracts, Vitalik Buterin, boy wonder of Ethereum, and Mike Hearn, one of the brightest minds behind blockchain who's now working on a permissioned distributed ledger product. I'd want Gavin Andresen, the guy Satoshi left in charge of developing the Bitcoin client software. I'd want David Chaum, who by many

Chapter 26:
If I were in charge

accounts is the father of Digital Cash, having first written a paper proposing the idea in 1982. I'd reach out to Jeff Garzik, one of the first widely respected Bitcoin developers to move on to found a company that focuses on commercial applications for Bitcoin. And I'd look for others who have shown solid thought leadership in digital currency technology or who have gained the respect of the crypto community as technology leaders.

These people offer thought leadership, and command respect within the crypto community. They might not be the actual developer team needed to engineer a global-scale digital currency, but they would know exactly who should be recruited to build that team.

I wouldn't stop there. I'm also reach out to some influential investors like Mike Novogratz, whose track record as a cryptocurrency speculator is almost unmatched. I'd also cautiously consider some of the Sand Hill Road venture capital crowd who have been involved in financing Fintech startups that build permissioned distributed ledger products. This second group would be people who understand business, and who would be more likely to understand and sympathize with my view that while cryptocurrency did a wonderful job of creating a small-scale *alternative* to the mainstream FRB system, there's no realistic way to re-engineer the mainstream system without government participation and sponsorship. I'd call on them to help conceive the right business model to structure Banco Nuevo to tap the best of the best in Silicon Valley to join the project, and to compensate them appropriately. This would probably involve equity participation in a *NuevoTech* start-up that would be contracted to develop the technology for *Banco Nuevo*.

I'd get them all together in one room and try to appeal to their sense of reason. I'd remind them that what Satoshi envisioned was a major improvement over the fractional reserve banking systems of yesteryear. I'd acknowledge that Satoshi saw governments and central banks as the enemy, but I'd make the argument that to be *effective,* if your goal is to *change what you cannot accept,* you have to be willing to also *accept what you cannot change.* I'd argue that state-sponsored digital currency is coming with or without our involvement. I'd make the case that our choice is either to participate and help the outcome look more like Satoshi's vision than Orwell's, or to stamp our feet, scream *down with the establishment*, and watch someone else develop what could become Orwell's worst nightmare.

I'd emphasize that even if the crypto community's vision of cryptocurrencies evolving to compete with major national currencies came true (something I think profoundly unlikely), that still does nothing to re-engineer the world's sovereign bond markets. I'd tell them they have the opportunity to change the world and alter the course of humanity by re-engineering fractional reserve banking and creating monetary policy tools that benefit society. Or they have the alternative to fight City Hall and play in their cryptocurrency sandboxes until they're outlawed. It's their choice to make.

I'd tell them bluntly that we need to use our collective bargaining power. Form a pact and come to terms with the fact that state-sponsored digital currency won't be designed with all of the values Satoshi envisioned for Bitcoin. I'd propose that we be realistic about what we can hope to change, and then sit down and figure out what we could actually *accept*. I'd suggest that we propose some sort of *digital currency Constitution* or bill of rights that defines certain guiding principles that governments cannot override, even in the name of "fighting terrorism". I'd suggest that we show the sponsors of *Banco Nuevo* our proposal, and use our willingness to all join a full-time effort *on terms we can accept* as a bargaining chip to get them to let go of any plans we cannot accept.

True, I'd be saying these things partly to appeal to their priorities in an effort to win their participation. But the bit about solidarity would be one hundred percent sincere. If I got that team of people ready to work full-time on building this system for *Banco Nuevo,* conditional on *Banco Nuevo* agreeing to some sort of Digital Currency Constitution to protect from an Orwellian outcome—I'd be the first to walk out the door if they wouldn't agree to the anti-Orwell clause.

Once I had a solid digital currency technology team recruited, my next hire would be Jeff Snider, Mr. Eurodollar. I'd tell Jeff his full-time job is to figure out what *benefits* the world gets out of the Eurodollar system that are actually of value to society, and to be in charge of making sure the *Nuevo* is designed to embrace those requirements.

Then I'd find the person who knows as much about the Tri-Party Repo system as Jeff Snider knows about Eurodollars, and hire them to figure out how the new system will replace what we use Repo for today. Same thing for a mortgage securitization guru, and so on, until every function of the modern-day fractional reserve banking system was represented by an expert who could help re-engineer it using digital currency technology.

I'd build a team of people that understand every facet of the current system, and I'd focus all my own energy on getting their heads *out* of

Chapter 26: If I were in charge

thinking about how to recreate current systems with digital technology, and to instead focus on defining what society actually gets out of the current system, which I'd then challenge the technology team to re-engineer in a completely new way using digital currency technology. Their designs would be subject to critical review by the finance staff, who would make sure they really do accommodate every need that the current system satisfies.

One of my biggest challenges would be to figure out how to compensate everyone so that their energy stayed focused on doing the right thing. The guys who truly know how the current banking system works well enough to lead an effort to re-engineer FRB all grew up in the woefully corrupt culture of finance, where everyone is self-serving and loyalty exists only to their own bank accounts. Meanwhile the technology team would include some of the most outspoken libertarians, who would be in constant emotional crisis over the fact we had to cave on some aspects of Satoshi's original vision. It would be an incredible management challenge, but I'd welcome it with open arms.

Growing the Organization

Banco Nuevo must have the culture of a major Silicon Valley software company, yet function as an independent supranational central bank. It would be unlike any organization that ever preceded it, and it would have more influence on the future of the world than the United Nations. Pulling it off would be an amazing feat, and I'd love to be part of it.

Eventually the innovation *Banco Nuevo* delivers to the world will be as important as the Internet. But it could also take a wrong turn at any moment and fall down a slippery slope into an Orwellian Nightmare.

Returning to Reality...

Well, that was a fun fantasy while it lasted. In reality as soon as governments are involved they'll spend more money and waste more time fighting turf battles than it would have cost the private sector to design and build the entire system. The *Defense-Industrial Complex* will be replaced by the *Fintech-Central Bank Complex*, and dirty dealing and politics will be the norm.

But I really do think we're on the cusp of a technology-driven monetary revolution.

I'd love to be part of it when it happens.

240 Beyond Blockchain: The Death of the Dollar and the Rise of Digital Currency

Please follow my work...

This is my first book, and my mentors tell me that nothing is more important for a new author than **Amazon reviews**. If you've enjoyed this book, I really hope you'll take a minute to write one. It's free, it's easy, and will only take a couple of minutes of your time. Just look this book up on Amazon, click where it says the number of reviews, and then click the button "Write a Customer Review". Thanks in advance for your help!

Please also stop by my personal website, www.eriktownsend.com. **You can buy the audiobook version of this book there if that interests you.** I'm planning to write several more books, and will announce my plans there as well.

The best way to follow my work is to subscribe to my free weekly podcast, *MacroVoices*. I give a brief summary of financial markets each week and then interview some of the smartest and most interesting people in the world of finance and investing. The show airs at 8:00 p.m. Eastern Time each Thursday night (but is available indefinitely after that). You can listen directly at www.macrovoices.com and you can also subscribe on iTunes to have the podcast downloaded to your mobile device automatically each week. If you register a free account at www.macrovoices.com, you'll also receive my free weekly e-mail newsletter which contains links to interesting articles and investment research on the Internet.

This book has focused on one specific scenario for how the U.S. dollar's hegemony over the global financial system could come to an end; with the advent of a global digital currency system designed to replace it as global reserve currency. But even if a digital currency is not the catalyst to bring about change, there are plenty of reasons to question how much longer the U.S. dollar can hold on to the title of global reserve currency. At the end of 2017 I produced a free five-part podcast series titled *The U.S. Dollar Endgame*[50] featuring Alhambra Investments CIO Jeffrey Snider, Forest For the Trees founder Luke Gromen, and Morgan Creek Capital founder Mark Yusko. If you found this book interesting, I think you'll find that series interesting as well, because it looks at the question of dollar hegemony from a completely different perspective.

---

[50] http://www.macrovoices.com/AIA

For more advanced finance buffs and investors, I also produced a seven-part series with Alhambra Investments CIO Jeffrey Snider titled *EuroDollar University*.[51] This series gives a thorough introduction to the history of the Eurodollar system and the role it plays in the global economy. This material is more advanced and may not appeal to novices in finance, but it's been super-popular with more experienced investors who seek more advanced material.

I've enjoyed writing this book, and already plan to write at least a few more. Please check my website for more information on my plans and future releases.

---

[51] http://www.macrovoices.com/EDU

Appendix A:
About the Author

I grew up in Concord Massachusetts, which is relevant only because my Junior High School was the first in the country to have a minicomputer donated to it. I was hooked instantly, and became a computer geek long before that phrase was coined. The idea of an eleven-year-old becoming an accomplished computer programmer is nothing exceptional today, but it was quite unprecedented in 1976. I spent most of my high-school years at MIT's Artificial Intelligence Laboratory, teaching myself more advanced aspects of computer programming, and learning all about the Internet, which was still called the ARPAnet back in those days.

To be clear, I'm not an MIT grad nor was I ever officially an MIT student. They had a program that allowed just about anyone to get a login account on the AI Lab's ITS Timesharing computers. It was intended for remote login use only. My dad gave me a Heathkit H-19 computer terminal kit for my 12th birthday, which I built myself. The idea was that I could use a dial-up modem (they were called *acoustic couplers* in the 1970s) to login to the AI Lab's computer from our home in Concord. I was only allowed to login after 8:00 p.m., during off-hours when the primary laboratory staff weren't using the computers.

I spent three years as a teen "sneaking in" to the AI Lab's computer room on the 9th floor of 545 Technology Square in Cambridge, Massachusetts. I grew a full beard and posed as a grad student doing research, but in reality I was just a self-taught teenager learning as much as I could about computer programming and networking technology. I met several real grad students while I was there, and learned quite a bit from them. I learned about networks and distributed computing from the very guys who literally invented the TCP/IP Protocol, and I learned to program in several languages including C, Lisp, and Assembly.

I incorporated my first software consulting company while still a sophomore in high school, and graduated high school a year early. My first 'real job' was working as a contract programmer at Digital Equipment, the same company that donated the computer to my Jr. High School. I'd never been so excited in my life as to start working at Digital—the company I thought of as the holy grail of computing at the time. I was still just a teenaged kid and really had no idea how lucky I'd been to have spent the time I did at MIT.

When I started at Digital, I assumed I'd be learning much more advanced things than I learned at MIT. After all, MIT was just a University (or it seemed that way to me at the time), and Digital was the place where they developed the latest technology. I assumed the people I'd meet there and the software development approach I'd be exposed to would be a whole step above and beyond MIT. Of course I actually had it backwards, but I was just a kid and didn't know anything about the world. *I had no clue that the researchers I'd been hanging out and drinking beer with at MIT late at night were literally among the smartest people in the entire computer industry.*

The group I worked in at Digital was developing factory shopfloor data collection systems. They were extremely proud of the work they were doing, and considered it to be bleeding edge—industry-leading stuff. The project was called the *Integrated Factory Information Network*. So cool, I thought. I get to work on a *Network*. I figured their network technology had to be much more advanced than what MIT had. To make a long story short, there was no network. They were developing application programs in BASIC that ran on a single VAX computer and logged simple information collected from a forms-driven user interface. It was 1,000 miles *behind* MIT's least impressive stuff.

By the end of my first month on the job, I commented in front of several co-workers that I was shocked that a company like Digital was still stuck in the dark ages of technology. They were quite sure they were on the bleeding edge, and I was a seventeen-year-old old kid with no college degree. Most of them weren't the slightest bit amused. Fortunately Mike Ronayne, my new boss, was far more open-minded than most. Anyone else probably would have fired such an obnoxious, outspoken *child* for so sharply criticizing the team's design work. Mike took me aside and explained that I should be careful how I come across to my elder co-workers. Then he told me to write him a white paper describing how I would have designed it differently.

I wrote the requested white paper and described an approach that was based loosely on how the distributed systems I learned about at MIT worked, but catered a little more to their vision of creating an extensible architecture of cooperating systems. My design was network-centric, and offered a way to build independent systems that would communicate and coordinate their activities in real time over the DECnet network. All of it was based on the way the guys at the AI Lab thought about distributed applications.

A year later in the spring of 1984, Mike tasked me with writing a more substantial document—he wanted a detailed functional specification for a new kind of software that would become known as *middleware*—the network plumbing that would be needed in order to build the kind of application software I'd described the year prior. The document I wrote would describe an approach that is known today as *Service-Oriented Architecture*, and it described a detailed functional specification for a style of communication between application programs that became known as *message queuing*, as well as an idea I called an *event server*, which would later be known in the IT field as *Publish & Subscribe Messaging*.

The group we worked for at Digital loved the design, and we began building the middleware and designing application software to use it. Nobody on earth besides Mike Ronayne would have listened to an obnoxious kid with no college degree telling an entire group of degreed engineers in their thirties and forties how to design distributed application software. But Mike didn't care about degrees or credentials. He knew that my design concept was what the project needed, and we marched ahead. I would work for Mike as a perpetually-renewed contract programmer for the next seven years, and we would become pioneers in a field that wouldn't even be given its name (*Service-Oriented Architecture*[52]) for almost two decades after we first started working with it.

I knew right then in 1984 that we were onto something that was going to change the IT industry. In hindsight I should have trusted my own instinct and left Digital much sooner to start a company to carry forward the approach to building distributed application software we began in 1984. But it wasn't until 1991 that I finally left Digital and went on to start The Cushing Group. Mike Ronayne would be my first employee and partner, after a long and arduous negotiation to persuade him that we could make it on our own and that we didn't need Digital, which had repeatedly refused to allow us to productize our ideas.

Wells Fargo Bank was our first major customer, and the application software we developed for them in 1993 was the first commercial application of *Service-Oriented Architecture* I am aware of. By 1998, we'd grown to thirty-five employees and $10 million in revenue, but the tech bubble was plain as day to me. I was scared it would burst before we could

---

[52] https://en.wikipedia.org/wiki/Service-oriented_architecture

sell the company in the summer of '98, but in the end, our timing was perfect. We sold The Cushing Group for $31 million. I'd bootstrapped the company (meaning no outside investors), so that money was all for us. Mike and I both made enough to retire.

My strong instinct and desire was to reinvent myself as a full-time investor. I'd always been fascinated with financial markets, and had been an avid retail investor over the years. I'd always been very quick to pick up new ideas, and wondered if I should become a venture capitalist and invest in software startups. I was talked out of the entire plan by the M&A lawyer who handled The Cushing Group's acquisition. He was so emphatic and persuasive, telling me I was a software guy, and that I had the opportunity to attract the talent of the private wealth management professionals at the world's most prestigious investment banks. He pleaded with me to reconsider, saying that I was not qualified to run my own money and that I should entrust it to professionals.

No worse advice has ever been given in the history of mankind. The world's most prestigious investment bank would soon lose half the money I'd made. I made the stupid mistake of taking business advice from a lawyer, something I'll never do again. The worst part was that at the lawyer's urging, I tried to be retired, and spent several years living on a yacht. Believe it or not that was the most miserable chapter of my life, and I'll probably write a separate book about it someday. For now, trust me that retiring in your early thirties and living aboard a yacht isn't nearly as much fun as it sounds.

After several miserable years of the yachting life, and losing half my fortune, I finally followed my own instincts and reinvented myself as a full-time private investor. At first I pursued angel investing in software startups, but quickly learned that wasn't for me.

I didn't even know what Macroeconomics was until I began reading Jack Schwager's *Market Wizards* book series. Jim Rogers' perspective on the world fascinated me, and I started learning more about his style of investing. A few years later I'd become quite skilled at trading, and was well on the way to making back the money I'd lost following the lawyer's advice to trust the Wall Street boys with my money.

Friends in the hedge fund business told me I was already doing all the work of running a hedge fund, and that I should organize myself as a fund to allow others to invest alongside me. I ran a small macro-focused hedge

Appendix A: About the Author

fund for five years, which I closed in 2018 after deciding that being responsible for other people's money wasn't for me.

I continue to produce my *MacroVoices*[53] weekly podcast, which has gained a reputation as one of the most-respected podcasts on the Internet for finance professionals and very sophisticated private investors.

I've wanted to write a book for many years, and have about five of them in my head. But while running my hedge fund it was simply impossible to make the time to write. I've enjoyed writing this book (my first), and look forward to writing a few more on a variety of different topics. I hope you've enjoyed this first one.

---

[53] http://www.macrovoices.com/

Beyond Blockchain: The Death of the Dollar and the Rise of Digital Currency

Acknowledgements

The idea for this book came from **Mike Ronayne**, my business partner and most trusted friend of over thirty-five years. I lamented to Mike in July, 2018 that I felt a sense of *déjà vu*. I said it felt exactly like I was back in 1984, when I knew the approach we developed for building distributed application software was going to change our industry. Mike's response: "Nobody's ever going to believe us that we invented *Service-Oriented Architecture* in 1984 (even though we did), and nobody's going to believe you saw this digital global reserve currency thing coming either unless you write a book so you can prove it."

I immediately asked Mike to elaborate … what good would writing a book do? How would that change the course of history or change anything else? Mike didn't miss a beat. "It won't. But at least I won't have to spend the next twenty years listening to you whine about how nobody believes you predicted a digital global reserve currency back in 2018 the way I've been listening to you complain about people not believing we invented SOA for the last twenty years!"

I started writing about a week later. And as with every other accomplishment in my professional life, I have Mike to thank for motivating me to make it happen.

Jeffrey Snider, chief investment officer at Alhambra Investments, was kind enough to review the monetary history chapters and offer considerable feedback. Unfortunately much of Jeff's feedback was too advanced for my target audience, but I appreciate the extraordinary detail just the same. One thing is clear—when the world recognizes the opportunity to re-engineer Fractional Reserve Banking using digital currency technology, Jeffrey Snider is the best man to head up the analysis of the role the Eurodollar system now plays in the global economy and how it should be redesigned in a digital currency system.

Jeff Parries, a thirty-year-old crypto millionaire and a dedicated MacroVoices listener, provided considerable input to the chapters on the culture and history of cryptocurrency, and has been a huge supporter of this book since the first day I mentioned it to him. Jeff was kind enough to review the entire book for accuracy of my statements relating to cryptocurrencies, which Jeff has considerable experience with.

Jonathan Tepper, founder of Variant Perception and author of two excellent books was kind enough to offer me considerable advice on publishing and book-writing, as well as encouragement to write the book in the first place.

Made in the USA
Middletown, DE
13 November 2018